Winning with Social Media 2.0

A Guide for Lawyers Using Social Media in Litigation and Trial

Winning with Social Media 2.0

A Guide for Lawyers Using Social Media in Litigation and Trial

Sydney Beckman

Professor of Law
Duncan School of Law
Lincoln Memorial University

With Contributions by
Michelle Sherman

NITA®
National Institute for Trial Advocacy

Address inquiries to:
Reprint Permission
National Institute for Trial Advocacy
325 W. South Boulder Rd., Ste. 1
Louisville, CO 80027
Phone: (800) 225-6482
Email: permissions@nita.org

ASPEN PUBLISHING

Official co-publisher of NITA.
aspenpublishing.com/NITA

ISBN 978-1-60156-934-9
FBA 1934
eISBN 978-1-60156-935-6
eFBA 1935

Library of Congress Cataloging-in-Publication Data

Names: Beckman, Sydney A. (Sydney Aaron). author.
Title: Winning with social media 2.0 : a guide for lawyers using social media in litigation and trial / Sydney Beckman, Professor of Law, Duncan School of Law, Lincoln Memorial University.
Description: Louisville, CO : National Institute for Trial Advocacy, 2023. | Includes bibliographical references and index.
Identifiers: LCCN 2022038336 (print) | LCCN 2022038337 (ebook) | ISBN 9781601569349 (paperback) | ISBN 9781601569356 (ebook)
Subjects: LCSH: internet in legal services--United States. | Trial practice--United States. | Social media--United States.
Classification: LCC KF320.I57 S54 2022 (print) | LCC KF320.I57 (ebook) | DDC 340.0285--dc23/eng/20221101
LC record available at https://lccn.loc.gov/2022038336
LC ebook record available at https://lccn.loc.gov/2022038337

Printed in the United States.

ACKNOWLEDGMENTS

Sydney Beckman

I wish to thank my friends, family, and colleagues who encouraged me through this and all of my writing endeavors. Both evidence and technology have long been passions of mine and this book represents how these two areas often intersect in the courtroom.

Michelle Sherman

Special thanks to my friends and professional colleagues, online and offline, who encouraged me to pursue my dream of writing about legal issues in the area of social media in 2010, and from there launch a blog, and speak to audiences of attorneys and judges about social media. I am especially thankful to Emily Aiken, Founder and Creative Brand Strategist of @The Story Studio, who helped me identify my passion for writing about new areas in the law; and to Professors Ben Lee and Jerry Swerling (ret.) of USC Annenberg School for Communication and Journalism, who helped me realize my dream of teaching.

NITA and Authors

The National Institute for Trial Advocacy and the authors wish to thank the following organizations whose branded screenshots appear in these teaching materials: Ashley Madison, Best Buy, Facebook, Google, Instagram, internet WayBack Machine, LinkedIn, Skadden Arps Flom LLP, and Twitter.

Authors' Note

Thank you for purchasing this book. It is designed by, and for, trial lawyers.

There are many references to applications, websites, software solutions, service providers, and more. No listing is intended to be an endorsement of any software, services, vendors, and the like from the authors or the National Institute of Trial Advocacy.

Social media changes quickly—between the first draft of this book and the final proofs, several citations had to be changed because the cited websites had moved or deleted documents. The websites referenced were visited as close to publication as possible, but we cannot guarantee that every link will still be active or accessible by the time you read this book.

Additionally, some screenshots may appear differently than those you encounter when visiting certain websites or using certain apps. Companies are constantly tweaking, revising, or completely changing the look and feel and functionality of their services.

If you have any questions or comments about the use of social media evidence at trial or wish to share feedback on the material in this book, we'd love to hear from you. Please contact Syd Beckman at SydBeckman@gmail.com.

Contents

PREFACE

Researchers estimate that over half of the worldwide population has at least one social media account.[1] Another report indicates that seven in ten Americans use social media to interact with each other.[2] One report indicates that in the United States, the average person spends over two hours each day on social media.[3] Social media, in many different forms, permeates our lives. Inevitably, it become intertwined with litigation. Whether it is through postings, interactions, publishing, or consumption, users across the country and the globe use social media with such regularity that their actions find their way into disputes; sometimes at the very heart of conflicts. As a result, it has also impacted the practice of law. Social media affects nearly every area of practice and increasingly figures (sometimes significantly) in legal cases, so lawyers who ignore social media evidence or dismiss its relevance do so at their clients' peril.

Judges frequently order a party to produce "private" social media content viewable only by the party's "friends" or followers and may also order the party to produce all of their social media activity by requiring them to provide to counsel login names and passwords for all accounts. This is tantamount to allowing a party to go through your corporate client's electronic and hard copy files with complete carte blanche. It's considered so intrusive a practice that many states now preclude employers and college admissions offices from asking applicants for their social media account login information.[4] Parties in litigation, however, are not so lucky.

Courts also don't take kindly to a party whose claims are completely at odds with public posts on their social media account. For example, in the widely noted case of *McMillen v. Hummingbird Speedway, Inc.*,[5] plaintiff McMillen claimed he suffered substantial injuries and loss of enjoyment of life after he was rear-ended on a stock car track. Hummingbird Speedway, the defendant, served interrogatories asking McMillen to identify the online social network sites he belonged to and, moreover, to provide his username, login name, and password for each account. McMillen

---

1. GWI, gwi.com (last visited Oct. 26, 2022).
2. Social Networking Fact Sheet, Pew Research Center—Internet, Science & Tech, https://www.pewresearch.org/internet/fact-sheet/social-media/ (last visited Oct. 26, 2022).
3. GWI, https://www.gwi.com/reports/social (last visited Oct. 26, 2022).
4. Privacy of Employee and Student Social Media Accounts (August 8, 2022), https://www.ncsl.org/research/telecommunications-and-information-technology/state-laws-prohibiting-access-to-social-media-usernames-and-passwords.aspx (summarizing bills that are pending, and have been passed on a state-by state-basis) (last visited Oct. 26, 2022); and Cal. Educ. Code § 99121 (2012); 14 Del. C. § 8103 (2012); 2012 N.J. Sess. Law. Serv. Ch. 75 (Assembly 2879) (some state laws applying to colleges).
5. McMillen V. Hummingbird Speedway, Inc., No. 113-2010 CD, 2010 Pa. Dist. Cnty. Dec. LEXIS 270 (Jefferson County, PA 2010).

responded that he was on Facebook and MySpace, but declined to provide his login information on the grounds that it was confidential. On a motion to compel, the court reviewed the public portion of McMillen's Facebook account, as provided by Hummingbird, and saw comments about McMillen going on a fishing trip and attending the Daytona 500 race in Florida. Hummingbird argued that the private pages might contain posts that impeach and contradict McMillen's disability and damages claims. The court granted Hummingbird's motion to compel on the grounds that there is no recognized privilege for social media posts. It also held that Hummingbird should have complete access to McMillen's accounts because there was evidence on the public pages that relevant posts existed on McMillen's social media accounts so that it was "reasonable to assume that McMillen may have made additional observations about his travels and activities in private posts not currently available to the defendants. If they do exist, gaining access to them could help to prove either the truth or falsity of McMillen's alleged claims."

The *McMillen* court is not an outlier. Other courts have issued similar orders when a party moving for discovery can show that the public pages of a social media account contradict claims that the party opposing discovery is making in the case.[6] These examples only begin to illustrate the impact of social media in the legal arena—and what's more, it's ever changing, ever morphing and evolving, nearly at the lightning speed of technology itself. Here are just a few things to anticipate:

1. The number of social media users will continue to grow because, according to a 2021 study by the Pew Research Center,[7] all demographics—gender, age, education level, or income—are highly active on social media, and 72 percent of the public uses some type of social media. Generally, people use a combination of social media sites and rarely limit their online presence to one or two sites. For example, 76 percent of thirteen- to seventeen-year-olds use Instagram (an immensely popular photo-sharing site owned by Facebook), 75 percent of teens use Snapchat and 66 percent use Facebook.[8]

2. Due to the popularity of social media, social media websites continue launching, meaning increased opportunities for lawyers to find potentially useful evidence.

---

6. *See, e.g.*, Largent v. Reed, No. 2009-1823, 2011 WL 5632688 (Pa. C. P. Nov. 8, 2011); Zimmerman v. Weis Markets, Inc., No. CV-09-1535, 2011 WL 2065410 (Pa. C.P. May 19, 2011); Gallion v. Gallion, No. FA113116S, 2011 WL 4953451 (Conn. Super. Ct. Sept. 30, 2011).
7. *See* n. 2, above.
8. *Instagram and Snapchat are Most Popular Social Networks for Teens; Black Teens are Most Active on Social Media, Messaging Apps*, APNORC (Undated), https://apnorc.org/projects/instagram-and-snapchat-are-most-popular-social-networks-for-teens-black-teens-are-most-active-on-social-media-messaging-apps/ (last visited Oct. 26, 2022).

3. Informal discovery, focusing on a few discrete sites that appeal to the masses, will be a regular part of the early development of any case, and detected social media activity will lead to follow-up formal discovery requests for all social media sites on which a party is active.

Social media has become integral to many cases. Once you become comfortable with social media, you will find that helpful evidence can be found on social networking sites. In the chapters that follow, you will see how social media evidence can be used in criminal and civil cases. You'll learn how to conduct informal discovery to make your case for getting social media discovery from the other side, and how to keep your client from sinking his case through "loose lips" on social media. You will learn how to use and monitor social media evidence from the onset of the case straight through to final judgment. Social media must be an important part of your discovery plan and trial preparation.

Do not dismiss the importance of the camera phone and the impulse of people to document and share every aspect of their lives. To underscore the popularity and staying power of the selfie era, consider these statistics:

> As of this writing, over 458 million posts tagged with "#selfie" have been posted to Instagram.[9] As of 2021, there are over 1 billion active users on Instagram and half of those are active daily; 35 percent of daily users report they access the service multiple times a day.[10]
>
> It is estimated that 92 million selfies are taken every day which would account for approximately 4% of all photos take daily. This same source estimated that individuals spend approximately seven minutes a day (54 hours a year) taking selfies with an average age of 24 years old.[11]

Social media, in the form of words and pictures, is woven into the fabric of our daily lives, and into the law as well.

This text is divided primarily into two parts. The first part is designed to inform you about social media and how to effectively use it and prepare for it in pretrial matters. The second part is intended to help you effectively use social media both offensively and defensively in trial. Good luck.

A word about the graphics in this book: the internet is a moving target, and websites are continually updating their interfaces. As of spring 2023, the graphics included here are screenshots of how these websites operate. By the time you read this, some of the features will inevitably have changed. Most times, however, those

---

9. https://www.instagram.com/explore/tags/selfie/?hl=en (last visited October 23, 2022).
10. https://www.wordstream.com/blog/ws/2017/04/20/instagram-statistics (last visited April 23, 2022).
11. Matic Broz, 28 *Selfie Statistics, Demographics, & Fun Facts*, PHOTOTUTORIAL (Jul. 19, 2022) https://photutorial.com/selfie-statistics/ (last visited October 26, 2022).

changes are more about "rearranging the furniture" than eliminating capabilities. Look around and you will find the feature renamed or relocated under a different heading.

PART ONE

PRETRIAL

By nature, litigation attorneys are curious people who relish the chance to drill down and become a subject matter expert on whatever case they are handling. Throw into this mix a trial lawyer's instinct for narrative and you will usually find a natural-born storyteller who enjoys the stage of the courtroom and the chance to tell their client's story to jurors. Almost every case has a trial theme that engages your jurors and makes your client someone they care about. Even when representing a large corporation that may come off as less sympathetic than an individual party, you can present the case so jurors will see your client in the context of its stakeholders—employees, customers, shareholders—all of whom are affected directly or indirectly by the trial outcome.

Coming up with a trial theme is one thing; developing evidence to support it is another matter entirely. This is especially true when you have a creative trial theme that asks jurors to look beyond the four corners of your case. For example, years ago when Michelle was a public defender in Los Angeles, she was involved in a criminal case in which the defendant was accused of prostitution and it was a "she said, officer said" situation. The jurors found for the defendant based on a trial theme that violence against women is such a legitimate problem that seemingly benign-looking men (like the arresting officer) pose a real threat of being a rapist or murderer. The defendant's reasonable fear of male strangers was used to explain why she may have appeared to be going along with or seeming to acquiesce to what the officer was saying or doing—until she had the opportunity to safely remove herself from the situation. Imagine how much more persuasive this theme could have been with some posts from the Facebook account of the officer making comments that are insensitive about college campus rapes or women in general or are just contrary to the image of a law enforcement professional he presented to jurors. Sound unlikely? In September 2011, a New Mexico State Police officer was fired after he allegedly posted a picture of himself having sex on the hood of a Honda.[1]

The chapters in Part One introduce you to the variety of social media websites frequented by online users, then move into an in-depth discussion of how to handle

1. *See* https://www.policemag.com/348295/n-m-police-fire-officer-who-had-sex-on-car-hood (Sept. 4, 2011) (last visited Oct. 26, 2022).

social media evidence at each phase of litigation and pretrial, from advising clients on social media activity to serving notice online, conducting informal and formal discovery, filing motions, and dealing with expert witnesses and anonymous online posters.

Select Statistics of Americans Using Social Media:*

Age Groups:
- 84% of those from 18–29 years of age
- 81% of those from 30–49 years of age
- 73% of those from 50–64 years of age
- 45% of those from 65 and older

Gender:
- 78% of women use social media
- 66% of men use social media

Education:
- 64% of those who have high school or less
- 76% of those who have some college
- 77% of those who have graduated college

Annual Household Income Levels:
- 69% of those who earn less than $30,000
- 76% of those who earn between $30,000 and $49,999
- 65% of those who earn between $50,000 and $74,999
- 78% of those who earn greater than $75,000

Pew Research, https://www.pewresearch.org/internet/fact-sheet/social-media/ (last visited 10/26/22)

Chapter One

Social Media Fundamentals

1.1 Defining Social Media

Social media refers to online platforms that enable users to chat with each other, create and share content, or participate in social networking. In 2021, a Pew Research Study found that 69 percent of adults were using Facebook, 40 percent were using Instagram, 31 percent were using Pinterest, 28 percent were on LinkedIn, 23 percent on Twitter, and 25 percent were using SnapChat.[1]

In January 2022, Facebook had an estimated 2.912 billion active users, WhatsApp had over 2.0 billion users, Twitter had 463 million users, Instagram had over 1.3 billion users, TikTok had 1.0 billion users, and Pinterest had 493 million users.[2]

When you develop your discovery strategy, remember there are literally hundreds of social networking sites and applications that may have discoverable information you can use to cross-examine witnesses. Here are some of the top platforms (note: in some cases, certain platforms have multiple features and may overlap):

Social Media: Facebook, MySpace, Twitter, MeetMe, Classmates, Nextdoor, Meetup (online social networking site that facilitates offline group meetings of like-minded people)

Video Sharing: YouTube, TikTok, Instagram, Snapchat (primarily a messaging app), Vine, DailyMotion, Vimeo, Veoh, Flickr, Vube, Meerkat, Periscope

Picture Sharing: Instagram, Pinterest, Photobucket, Flickr, Yogile, Shutterfly, ThisLife

---

1. *Social Networking Fact Sheet*, Pew Research Center—INTERNET, SCIENCE & TECH, https://www.pewresearch.org/internet/fact-sheet/social-media/ (last visited Oct. 26, 2022).
2. *Ranked: The World's Most Popular Social Networks, and Who Owns Them*, Visual Capitalist, https://www.visualcapitalist.com/ranked-social-networks-worldwide-by-users/ (last visited Jan. 15, 2022).

Messaging:	WhatsApp, Facebook Messenger, iMessage, SnapChat, Telegram, Skype, Zoom, Microsoft Teams, WeChat, QQ
Blogs:	Tumblr, Reddit, Medium, Blogger, Weebly, TypePad, Xanga, MyBlogLog, Vox, Sina Weibo
Dating:	Match, Tinder, Plenty of Fish, OurTime, Grindr, Zoosk, JDate, ChristianMingle, eHarmony, Ashley Madison, Minder (*Note*: Dating site profiles can be especially helpful for impeachment purposes because people try to look and sound happy, active, and socially engaged on them.)
Review Sites:	Yelp, Quora, TripAdvisor (reviews often include how people spent their time on vacation, and the time period for doing it)
Professional:	LinkedIn, Microsoft Teams, Skype, Zoom, Doximity and SERMO (networking for physicians), RallyPoint (military services networking site), AngelList (thousands of startups seeking skills, talent and angel investors), Zerply (talent in production, films, games, and virtual reality)

Due to the sheer number of people who are using social media, lawyers may have an ethical obligation to include social media in their discovery plan and trial strategy.[3] Judges as well may find it worthwhile to understand social media, and the various impacts social media will have on the trials before them. In one case, a federal district court was reversed because the judge apparently did not appreciate that to "like" something on Facebook is a form of nonverbal communication that is protected speech under the First Amendment.[4] This judge's oversight was widely discussed in the mainstream news and legal community and is a mistake that could have been avoided with some understanding of social media. So, let's begin with some basics.

1.2 Social Media Basics

Social media sites are usually free and quite easy to use. Most accounts can be established with only an email address and password. The sites make their money from advertising dollars and are geared toward people building the number of their

3. *Cf.* In Johnson v. McCullough, 306 S.W.3d 551 (Mo. 2010) (en banc) (per curiam), the Missouri Supreme Court discussed how attorneys should take advantage of technological advancements and research their prospective jurors in order to avoid the need for a motion for new trial because a juror deliberately concealed his personal bias in order to stay on the jury.
4. Bland v. Roberts, 730 F.3d 368 (4th Cir. 2013).

connections and using algorithms to help users connect with more people. The more active users on the sites, the more advertising revenue these sites generate. On the sites themselves and elsewhere on the internet, there are many of how-to guides (both free and paid) for getting started and using all of the features. Here, we will discuss some basic features that are helpful when using social media as a discovery tool and getting it admitted into evidence.

1.2.1 Facebook

As of this writing, Facebook (owned by Meta) is the social media network used by more people than any other, with the number of users as of January 2022 estimated to be 2.912 billion. Facebook users create an account using their real name, although some people do use fictitious names in an effort to remain anonymous or to avoid exposure to employers, family members, or other potential undesirable viewers. Once they have a Facebook account, users connect to "friends" by sending them a friend request. There are several ways to find people that users might know, including searching by a person's name or email address, looking at the list of friends of other users, and connecting with people who Facebook identifies through its "people you may know" feature.

Facebook account users can post comments, "like" what their friends post, "like" Facebook pages created by businesses and individuals, post pictures, tag friends in those pictures (which, if allowed by the friend, will then automatically show up on the friend's Facebook page), be tagged in pictures posted by their friends (which, again, if allowed, will automatically be posted on their page for their other friends to see), and share links of stories or posts by other Facebook users. Depending on a user's privacy settings, this can range from a small, defined subset of their Facebook friends—i.e., close friends and family only—to a public page that anyone with a Facebook account can see. You would be surprised at how many people still have publicly viewable Facebook accounts. And yet, even if their Facebook account is only visible to their friends, there are ethical "backdoor" ways of seeing enough of their social media footprint that you may be able to persuade a court to grant a motion to compel discovery of their private social media activity. We'll discuss creative ways to explore social media in Chapter Four.

Facebook users post about their vacations, activities, and major life events such as graduations, engagements, marriages, new jobs, new babies, and deaths. It's common for people to overshare on Facebook as much as it is a documented phenomenon that most people will paint their lives very positively to enhance their personal "brand." Sherry Turkle, an MIT psychologist who studies online services and their usage, remarked that Facebook is "where you show your best self. It's a place for good news, not the place where you talk about your most vulnerable self."[5] This

---

5. Hannah Seligson, *Facebook's Last Taboo: The Unhappy Marriage*, NEW YORK TIMES (Dec. 26, 2014), http://www.nytimes.com/2014/12/28/fashion/facebook-last-taboo-the-unhappy-marriage.html?_r=0 (last visited Oct. 26, 2022).

overly rosy spin on Facebook is very useful in litigation cases in which a party often complains about terrible personal and financial consequences and seeks compensation for them from the other party. The same can be said about company pages on Facebook in which businesses spin the news about great financial results, the success of a product launch, or the long-term viability of the company.

1.2.2 Twitter

Twitter, owned by Elon Musk, is an online social networking site that enables users to send and read short, 280-character messages called "tweets." The United States has more Twitter users than any other country at approximately 73 million.[6] Tweets are frequently short comments that often include links to articles, websites, or pictures. Registered users can read and post tweets, but unregistered users can only read them. Users can make their tweets private so they can be viewed only by followers they've accepted. Otherwise, it's possible to view anyone's tweets and they will not know you have viewed them unless you "favorite" or "retweet" a particular tweet. Hashtags "#" are used in front of short descriptive comments—one to three words with no spaces—within a tweet, and are often used so users can tweet on the same subject, frequently on "trending" topics like a presidential election, current events, and the like. To find tweets on a particular subject, users can search using a hashtag (#) and the subject they are interested in—e.g., #greatdanes. Users can be found by searching for their full name or their username, which is preceded by the "@" symbol. Twitter is a very fast-paced site (about 6,000 tweets per second, 500 million a day, according to a December 2014 estimate), with each tweet appearing with a time stamp showing how many seconds, minutes, or hours ago it was posted.[7] It's a continuous, fast-moving stream of information, with users seeing on their "timeline" all tweets they post as well as whomever they "follow" and the posts those people retweet.

A 2010 study of Twitter activity found that a number of jurors were ignoring the court's instruction not to discuss an ongoing trial. Reuters Legal found during a three-week period of monitoring Twitter for use of the phrase "jury duty" that people were posting at an alarming rate of one post nearly every three minutes to describe themselves as prospective or sitting jurors. Reuters Legal also found that between 1999 and 2010, at least ninety verdicts were the subject of challenges because of alleged internet-related misconduct by jurors and that judges granted new

6. Adam Connell, *35+ Top Twitter Statistics For 2022 [Users, Demographics & More]*, BloggingWizard (Apr. 16, 2022), https://bloggingwizard.com/twitter-statistics/ (last visited Oct. 26, 2022).

7. Internet Live Stats, *Twitter Usage Stats*, http://www.internetlivestats.com/twitter-statistics/ (last visited Aug. 9, 2022). On the day of the last visit, the tweet counter for the day was over 600,000 at 4:30 a.m. Eastern Time.

trials or overturned verdicts in twenty-eight criminal and civil cases.[8] The numbers of jurors posting about trials, and conducting independent online research outside the courtroom, undoubtedly has increased along with the continuing growth of social media users. There are proactive steps lawyers and the courts can take to minimize the risks of it happening in their cases. These steps are discussed fully in Chapter Seven.

1.2.3 Instagram

Instagram (owned by Meta) is an online photo-sharing site. Users create an account with a username and password, and from there can follow other users' photo and video streams so that what they post appears in the users' "feed." Users can "like" and comment on other users' posts. Instagram's photo filters allow users to play with the color, texture, and overall look of their pictures at the touch of a button. The site allows users to preview the different possibilities before posting the final picture. Instagram also enables users to post their picture or video onto other social media platforms such as Twitter, Facebook, Tumblr (a social media site for blogs), and Flickr. Users can "tag" the photo's geographical location, as well as comment on what they've posted using a hashtag before each comment, such as #photooftheday, #love, or #sunset. Hashtags are a way to search for related pictures on Instagram, akin to the hashtags used on Twitter.

When you see a picture posted on Facebook with a series of short comments all preceded by a hashtag, search Instagram for the person's account because, typically, a hashtag-riddled post is a good indicator that the person posted the picture via their Instagram account.

Instagram users can follow other users and also have their own followers. Instagram accounts can be made private, such that new followers must send a "follow" request and be accepted before they can view the content of a private account.

1.2.4 LinkedIn

LinkedIn (owned by Microsoft) is a platform used for professional networking, business development, and job searches. A polling company performed a nationwide survey of thousands of adults in 2021 and found that job searchers use social media as one means of looking for jobs. Of the job boards used (including LinkedIn, Indeed, Facebook, and Career Builder), those seeking a job used LinkedIn about 17 percent of the time.[9]

8. Brian Grow, *As jurors go online, U.S. trials go off track*, Reuters Edition (Dec. 8, 2010), https://www.reuters.com/article/us-internet-jurors/as-jurors-go-online-u-s-trials-go-off-track-idUSTRE6B74Z820101208 (last visited Oct. 26, 2022).
9. Job Seeker Nation Study 2022, Jobvite, https://www.jobvite.com/wp-content/uploads/2022/03/JSN-2022-3-25.pdf (last visited Oct. 26, 2022).

Users on LinkedIn use their real names and create online profiles very similar to a resumé, with their work experience, jobs held, educational background, and online recommendations from their connections. They can even upload writings they have authored. Users build networks, facilitated by LinkedIn's algorithm, which recommends connecting with other users based on a number of variables, including places they've worked or schools they've attended—"People You May Know."

When you look at someone's profile, LinkedIn suggests other people whose profiles users have looked at when pulling up the profile you are viewing. Users can also join groups (some of which are closed groups with membership requirements), participate in group discussions, and post status updates.

Unlike Facebook and many other social media sites, LinkedIn enables users to see who's looked at their profile. It is, however, possible to adjust your default settings so your profile remains hidden from users and you can conduct your searches anonymously. When researching people on LinkedIn for litigation, I strongly recommend you go into "Privacy & Settings" and make your profile "totally anonymous" so those you're researching cannot see that you've viewed their profile. While it is possible that you, as a consequence of looking at their profile anonymously, may get picked up in an algorithm that LinkedIn uses to suggest people that a user may know or want to connect with, this is a risk worth taking to do your research. I do not know of anyone who zeroed in on me researching them, because I always search anonymously.

Steps to Conducting a LinkedIn Search Anonymously

Select:

Settings & Privacy
Visibility
Visibility of Your Profile and Network
Profile Viewing Options
What Others See when You've Viewed Their Profile
"Private Mode"
"Back to LinkedIn"

In terms of litigation, LinkedIn is a good resource for locating witnesses, researching prospective jurors, and preparing for fact witness and expert witness depositions. For example, users sometimes embellish their LinkedIn profile, which can then be used to impeach their credibility. It is also helpful to see the people with whom they are connected, who has recommended them, and what LinkedIn groups they have joined. They may have participated in a group discussion that's helpful for impeachment purposes in your case.

LinkedIn was used in a case with which one of the authors was personally involved. In that case, the social media network was used to develop a corporate alter ego theory to impute the acts of the corporate parent to the subsidiary company, which was subject to certain contractual obligations. In depositions of key employees of the subsidiary, counsel found that one manager-level employee had listed on LinkedIn her employer as the parent company and viewed herself as an employee acting on behalf of the parent company. She made this representation because the parent company was well known in the industry, so it elevated her professional profile by association. It was also helpful that she was connected to managers and executives at the parent company, so an argument could be made that her description of her employer was tacitly accepted by the parent company because no one asked her to correct it.

1.2.5 Pinterest

Pinterest is an online photo "pinboard" site that allows users to create an unlimited number of themed "boards" on which they can post photos they've taken, found elsewhere on the internet, or were posted by other Pinterest users. These photos are often accompanied by links to websites so that Pinterest serves as a kind of visual "Favorites" bar. Users can follow all or some of the themed boards of other users and get updates when users they follow have created a new board, added new pictures, or liked the pins of another user. Because Pinterest users create their own boards, it sometimes presents useful information. Once you have created a Pinterest account, you can anonymously view the boards of other users—and, generally, users' boards are public. One estimate is that 77.1 percent of Pinterest users are women.[10]

Users also have the option of creating an unlimited number of secret boards that are not publicly viewable unless the user chooses to make them visible or makes the secret board viewable by a discrete group of friends. There are a number of reasons for creating a secret board: the user may have a particular health issue and uses their board to track different treatment options, they may be planning a vacation or party and do not want to publicize it, or they may have secret pleasures.

The default settings on Pinterest are similar to Facebook and Twitter, with you being able to see who a user follows, the user's followers, and the boards of all these other users without any of them being notified that you've viewed their boards.

1.2.6 SnapChat

SnapChat (owned by Snap, Inc.) is primarily a messaging app, although people may send video clips, photos, and the like to other users. SnapChat was designed,

10. Salman Aslam, "51 Pinterest Statistics You Need to Know in 2022," Omnicore, https://www.omnicoreagency.com/pinterest-statistics/ (last visited March 3, 2022).

however, so that whatever was sent from one user to another ultimately disappears. This, of course, makes obtaining evidence from SnapChat difficult.

SnapChat does have some features to save the information sent from one user to the next. But doing so alerts the sender that the information was saved. This is designed to inform the sender and also to discourage the retention of the information. So too, when a user takes a screenshot of a message or photo on SnapChat, the sender is notified that a screenshot was taken. As a result, attempts to discover this information are generally futile.

Although the information passes through SnapChat's servers, it is not retained for long. Snap's privacy policy provides that:

> [M]ost messages—like Snaps and Chats—sent in Snapchat will be automatically deleted by default from our servers after we detect they've been opened by all recipients or have expired. Other content, like Story posts, are stored for longer."

Therefore, obtaining the information directly from SnapChat is also unlikely.

1.3 Messaging Apps

There are numerous messaging apps. The most frequently used apps are WhatsApp, iMessage, and Facebook Messenger. Twitter and Google Mail also have private message functions. These messaging apps are fairly straightforward communication tools. Unfortunately, you generally need to access these applications from a logged-in account to view messages sent or received. Depending on the device, extraction of these messages may be tricky. See Chapter 11 for tools that will assist you in extracting this type of data.

1.4 Privacy Concerns

Lawyers and judges are sometimes reluctant to have social media accounts of their own because of privacy concerns. This is understandable. However, having an account does not mean you need to have a social media presence. If you're simply using it for work-related purposes so you can perform searches on the various sites, you can maintain an account and not even have a profile picture of yourself. When you receive requests to connect from people, just ignore them or explain offline that you aren't connecting with people at this time because you use your account strictly for limited purposes.

Most sites also offer privacy options so users can restrict who sees their social media posts or, as demonstrated below, who can reach out and connect with them. These settings are usually under the "Privacy" tools for the site.

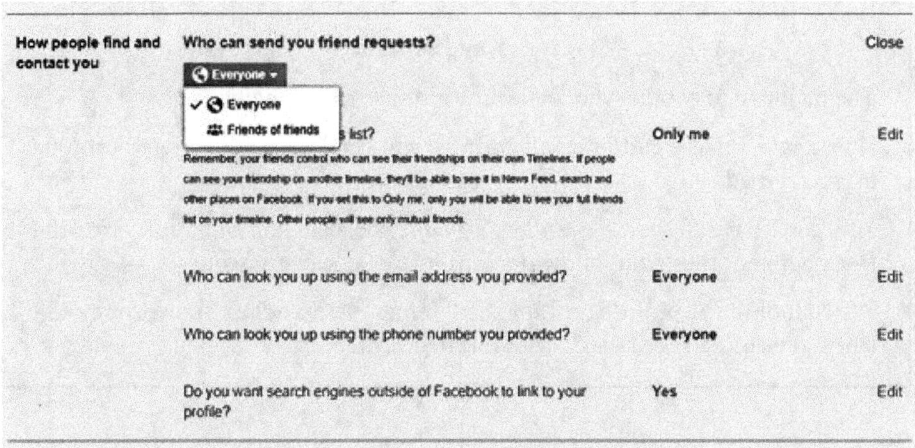

Settings for Determining Who May
Send You Friend Requests in Facebook

Facebook and other sites also allow users to restrict who sees their posts, with Facebook going as far as allowing users to lock their account so their posts are only viewable by themselves.

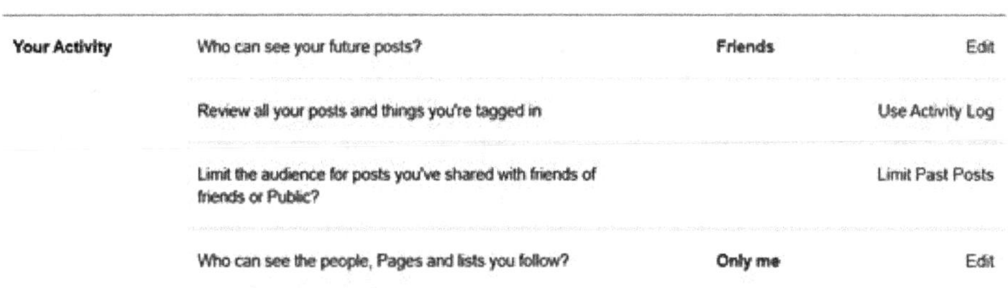

Managing Privacy Settings in Facebook

Privacy concerns or other personal objections to social media should not be an obstacle to taking advantage of the fact that many people use social media as an online diary where they share more information than they should and in terms that reflect favorably upon themselves. You don't want to miss out on evidence that may be very helpful to your case.

Key Points

The majority of people who are online also use social media.

If you have a name and/or email address, you can locate most users' accounts on social media.

You don't have to search every conceivable social media site. Start with the most popular ones, and follow up with formal discovery requests.

When looking at profiles on LinkedIn, remember to adjust your privacy settings so users can't tell you've viewed their profile.

Chapter Two

Prelitigation Steps

2.1 Clients and Social Media

In Chapter I, we discussed some of the good things about social media. People share many details of their lives on it and often post about their lives in the most glowing ways. People tend to post pictures when they are being physically active, are on vacation, or are just generally happy. Even when they post about negative events—the loss of a job, death of a loved one, health problems, parenting challenges—they are seeking emotional support: affirmations that they are good, that others care about them, and that everything will be better in the long run. Even in tragedy, we have an optimistic outlook.

Unfortunately, your individual clients may be oversharing on social media, and your corporate clients have employees who are saying things that are ill advised, not well thought out, and which may hurt the personal brand of the company or its active litigation matters.

Many companies still don't have a social media policy for their employees—and even when they do, it's often just another human resource policy that no one reads. Further, even the most well-meaning employee can make a mistake on social media. Who among us hasn't said something we wish we could take back?

On top of this, people don't generally end up in court because they are happy and optimistically confident that things will keep getting better. No! They're in court because they believe they've been damaged and want compensation.

Here is some more bad news. Social media is discoverable, and private pages and accounts are not subject to constitutional privacy protection. Courts recognize that what is posted on social media can be shared, retweeted, and go viral, with the original posters quickly losing control over who sees their original post.

2.1.1 No Expectation of Privacy

There is no reasonable expectation of privacy in material posted on Facebook. When a user communicates on Facebook, her posts may be shared with strangers.

And making a Facebook page "private" does not shield it from discovery Only the uninitiated or foolish could believe that Facebook is an online lockbox of secrets.[1]

Social media activity should be thought of as an extension of electronically stored information (ESI) and subject to the discovery rules that apply when a company is in a legal dispute that would trigger a duty to preserve company emails and electronic documents. When the Federal Rules of Civil Procedure were amended in 2006 to include ESI, the term was "intended to be read expansively to include all current and future electronic storage mediums."[2] It does not matter how brief the storage period; courts will treat the information as discoverable. Accordingly, even digital data stored in "the cloud" (i.e., saved online, rather than locally to your hard drive or a thumb drive) or on a social networking site will be treated as discoverable ESI.

As you work with social media throughout your case, it helps to think of social media as another form of ESI similar to a text message. This analogy will come up again as we look at ways to lay a foundation, authenticate, and get social media activity admitted into evidence.

2.1.2 Take Initiative in the First Intake Meeting

Take some time to talk to your new client about what social media accounts they have. Ask them to print or share their username for each and every account they have. A variety of checklists have been provided at the end of the book to assist you. Ask them to print out (or save in a digital file) all of their posts for any relevant period of time. Review all their posts so you can get an idea of what they have been posting, as well as what posts should be printed because they may need to be produced later.

Encourage new individual clients to enter a self-imposed "blackout" on social media. After all, you cannot be looking over their shoulder to monitor what they post and it's hard to cover all of the posts that could be used against them. Here are

1.Largent v. Reed, No. 2009-1823, slip op. (Pa. C.P. Franklin Co. Nov. 8, 2011). *See also* Palmieri v. United States, 2014 U.S. Dist. LEXIS 155613, at *36 (D.D.C. Nov. 3, 2014) (in a case in which a military contractor was objecting to the loss of his security clearance after the government's investigation of him, the court held that the government contractor plaintiff had no expectation of privacy in his Facebook posts because once the information was shared with "friends," those friends were free to use the information as they desired, including sharing it with the government); Higgins v. Koch Dev. Corp., 2013 U.S. Dist. LEXIS 94139, at *7–8 (S.D. Ind. July 5, 2013) (the court overruled a variety of privacy objections, including that the plaintiffs had set their Facebook pages to the highest of privacy settings, and also that nonparties who posted on plaintiffs' Facebook pages or tagged plaintiffs in photos (thereby resulting in the pictures appearing on the tagged plaintiff's Facebook page) retained a privacy interest in posts that were now in the "possession, custody, or control" of plaintiffs. The court noted that this is consistent with Facebook's privacy policy, which provides that all posting is done at one's own risk).

2. Fed. R. Civ. P. 34 advisory committee's note to 2006 amendment.

some examples of situations one author has come across in which social media posts can and have been used against plaintiffs in a lawsuit.

- In a personal injury action involving a bicyclist hit by a car, the plaintiff, a cyclist, downplayed his injuries on Facebook and talked about how quickly he expected to return to training for his next triathlon.
- In a wrongful termination case, the plaintiff employee posted about the progress of his recovery from cancer, saying that he could not even begin to return to work until more than a year had passed since his termination. His case was premised on him being able to work and perform the duties of his job with reasonable accommodations.
- In an ERISA case concerning whether the employer pension fund properly found that the plaintiff employee was not permanently disabled, the plaintiff had to explain date-stamped photos that showed her vacationing in Cancun with her family during the same period in which she claimed she suffered from debilitating headaches and was permanently disabled.
- In a disability discrimination case, the plaintiff employee was cross-examined using Facebook photos of him participating in competitive, long distance, and high-altitude bike rides. These public pictures would have been used to support a motion to compel discovery of his other, nonpublic social media activity if the case had not settled.
- In a sexual harassment lawsuit filed against a law firm partner by an associate following an alleged sexual assault on the night of the firm's holiday party, the plaintiff was cross-examined about Google Chat[3] messages she sent to friends and family, including 1) calling her case against the law firm and firm partner as "her experiment with the legal system"; 2) sharing her hope that the law firm "will pay [her] to go away"; and 3) talking with a friend about moving to Hawaii if she got a big settlement from the case.[4]
- To support a statute of limitations defense or statutory time bar, if the social media posts indicate a belief that the plaintiff has been wronged but did not take certain acts early enough, such as filing a charge of discrimination with the EEOC within the statutory time period.[5]

---

3. Google Chat (Gchat) is a web-based video chat and instant messaging service provided by Google.
4. David Lat, "Alexandra Marchuk v. Faruqi & Faruqi: 5 Observations From Inside The Courtroom" (Jan. 14, 2015); http://abovethelaw.com/2015/01/alexandra-marchuk-v-faruqi-faruqi-5-observations-from-inside-the-courtroom/ (last visited Oct. 26, 2022).
5. The statutory time period is 180 calendar days, but is extended to 300 days if there is a state or county agency that enforces a statute that prohibits discrimination of the same kind. For age discrimination claims, there must be a local or state agency enforcing a state statute prohibiting age discrimination to have the time period extended to 300 calendar days. The time period is

- In a False Claims Act case, the public disclosure bar may possibly apply where the *qui tam* plaintiff has already posted on personal blogs about the alleged wrongdoing, or alternatively, if the plaintiff's allegations are already being reported and shared on Twitter, which is now viewed as a real-time news source reporting on events before mainstream media. The public disclosure bar provides that courts shall dismiss *qui tam* suits when the relevant information has already entered the public domain through certain channels, including the news media, unless the action is being brought by the Attorney General or by a person who is the original source of the information.[6]

Photographs can undermine a case just as much as a written post, so be sure to talk about both in your prelitigation discussions with clients.

Exercising such caution doesn't mean your client cannot "like" and share the posts of other users on social media during his self-imposed blackout period, but it does mean that adding comments of a personal nature in the form of an opinion or sharing information are probably not a good idea. For a business client, it is unrealistic to recommend a blackout period. However, it is realistic to recommend topics that are off-limits; this will vary on a case-by-case basis.

2.1.3 Develop Your Theory of the Case Informed by the Client's Online Profile

Develop the theory of your case and your trial theme with some awareness of and sensitivity to how it fits with your client's online profile. Lawyers have often been surprised, and sometimes embarrassed, to find that their client is not as innocent or naïve as they appeared to be once they've factored in their client's online profile. For example, in a Title VII sexual harassment case, the plaintiff alleged that one of the defendant's employees masturbated in front of her in the staff break room at the defendant's movie theater and that the incident left her in a bedridden and vegetative state. In *Cajamarca v. Regal Entertainment Group*,[7] the court ordered the plaintiff's lawyer to pay $3,000 in sanctions, based, in part, on making these allegations when he should have known from the plaintiff's Facebook account that,

---

not extended if there is only a local statute prohibiting age discrimination. http://www.eeoc.gov/employees/timeliness.cfm (last visited Oct. 26, 2022).

6. 31 U.S.C. § 3730(e)(4)(A). With the exponential growth of the internet, the meaning of news media has expanded and, thereby, created more opportunities for a company to assert the public disclosure bar. The definition of "news media" in Wikipedia highlights this broad scope: "The news media are those elements of the mass media that focus on delivering news to the general public or a target public. These include print media (newspapers, newsmagazines), broadcast news (radio and television), and more recently the Internet (online newspapers, news blogs, etc.)." *See* https://en.wikipedia.org/wiki/News_media (last visited Oct. 26, 2022).

7. Cajamarca v. Regal Entertainment Group, 2012 U.S. Dist. LEXIS 124485 (E.D.N.Y. Aug. 31, 2012).

during the period of time in which she was allegedly highly traumatized, she was enjoying an active travel and social life and engaged in sexual banter with her Facebook friends.[8] The court referred to the intake interview and what a terrible job the plaintiff's lawyer seems to have done:

> [P]laintiff 's lawyer should be roundly embarrassed. At the very least, he did an extraordinarily poor job of client intake in not learning highly material information about his client, and setting up an expert psychiatric interview where the psychiatrist, charged with diagnosing a claim of PTSD solely as a result of an alleged five minute instance of exhibitionism, had no idea that plaintiff was a former prostitute.[9]

In another case from New York, the plaintiff was injured when she, as a pedestrian, got into an altercation with a driver. The defendant driver started driving while the plaintiff stood on the vehicle's running board, and the plaintiff was injured when she fell or jumped from the vehicle. The plaintiff claimed she suffered from vertigo, constant migraines and pain, and anxiety that kept her from going out and socializing with friends for about two years after the accident. Over the plaintiff's objection, the court admitted about twenty Facebook photos that, taken over a year-and-a-half-long period that began immediately after the accident, showed the plaintiff out drinking with friends, dancing, vacationing, and drinking beer in an inverted position described as a "keg stand."[10]

Needless to say, there is no upside to pursuing an action only to have social media evidence sink the case or the court grant a motion for sanctions.

2.1.4 Put a Litigation Hold on Social Media Activity

Because social media is ESI, it must be preserved. It cannot be deleted or altered once a party knows, or has a reasonable belief, that it may be discoverable evidence. In addition, it must be addressed in a company document retention policy.

To summarize the e-discovery rules, there is a duty to preserve relevant or potentially relevant information once litigation is pending or reasonably anticipated as long as that evidence is in your custody or control. The party filing the legal action should trigger the litigation hold and "do not destroy" notice before the complaint is filed.[11]

How to best preserve social media activity will vary from site to site. Facebook makes it fairly easy with a feature that allows users to download their social media

---

8. *Id.* at *3.
9. *Id.* at *5.
10. Johnson v. Ingalls, 944 N.Y.S.2d 654 (N.Y. App. 2012).
11. "A duty to preserve evidence arises when there is knowledge of a potential claim." Micron Tech v. Rambus, 255 F.R.D. 135 (D. Del. 2009), *aff'd*, 645 F.3d 1311 (Fed. Cir. 2011).

activity from the desktop application. Under Settings, select the tab on the right that is labeled "Your Facebook Information."

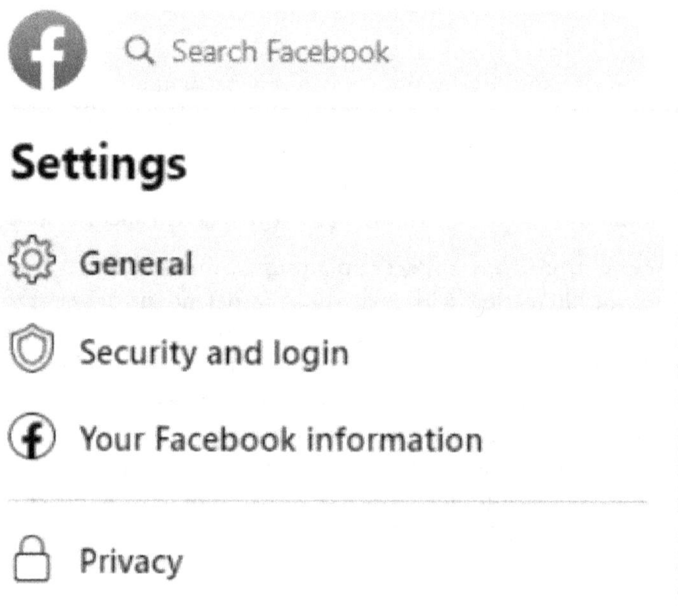

Then select "Download Your Information" from the right side of the screen.

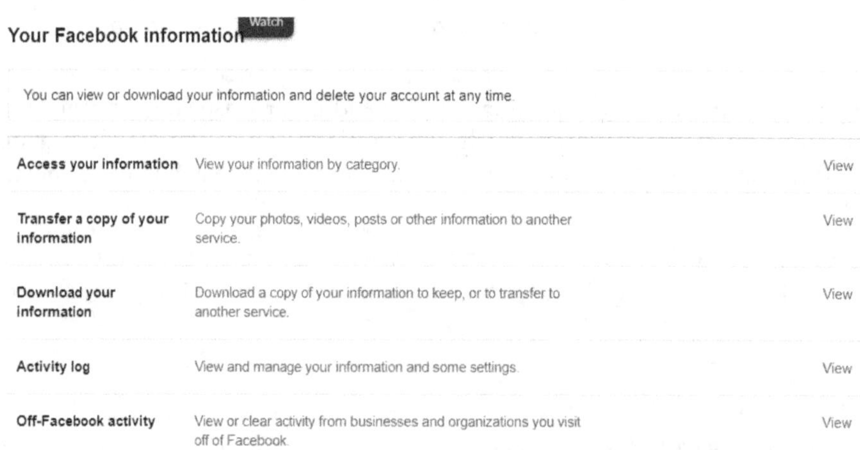

There is also a View Activity Log option that shows your own posts and what you have liked or commented on in other users' posts. You can access this feature from your home page or from the settings page.

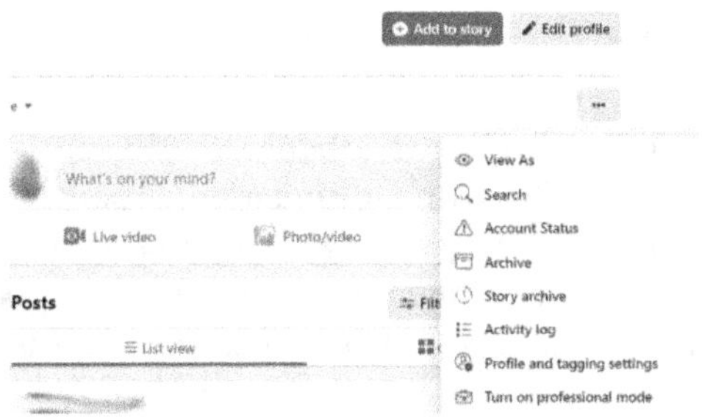

Accessing the Activity Log from the Home Page

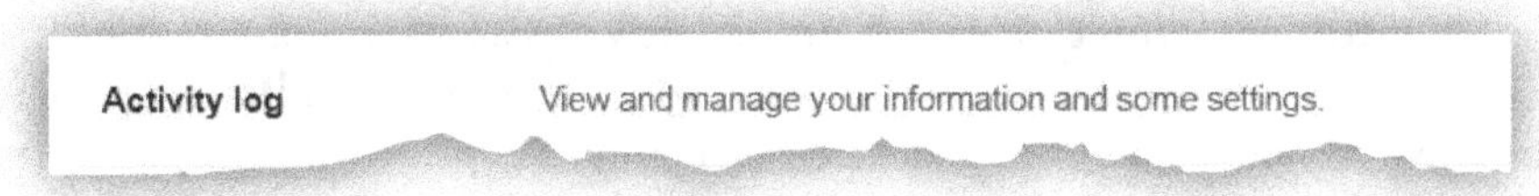

With the Activity Log, you can download everything (choose "all" in the Activity Log) or any of a multitude of categories. These are features that cannot be accessed by anyone other than the Facebook user himself. This image shows a portion of the categories available for download:

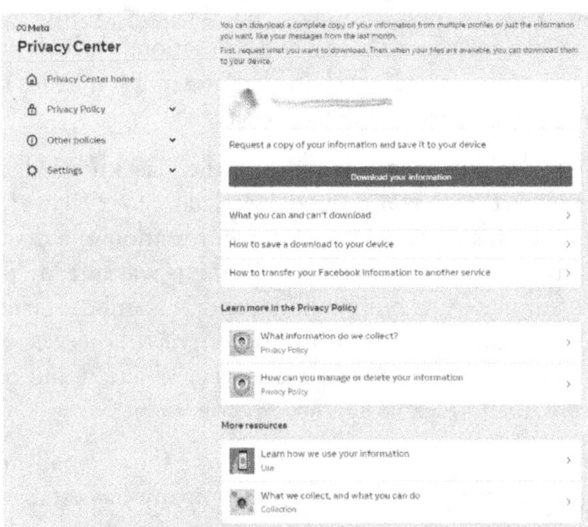

Accessing the Activity Log from Settings

In Twitter, Instagram, and Pinterest, it is possible to pull up a URL link to a user's activity, and this can be done by someone other than the account owner.

For businesses that use social media to communicate with their customer base or businesses in a highly regulated industry like insurance or financial services, the need for an established method of capturing their business's social media activity is higher.

Fortunately, there are a number of vendors offering social media compliance software and services, including without limitation Actiance, Inc.; Hearsay Social; and Smarsh. Some terms worth negotiating with a vendor include: 1) that the client company owns the data; 2) strict limitations on who can have access to the data; 3) the holding period for the data; and 4) that personal data is stored in encrypted form.

2.1.5 Update Your Client's Document Retention Policy to Include Social Media

Social media communications and online activities are an extension of ESI. The discovery rules that apply when a company is in a legal dispute also trigger a duty to preserve company emails and electronic documents. When the Federal Rules of Civil Procedure were amended in 2006 to include ESI, the term was "intended to be read expansively to include all current and future electronic storage mediums." No matter how brief the storage period may be, courts will treat the information as discoverable. Accordingly, even storage in the cloud or on a social networking site is treated as discoverable ESI.

Explore with your business client whether its document retention policy includes its social media activity. If not, recommend that the policy be updated sooner rather than later in the litigation. You want to avoid a situation in which it appears that the document retention policy was drafted around preservation issues that the business client has with regard to its social media activity.

"A duty to preserve evidence arises when there is knowledge of a potential claim."[12] In *Micron Tech v. Rambus*, the district court for Delaware held that there was evidence of spoliation because 1) the implementation of a document retention policy was around the time that defendant Rambus was already preparing its litigation strategy to enforce its patent portfolio, and 2) Rambus started, and was continuing, to destroy documents until just prior to receiving service of Micron Tech's suit. The court imposed the most severe discovery sanction and declared that the patents in suit were unenforceable against Micron Tech.

The procedures your corporate client is following for its email storage and retention may be a good starting point. When a company has established procedures

12. Micron Tech. v. Rambus, 255 F.R.D. 135 (D. Del. 2009), *aff'd*, 645 F.3d 1311 (Fed. Cir. 2011).

and follows them, adversaries in litigation will have a hard time arguing that the company has destroyed relevant and possibly damaging information. In deciding whether to impose sanctions up to and including terminating sanctions for lost ESI, federal courts apply Federal Rule of Civil Procedure 37(e). The best "safe harbor" a party can have under Rule 37(e) to avoid sanctions is being able to show that the party took responsible steps to preserve the information.

Revisions to the document retention policy should also take into consideration any industry regulations, such as state laws governing real estate brokers, and Securities and Exchange Commission (SEC) and Financial Industry Regulatory Authority (FINRA) recordkeeping rules for the financial services industry. By way of illustration, FINRA issued guidance in January 2010 for blogs and social networking sites and set forth the recordkeeping responsibilities in the financial broker-dealer business.[13]

2.1.6 Discuss the Serious Potential Consequences of Deleting or Altering Social Media Activity

To summarize the discovery rules, you have a duty to preserve relevant or potentially relevant information once litigation is pending or reasonably anticipated as long as it is in your custody or control. For the party filing the legal action, the litigation hold and "do not destroy" notice should be triggered before the complaint is filed.

To underscore to your client how important it is that they not delete or alter social media posts that they believe may reflect poorly on the or their case, tell them about a wrongful death case in which the trial court awarded about $700,000 in sanctions for destruction of a Facebook page.[14] The sanction was levied against the widower of a woman killed in a car accident and the widower's lawyer. The plaintiff widower had previously won a $10 million wrongful death suit against the truck driver whose truck overturned and killed plaintiff's wife and against the driver's employer at the time of the accident. According to the court order, plaintiff's counsel received a discovery request for the contents of the plaintiff's Facebook account, with a copy of a photo that defense counsel downloaded from the plaintiff's Facebook account.[15] The photo depicted the plaintiff holding a beer can

13. FINRA, Regulatory Notice 10-06, *Social Media Web Sites, Guidance on Blogs and Social Networking Web Sites* (Jan. 2010), http://www.finra.org/sites/default/files/NoticeDocument/p120779.pdf (last visited Oct. 26, 2022).

14. Lester v. Allied Concrete Co., No. CL08-150 (Va. Cir. Ct. Sept. 1, 2011), *aff'd*, No. 120074 (Va. Ct. App. Jan. 10, 2013); http://www.courts.state.va.us/opinions/opnscvwp/1120074.pdf (last visited Oct. 26, 2022).

15. The defendant trucking company learned of and had access to the plaintiff's Facebook account after the plaintiff sent a message through Facebook to an attorney for the trucking company.

and wearing a t-shirt emblazoned with "I [heart] hot moms" while standing next to other individuals.

Plaintiff's counsel allegedly instructed a paralegal to tell the plaintiff to "clean up" his Facebook page because "we don't want blowups of this stuff at trial." The paralegal reportedly emailed that message to the plaintiff the next day and also told him that there are "some other pics that should be deleted" from his Facebook page. There was more back-and-forth with the plaintiff allegedly deleting his Facebook page, followed by sending discovery responses denying that he had a Facebook page on the date he sent his discovery responses, and then reactivating his Facebook account after the defendant trucking company filed a motion to compel. Ultimately, the court found that the plaintiff deleted sixteen photos from his Facebook page.

While these facts are especially egregious, given the measures that the plaintiff and his counsel used to avoid discovery of the plaintiff's Facebook page, it sends an important message that courts will issue strong sanctions for the intentional destruction or alteration of social media evidence. The plaintiff's undoing was that the defendant trucking company already knew that the plaintiff had at least one embarrassing picture on his Facebook page. Similarly, parties should realize that there is a good chance that a party serving discovery seeking social media activity already has some idea of what the party responding to the discovery has been posting on social media.

Deleting or altering social media activity is enough of a problem in litigation that it is worth listing more examples. Use these to really drive home the message that your client needs to leave their social media posts alone. Alternatively, these examples can be used in support of sanctions motions for parties who believe that social media evidence has been altered or deleted by the other side.

- In *Katiroll Company, Inc. v. Kati Roll and Platters, Inc.*,[16] the federal district court held that the defendant was technically in the wrong for changing his Facebook profile picture, which allegedly showed the infringing trade dress. However, the court did not impose discovery sanctions because the plaintiff had not expressly requested that the defendant preserve his Facebook account as evidence. The court concluded that it may not have been obvious to the defendant that changing his profile picture would be destroying discoverable evidence. The court's remedy was to order the defendant to briefly restore his profile picture to the allegedly infringing trade dress so the plaintiff could grab screenshots of it and any posts concerning it.
- In *Federico v. Lincoln Military Housing, LLC,*[17] the defendant contractor, who was being sued for damages related to the presence of mold in military

16. Katiroll Co., Inc. v. Kati Roll and Platters, Inc., No. 10-3620 (GEB) (D.N.J. Aug. 3, 2011).
17. Federico v. Lincoln Military Hous., LLC, 2014 U.S. Dist. LEXIS 178943 (E.D. Va. Dec. 31, 2014).

housing, was unsuccessful in having the court order terminating sanctions. However, the court ordered the plaintiffs to pay a portion of the attorney fees the defendant incurred in filing its motion to compel and to cover the $29,000 charge for the forensic examination and production of their electronic media (rather than shifting any of the cost to the defendant contractor). The defendant filed its motion to compel after the plaintiffs produced very little electronic media and no social media activity in response to the defendant's discovery requests. Because defense counsel had done his homework in advance, he was able to show the court that there were a number of publicly available Facebook posts by the plaintiffs, including special interest pages such as "Families Affected by Military Housing Mold" and "Victims of Toxic Mold," that should have been produced—and, further, that plaintiffs' counsel had been sent a letter asking him to preserve certain social media evidence.

2.2 Dealing with "Doe" Defendants

The exponential growth of the internet has resulted in an increase in the number of legal actions against "John Doe" defendants. John Doe is the appellation used for an anonymous speaker (blogger), who may be liable for claims such as copyright infringement, trademark infringement, or defamation. Fortunately, there is guidance from the courts, so you can improve the chances of your client being able to identify and sue these anonymous bloggers.

If you are fortunate enough to have the anonymous blogger's internet Protocol (IP) address, you can utilize various online services through which you can learn information about the computer, tablet, or smartphone from which the post was made, such as the city and possibly even the name of the subscriber. However, to obtain the name on the account with the internet service provider (ISP), such as WordPress or Google, you must get a court order. ISPs are not required to connect the dots for you.[18]

The most common approach for identifying an anonymous blogger is typically 1) a motion for leave to take discovery prior to the Federal Rules of Civil Procedure Rule 26(f) conference of the parties, and 2) an order allowing discovery from the ISP through a subpoena served on the ISP. In the discovery order, courts generally require the ISP to give notice to its subscriber (i.e., the anonymous blogger) before turning over the subscriber's contact information. The discovery order typically includes a cutoff date for the notice to be given and for the subscriber to file a motion to quash the subpoena. Alternatively, some states have statutes that allow for pre-action discovery.

---

18. *See* 18 U.S.C. Ch. 121 §§ 2701–2712 (Stored Communications Act); Crispin v. Christian Audigier, Inc., 717 F. Supp. 2d 965 (C.D. Cal. 2010).

For example, Carla Franklin, a former actress/model turned businesswoman in New York, entered into a joint stipulation with Google and YouTube to set a briefing schedule for a motion to compel the disclosure of an unidentified person who was posting what Franklin described as unauthorized videos of her and also making online comments that hurt her reputation. The motion was filed pursuant to New York Civil Practice Law and Rules 3102(c) and granted by the court after the anonymous poster failed to file any opposition and the court found that Franklin had "made an appropriate showing that the info is needed to frame a complaint."[19]

It cannot be overemphasized that the First Amendment protections afforded to anonymous speech on the internet present a genuine hurdle for getting relief from the courts. At the same time, courts are issuing discovery orders in recognition that speech is not absolutely protected. As the essence of the First Amendment, political speech receives the highest level of protection. Speech that can be characterized as "commercial" speech does not receive the same protections and is protected only so long as "the communication is neither misleading nor related to unlawful activity."[20] "Fighting words" and obscenity are not protected forms of speech. Thus, how the speech is characterized will affect the merits of your discovery motion.

2.2.1 Factors that Favor Identification of Anonymous Bloggers

- **The Popular Prima Facie Standard**

Your client can make a prima facie showing of its claim against the anonymous speaker. There is not a single standard that is applied uniformly by all of the federal district courts. Many courts apply the prima facie case standard, however, including California district courts. This need for a prima facie showing was one of the deciding factors in a New York state court defamation case. The state court of appeal sustained an order denying a motion to compel the identity of the person or persons who posted negative comments about the petitioner (a financial services business) on a website called PissedConsumer.com. The statements at issue included complaints that the petitioner failed to follow through on a promise to give a $500 gas card and that the petitioner "will forget about you and . . . all the promises they made to you" once "you sign on the dotted line." The court held that the lower court properly denied the motion to compel the identity of the anonymous (and unhappy) customer because the posts were essentially that: very obvious complaints, and not actionable defamation:

> Nothing in the petition identifies specific facts that are false and when the statements complained of are viewed in context, they suggest to a reasonable reader that the writer was a dissatisfied customer who utilized respondent's consumers' grievance website to express an opinion.

---

19. Oct. 14, 2010, Order issued by Hon. Judith J. Gische, Index No. 110892-10.
20. Central Hudson Gas & Elec. Corp. v. Public Serv. Comm'n of N.Y., 447 U.S. 557, 564 (1980).

> Although some of the statements are based on undisclosed, unfavorable facts known to the writer, the disgruntled tone, anonymous posting, and predominant use of statements that cannot be definitively proven true or false, supports the finding that the challenged statements are only susceptible of a non-defamatory meaning, grounded in opinion.[21]

The court also noted that the petitioner had failed to allege facts showing that its business reputation was damaged as a result of these posts. In other words, making a prima facie showing of your claim will be important in many federal and state courts.

- **The Lower, More Relaxed "Motion to Dismiss" Standard**

The lowest standard that courts apply is the "motion to dismiss" or good faith standard.[22] This standard is usually applied in commercial speech cases, in which the level of First Amendment protection of anonymous speech is a little more relaxed, for the same reasons that the constitutionality of government regulations of commercial speech are analyzed under the *Central Hudson* test and not the "strict scrutiny" test for political speech or content-based regulations.[23] Under this motion-to-dismiss standard, the party trying to discover the identity of Doe defendants must show that its claims would survive a hypothetical motion to dismiss and demonstrate that the party has alleged all elements of their claim.

- **The Higher, Less Common "Motion for Summary Judgment" Standard**

With the prima facie standard in the middle, at the other end of the spectrum is the "motion for summary judgment" standard applied by a few circuits. Under this standard, the party seeking discovery must demonstrate that its claim would survive a hypothetical motion for summary judgment. In other words, the party must show that they have met the threshold of a "concrete showing of a prima facie claim of actual harm" on which their discovery motion is based, i.e., in a copyright infringement action, and that the party has admissible evidence in support of his claim.[24] In *First Time Videos, LLC v. Doe*, for example, the court allowed the discovery because it found that:

> FTV has alleged that each of its creative works at issue in this action "has an application for registration pending in the United States

21. Matter of Woodbridge Structured Funding, LLC v. Pissed Consumer & PissedConsumer.com, 2015 N.Y. App. Div. LEXIS 1485, at *2 (N.Y. App. Div. 1st Dep't Feb. 19, 2015).
22. Taylor v. Doe, 2014 U.S. Dist. LEXIS 63789 (E.D.N.C. May 8, 2014).
23. Central Hudson Gas & Electric Corp. v. Public Service Comm'n of New York, 447 U.S. 557 (1980).
24. First Time Videos, LLC v. Doe, 276 F.R.D. 241, 249, 2011 U.S. Dist. LEXIS 89044 (N.D. Ill. 2011).

> Copyright Office" and "contains a copyright notice and a warning regarding unauthorized reproduction and redistribution." FTV has also adequately pleaded the Doe Defendants' infringement of FTV's copyrighted materials, alleging that "each Defendant copied, reproduced, and distributed [FTV's] owned and copyrighted work as described on Exhibit A." FTV has submitted supporting evidence in the Exhibit attached to its complaint, specifying the dates and times at which Doe Defendants allegedly copied its copyrighted materials, as well as the IP addresses assigned to the Doe Defendants at the time of copying.[25]

Put simply, where you file your action may affect your chances of identifying the anonymous blogger and the very nature of your claims. The Ninth Circuit, citing to a Supreme Court decision, has held that the type of speech at issue (political versus commercial) should be considered in deciding what standard to apply, with a more relaxed standard being applied to commercial speech: "[W]e suggest that the nature of the speech should be a driving force in choosing a standard by which to balance the rights of anonymous speakers in discovery disputes."[26]

- **Anonymous Poster as Nonparty, Not Defendant**

Courts are much more inclined to order discovery of an anonymous blogger or social media poster when the online activity is made by a Doe defendant. Put simply, you will be hard pressed to get an order naming an anonymous blogger who is a nonparty witness in the legal action.

- **Nature of the Claim and Interest Being Protected**

Courts have held that when a plaintiff has made a prima facie claim of copyright infringement, the plaintiff's need for disclosure outweighs any First Amendment rights.[27] Cases involving the online disclosure of confidential insider information are another area in which courts seem more inclined to issue a discovery order. In defamation cases, it is more difficult to overcome the First Amendment protections. However, courts are issuing discovery orders in these cases as well.

In cases involving commercial speech, such as a competitor who is believed to be defaming the plaintiff on a review site, courts apply the more relaxed motion-to-dismiss standard.[28] Under this standard, a court will order the ISP to identify the

25. *Id.* Internal citations omitted.
26. Anonymous Online Speakers v. United States Dist. Court (In re Anonymous Online Speakers), 661 F.3d 1168 (9th Cir. 2011).
27. Arista Records LLC v. Does 1–19, 551 F. Supp. 2d 1, 8 (D.D.C. 2008) ("a defendant's First Amendment privacy interests are exceedingly small where the 'speech' [at issue] is the alleged infringement of copyrights").
28. Taylor v. Doe, 2014 U.S. Dist. LEXIS 63789 (E.D.N.C. May 8, 2014).

anonymous speaker if the plaintiff can demonstrate that its complaint would survive a hypothetical motion to dismiss.

2.2.2 Less Intrusive Sources of Identity

Because of the constitutional bias in favor of protecting anonymous speakers, courts will want to explore methods short of a court order to identify an anonymous blogger/poster, etc. In other words, expect to argue that the identity of the anonymous individual is not available from other, less intrusive sources, such as deposing the person who is reasonably believed to have posted the objectionable material, or finding some means (other than serving a subpoena on the ISP) to identify which user is assigned to a specific IP address.

Cases evaluating subpoenas seeking identifying information from ISPs regarding subscribers who are parties to litigation have considered a variety of factors to weigh the need for disclosure against First Amendment interests. These factors include:

1. a concrete showing of a prima facie claim of actionable harm;
2. specificity of the discovery request;
3. the absence of alternative means to obtain the subpoenaed information;
4. (a central need for the subpoenaed information to advance the claim; and
5. the party's expectation of privacy.[29]

Frequently, only the ISP has any record of which IP addresses were assigned to which users. To other entities online, those users would appear only as their IP addresses.[30]

When seeking the identity of the unknown defendant, set forth what steps you took to identify the defendant through less intrusive means.[31]

2.2.3 Giving Notice to Doe Defendants via Online Public Forums

Make some effort to notify a poster of the subpoena before filing the motion to compel discovery. For example, one court held that the party seeking the discovery should post the subpoena on online discussion boards that are likely to be frequented by the Doe defendants. What first comes to mind is a comment on the post(s) at the center of the legal action or, alternatively, posting the subpoena on that site, with a clear heading that it is being directed at the person who authored the objectionable

29. Sony Music Ent. Inc., v. Does 1–40, 326 F. Supp. 2d 566 (S.D.N.Y. 2004).
30. London-Sire Records, Inc. v. Doe 1, 542 F. Supp. 2d 153, 179, 2008 U.S. Dist. LEXIS 38817 (D. Mass. 2008).
31. Anonymous Online Speakers v. United States Dist. Court (In re Anonymous Online Speakers), 661 F.3d 1168 (9th Cir. 2011).

post, and clearly stating the date and time of the post (without repeating, of course, the parts that are allegedly defamatory or otherwise actionable).[32]

2.2.4 Grounds for Courts to Deny Discovery Motions

Courts will override First Amendment free speech concerns when the aggrieved plaintiff's interests outweigh the interests of the defendant to remain anonymous. However, courts have found a number of grounds to deny the plaintiff's efforts to discover who the unknown person is:

1. The anonymous blogger is being sued for speech that can be characterized as political speech, which is entitled to the highest level of First Amendment protection.

2. The blogger is someone whose identity should be protected under the relevant state shield law: reporter's privilege. Blogs, chatrooms, and websites potentially can be encompassed within the spectrum of a shield law extended to the news media. For example, the Drudge Report has successfully asserted the reporter's privilege. Media companies have also asserted the reporter's privilege in response to subpoenas seeking the identity of anonymous posters, with some success in states such as Colorado, Florida, Illinois, Montana, North Carolina, and Oregon.

3. The basis for the subpoena is stated in a cursory manner without any evidence to support the elements of the claim on which it is based.

4. The subpoena is overbroad and does not specifically seek information that is necessary to identify the anonymous blogger.

5. The subpoena seeks information that is cumulative of other evidence. For example, your client has a reasonable idea about who posted the speech at issue and can confirm its suspicions by deposing the person or serving less intrusive discovery.

In *Music Group Macao Commercial Offshore Ltd. v. Doe*,[33] the court ordered Twitter, a nonparty to the action, to identify the persons behind the accounts that had posted tweets accusing the plaintiff company of encouraging domestic violence and misogyny and saying its CEO visited prostitutes. Twitter was ordered to

---

32. Indep. Newspapers, Inc. v. Brodie, 966 A.2d 432 (Md. 2009) (plaintiff must notify the anonymous speakers that they are the subject of a subpoena for an order of disclosure, including "posting a message of notification of the identity discovery request on the message board");" cf. Taylor v. Doe, 2014 U.S. Dist. LEXIS 63789 (E.D.N.C. May 8, 2014) (court denied motion to enforce subpoena because some of the Does had not been notified that the website had received a subpoena seeking their identity, so they did not have an opportunity to protest their identification).
33. Music Group Macao Commercial Offshore Ltd. v. Doe, 2015 WL 75073 (N.D. Cal. Jan. 6, 2015).

provide the name, address, email address, and any proxy address for each Twitter account user. The plaintiff company was suing for defamation, copyright infringement, unfair competition, and breach of contract. It is generally the case that the nonparty ISP (in this case, Twitter) will refuse to produce the requested documents unless and until a court finds that the production will not violate the user's First Amendment rights. Sometimes, the ISP may notify the user whose account is the subject of the discovery motion so the user has the opportunity to oppose the discovery on the merits. Or, alternatively, what the court did in *Music Group Macao* was to grant the motion to compel, and then give Twitter time to serve the subpoena and order on the user so the user could have time to file a motion to contest the subpoena (including a motion to quash or modify the subpoena). If the time to contest the subpoena passes without a motion being filed, then the ISP must provide the account information within a set number of days. In *Music Group Macao*,[34] the district court applied the Ninth Circuit "prima facie case" framework for identifying anonymous internet speakers as set forth in *Perry v. Schwarzenegger*:[35]

> The party asserting the privilege must demonstrate a prima facie showing of arguable first amendment infringement. This prima facie showing requires [the requesting party] to demonstrate that enforcement of the discovery requests will result in (1) harassment, membership withdrawal, or discouragement of new members, or (2) other consequences which objectively suggest an impact on, or "chilling" of, the members' [First Amendment] rights. If [the party opposing discovery] can make the necessary prima facie showing, the evidentiary burden will then shift to the [party seeking discovery] to demonstrate that the information sought . . . is rationally related to a compelling governmental interest and the least restrictive means of obtaining the desired information. More specifically, the second step of the analysis is meant to make discovery that impacts the First Amendment rights available only after careful consideration of the need for such discovery, but not necessarily to preclude it.

Courts will rarely order discovery from an ISP that goes further than giving sufficient information to identify the account user.

---

34. *Id.* at *5. *See* Drummond Co. v. Collingsworth, 2013 WL 6074157 (N.D. Cal. Nov. 18, 2013) (applying Perry to subpoena seeking identity of anonymous Internet service users); Chevron Corp. v. Donziger, 2013 U.S. Dist. LEXIS 49753 (N.D. Cal. Apr. 5, 2013) (same); AF Holdings LLC Doe, No. 12-2206, 2012 U.S. Dist. LEXIS 159990 (E.D. Cal. Nov. 7, 2012) (Does identified in a copyright infringement action). See also Thomson v. Doe, 2015 Wash. App. LEXIS 1434 (Wash. Ct. App. July 6, 2015), in which the court reviewed the different tests, and included a thorough list of state and federal court case citations that legal professionals may find helpful. In Thomson, court applied the prima facie test and denied the plaintiff attorney's motion to compel AVVO, an online attorney review and rating site, to identify the anonymous poster of a detailed, negative review of the plaintiff's alleged representation of the poster in a divorce case.

35. Perry v. Schwarzenegger, 591 F.3d 1126 (9th Cir. 2009).

2.2.5 Digital Millennium Copyright Act

In certain contexts, The Digital Millennium Copyright Act (DMCA) may apply to infringing content that is posted online. The DMCA provides for copyright holders to serve a subpoena with a takedown notice to an ISP asking it to identify the person who posted the allegedly infringing content.

Section 512 provides in pertinent part:

> (h) Subpoena To Identify Infringer.—
>
> (1) Request.—A copyright owner or a person authorized to act on the owner's behalf may request the clerk of any United States district court to issue a subpoena to a service provider for identification of an alleged infringer in accordance with this subsection.
>
> (2) Contents of request.—The request may be made by filing with the clerk—
>
> (A) a copy of a notification described in subsection (c)(3)(A);
>
> (B) a proposed subpoena; and
>
> (C) a sworn declaration to the effect that the purpose for which the subpoena is sought is to obtain the identity of an alleged infringer and that such information will only be used for the purpose of protecting rights under this title.
>
> (3) Contents of subpoena.—The subpoena shall authorize and order the service provider receiving the notification and the subpoena to expeditiously disclose to the copyright owner or person authorized by the copyright owner information sufficient to identify the alleged infringer of the material described in the notification to the extent such information is available to the service provider.
>
> (4) Basis for granting subpoena.—If the notification filed satisfies the provisions of subsection (c)(3)(A), the proposed subpoena is in proper form, and the accompanying declaration is properly executed, the clerk shall expeditiously issue and sign the proposed subpoena and return it to the requester for delivery to the service provider.
>
> (5) Actions of service provider receiving subpoena.—Upon receipt of the issued subpoena, either accompanying or subsequent to the receipt of a notification described in subsection (c)(3)(A), the service provider shall expeditiously disclose to the copyright owner or person authorized by the copyright owner the information required by the subpoena, notwithstanding any other provision of law and regardless of whether the service provider responds to the notification.

A party relying on this statute to identify the alleged copyright infringer needs to act expeditiously to serve the subpoena because if the alleged infringing content has already been removed when the DMCA takedown notice is served, then Section 512(h) does not apply and the subpoena is not effective:

> To be clear, the Court finds that a DMCA subpoena is valid whether served simultaneously with a satisfactory DMCA notification or after a satisfactory DMCA notification is served. A satisfactory DMCA notification requires that the allegedly infringing material is present at the time the notification is served. The subpoena is valid and enforceable regardless of whether the provider acts in response to the notification.[36]

Key Points

Social media activity is discoverable ESI that needs to be covered by a litigation hold.

Talk to clients about their social media activity so they are forewarned about posting anything that can be used against them.

For individual clients, recommend a social media blackout period. For corporate clients, remind them to exercise care in connection with their social media posts and to avoid discussing the litigation absent your prior approval.

Conduct your social media research early. Google the other side to see if they're active on social media. Search for them on Facebook, LinkedIn, Instagram, and Twitter. Print and save their public posts.

If feasible, state an intellectual property claim to increase your chance of a court ordering an ISP to identify an anonymous poster.

36. In re DMCA Subpoena to eBay, Inc., 2015 U.S. Dist. LEXIS 7334, at *8 (S.D. Cal. June 5, 2015).

Chapter Three

Personal Jurisdiction and Service of Process

3.1 Service

If you have exhausted traditional methods for serving a party in your case, don't despair. While it's by no means an accepted practice as of now, courts are warming up to the idea of elusive parties being served a summons and complaint through social media. It is not without precedent. State courts have permitted, in extraordinary circumstances, for service to be effected via email.[1] Here are some "nuts and bolts" that might assist in persuading a court to permit this unorthodox method of service.

3.1.1 Making Your Argument for Unorthodox Ways of Serving a Complaint

There are a number of reasons why it may be harder these days to serve a summons and complaint by personal or substitute service at a physical address. First, we are seeing more virtual businesses that may not even have a brick-and-mortar address. Second, we communicate so much by email and text message that some people have dropped mailing addresses from their business cards, websites, and other forms of designating their location. Third, people pick up and move and, oftentimes, we can only find them through emails or social media. And finally, especially since the pandemic, many people operate their businesses virtually without any specific permanent location, often traveling from place to place with no real "home" to speak of.

However, just because it is harder to find a physical address for someone doesn't mean courts are abandoning the requirement of either personal service of a summons and complaint or substitute service on someone who can be trusted to deliver a copy of the complaint to the named defendant. These are still the most accepted ways of serving someone because we can say with some degree of confidence that the defendant had notice of the complaint and an opportunity to defend himself.

---

1. While there are not many cases surrounding service via social media, there is a great deal of discussion about it. One recent article goes into some detail: Emily Davis, *Social Media: A Good Alternative, for Alternative Service of Process*, 52 CWRJIL 573 (Spring 2020).

In other words, he is not being deprived of something (such as money, real property, or custody rights) without due process of law.

Fortunately, as mentioned, courts are becoming amenable to allowing service through less traditional means. Courts recognize that the focus should be on giving notice to the named defendants, and not giving a free pass to people who try to evade service or hide their physical footprint. Courts also recognize that "notice" can be effected through modern means that were not contemplated by the original service requirements. Courts are generally reasonable about balancing the due process interests of a defendant against the interests of a plaintiff, who believes they have been damaged and should be compensated for it.

In other words, keep in mind the arguments cutting against nontraditional methods for service to argue persuasively that these concerns are not a problem in your case. Here are some arguments for not allowing unconventional methods of service, like service via email or social media. First, we won't have finality of judgments. Parties will just come into court and deny knowing of the complaint after a default judgment is entered and the plaintiff starts enforcing it. The party can move to set aside the default judgment and argue that their due process rights have been violated. Second, it can become a matter of "he said, she said," with the defendant denying they received a copy of the summons and complaint, and the plaintiff having no way to demonstrate actual service. Third, people may lose faith in the legal system and turn more to "self-help" (think vigilante justice) to solve their legal problems. (This last argument cuts both ways in favor of and against allowing service of process through nontraditional methods.)

Luckily, these arguments are not keeping courts from allowing alternative methods of service in unusual cases. For example, we're seeing more cases in which the court has allowed the summons and complaint to be served via email. However, we are not seeing many courts that allow a party to be served through their social media account. The few cases in which it has been allowed are worth considering and using if you have a party that is especially difficult to serve through mainstream methods.[2] This slowly-building trend is happening in countries outside the United States and in cases filed in the United States where a pleading (other than a summons and complaint) is being served on a defendant outside the United States. In these cases, the social media service is used in combination with serving the other party through substitute service.

This chapter provides the arguments for why a court should allow service of a complaint and summons through social media in exceptional cases. If you cannot otherwise serve the party, it's an argument worth making. Cases addressing service of process via email are a good benchmark from which to make your argument. As

2. *See, e.g.*, Baidoo v. Blood-Dzarku, 2015 N.Y. Slip Op. 25096 (March 27, 2015), http://bit.ly/1H3NEJt (last visited Mar. 18, 2022).

federal and state courts have recognized, the courts "cannot be blind to changes and advances in technology."[3] Thus, federal and state rules allowing for some flexibility "unshackles the federal courts from anachronistic methods of service and permits them entry into the technological renaissance."[4] When you think about it, serving someone by publication is less in accord with due process considerations than serving parties via a social media account they use on a regular basis and which you have good reason to believe is, in fact, their account. In other words, people may raise their eyebrows in disbelief at the thought of courts granting motions to serve a party through social media, but it's not that radical an idea, as you will see from the case discussions that follow.

The Federal Rules of Civil Procedure give courts flexibility to allow for alternative forms of service. Rule 4(e) sets forth the methods by which service can made on parties located in the United States, with the bright line rule being that it needs to be a method likely to give actual notice to the person being served.

> (e) Serving an Individual Within a Judicial District of the United States. Unless federal law provides otherwise, an individual—other than a minor, an incompetent person, or a person whose waiver has been filed—may be served in a judicial district of the United States by:
>
> (1) following state law for serving a summons in an action brought in courts of general jurisdiction in the state where the district court is located or where service is made; or
>
> (2) doing any of the following:
>
> (A) delivering a copy of the summons and of the complaint to the individual personally;
>
> (B) leaving a copy of each at the individual's dwelling or usual place of abode with someone of suitable age and discretion who resides there; or
>
> (C) delivering a copy of each to an agent authorized by appointment or by law to receive service of process.

It is through Rule 4(e)(1) that parties are trying to stretch the methods for serving a summons.

Many states allow a plaintiff to seek leave of court to serve a defendant using nontraditional methods when the plaintiff demonstrates that service cannot be

---

3. New England Merchs. Nat'l Bank v. Iran Power Generation and Trans. Co., 495 F. Supp. 73, 81 (S.D.N.Y. 1980); *see also* Rio Prop., Inc. v. Rio Int'l Interlink, Inc., 284 F.3d 1007, 1018 (9th Cir. 2002) (in which the court recognized that due process concerns can be satisfied where the use of new technology to serve a defendant was reasonably calculated to give interested parties notice of the action and afford them an opportunity to present their objections).
4. Rio Prop., Inc., 284 F.3d at 1017.

completed by serving the defendant individually or through another adult resident at the defendant's personal residence. Or, in the case of a corporate or entity type of defendant, the business has not registered to do business in the state and, therefore, has not designated an agent for service of process.

This situation is best highlighted by a few cases. In *Safadjou v. Mohammadi*,[5] the Supreme Court of New York affirmed the trial court's decision allowing service via email on the wife in a divorce proceeding. New York Civil Practice and Laws (CPLR) 308(5) (personal service upon a natural person) allows for service "in such manner as the court, upon motion without notice, directs, if service is impracticable under paragraphs one, two and four of this section."[6] In this family law case, the husband was having trouble serving his wife because she had permanently relocated to Iran with the couple's child. To get the order allowing him to serve her by email, the husband had to demonstrate that even attempts to serve his wife in Iran at the home where she was staying had been unsuccessful. In other words, the express methods under the rules were impracticable. The husband also demonstrated that he and his wife had been communicating via email a few months before, so it was likely that one of several email addresses would be an effective way to inform her of the divorce proceeding. The court affirmed the order allowing service by email because the wife admittedly received case-related documents via one of the email addresses—although, interestingly, she denied having received a service copy of the summons and complaint.

In a business dispute, *Snyder v. Alternate Energy Inc.*,[7] the court allowed the plaintiff LLC to serve the defendant corporation and its president via email because the corporation had not registered to do business with the New York Secretary of State. The plaintiff was able to show reasonable efforts to obtain an address where he could serve the defendant corporation or its president: he demonstrated that he had tried a number of avenues, such as looking at public records, online phone books, and other such "people locators" and none of them had produced an address for the defendant corporation. The plaintiff demonstrated that he left voicemails asking the president for a physical address, but his messages were ignored. The plaintiff demonstrated that the email address was, in fact, being used by the president, so the complaint would reach the president. The conditions set for serving the defendants by email were 1) to send the summons and complaint on two consecutive days; 2) to give clear and prominent notice in the subject line that legal papers that should be opened immediately were attached to the email; 3) that copies had to be mailed to the last known physical addresses; and 4) the plaintiff must leave a follow-up voicemail on the president's cellphone , telling him of the legal action.

5. Safadjou v. Mohammadi, 964 N.Y.S.2d 801 (N.Y. App. Div. 2013).

6. State statutes allowing alternative service upon order of the court include Arkansas (Ark. R. Civ. P. 4(e)(5)), California (Cal. Code of Civ. Proc. § 413.30 ("in a manner which is reasonably calculated to give actual notice to the party to be served")), and Michigan (M.C.R. 2.105(I)), among others.

7. Snyder v. Alternate Energy, Inc., 857 N.Y.S.2d 442 (N.Y. Civ. Ct. 2008).

In *Noel B. v. Anna Maria*,[8] a New York family court judge ruled that Facebook was an acceptable form of "alternate service" where Noel B.'s ex-wife, Anna Maria, could not be located. The matter involved a request to stop paying child support because the divorced couple's child had reached the age of twenty-one. The judge noted that even though Anna Maria could not be located, she was active on Facebook. Among other things, Anna Maria had "liked" posts by her ex-husband's current wife. The court concluded that the order may be served by way of Facebook on the condition that plaintiff Noel B. also mailed a copy to Anna Maria's last known address.

Similarly, in another family court matter, a Minneapolis court allowed service of divorce proceedings through email, MySpace, Facebook, or another social networking site because it was believed the husband had left the country. The order stated that while the court allowed service by publication in a legal newspaper, it was unlikely the respondent would see it. "The traditional way to get service by publication is antiquated and is prohibitively expensive," the court wrote. "Service is critical, and technology provides a cheaper and hopefully more effective way of finding respondent."[9]

A New York court, even with the defendant possibly somewhere in the United States, allowed service via Facebook in a divorce case.[10] *Baidoo v. Blood-Dzarku* was particularly trendsetting because unlike previous cases allowing service via social media, the court recognized that social media was the only way to serve the defendant. In other words, the court did not and could not treat social media as a "supplemental" method of service in addition to accepted substitute methods of service.

The *Baidoo* court noted that while service by email is still not a statutorily recognized form of service of process, courts increasingly are allowing it as an alternative means of service. Not far off, the court predicted, is allowing service via social media. In *Baidoo*, the plaintiff wife filed an ex parte application pursuant to New York Civil Practice Law and Rules 308(5) (which allows the court to direct an alternative form of service) seeking permission to serve her ex-husband by sending service of process to him through a direct message to his Facebook account. Before granting her application, the court required the plaintiff to show that 1) she could not effect personal service on her soon-to-be ex-husband; 2) neither "substitute service"—serving someone of suitable age and discretion—nor "nail and mail"

---

8. Noel B. v. Anna Maria A., File No. 28088, Docket No. F-00787-13/14B (NY Family Court, Sept. 12, 2014); see http://nylawyer.nylj.com/adgifs/decisions14/091714gliedman.pdf (last visited Oct. 26, 2022).
9. Mpafe v. Mpafe, Hennepin County, MN No. 27-FA-11-3453 (May 10, 2011), http://www.scribd.com/doc/70014426/Mpafe-v-Mpafe-order#scribd (last visited Oct. 26, 2022).
10. Baidoo v. Blood-Dzarku, 2015 N.Y. Slip Op. 25096 (Mar. 27, 2015), http://bit.ly/1H3NEJt (last visited Oct. 26, 2022).

service were feasible; and 3) "sending the summons through Facebook can reasonably be expected to give him actual notice that he is being sued for divorce."[11]

The *Baidoo* court was satisfied by the plaintiff's showing that she could not locate the defendant husband despite making a reasonable effort to find him. The plaintiff and defendant never lived together, and in sporadic conversations with him, the defendant told the plaintiff he didn't have a fixed residence or place of employment and, further, declined to make himself available for personal service. The last address that the plaintiff had for her husband was for an apartment he vacated in 2011. Investigative firms she'd hired could not locate him: the post office had no forwarding address for him, there was no billing address linked to his prepaid cellphone account, and the Department of Motor Vehicles had no record of him. She was, however, able to make a reasonable case to the court that her husband had a Facebook account. She submitted a declaration and attached exchanges she'd had with her husband via his Facebook account and printed and attached pages of photos of himself that he'd posted on the account. While not "absolute proof" that the Facebook account belonged to the defendant, the court was sufficiently satisfied. Next, the plaintiff had to demonstrate that the defendant logged into his Facebook account with regularity and that she and her lawyer would alert him that a divorce action had been initiated by 1) texting him and 2) leaving him voicemail instructions to check his Facebook account. In this way, the plaintiff was able to assure the court that the defendant would have the statutory time in which to respond to the complaint. He would be alerted of the summons and complaint through the text and voicemail messages.

The *Baidoo* court appreciated how groundbreaking a decision it was making and answered the anticipated question of why the court allowed for service via social media when service by publication is a substitute form of service that has been used as a backup method since colonial times. Hopefully, the court's sound reasoning for rejecting service by publication will be adopted by more courts and this antiquated method will finally fall by the wayside:

> The problem, however, with publication service is that it is almost guaranteed *not* to provide a defendant with notice of the action for divorce, or any other lawsuit for that matter. [In divorce cases] brought in New York County, plaintiffs are often granted permission to publish the summons in such newspapers as the *New York Law Journal* or the *Irish Echo*. If that were to be done here, the chances of defendant, who is neither a lawyer nor Irish, ever seeing the summons in print, either in those particular newspapers or in any other, are slim to none. The dangers of allowing somebody to be divorced and not know it are simply too great to allow notice to be given by publication,

11. *Id.* at *3.

> a form of service that, while neither novel or unorthodox, is essentially statutorily authorized nonservice. This is especially so when, as here, there is a readily available means of service that stands a very good chance of letting defendant know that he is being sued.[12]

The court also outlined how the service had to be executed. Because a party is not allowed to effect service themselves on another party, the plaintiff's lawyer needed to access the plaintiff's Facebook account and message the defendant by first identifying himself and then including either a website address with the summons or pasting an image of the summons in his Facebook message. The plaintiff's lawyer was ordered to repeat this process for three consecutive weeks or until the message was acknowledged by the defendant. After sending the initial message through Facebook, the plaintiff or her lawyer had to call and text the defendant to inform him that a summons for divorce proceedings had been sent to him via Facebook.

This opinion received lots of news coverage when it was issued, so it is worth citing and looking for other cases that followed it,[13] in cases where substitute service cannot be effected and social media is the only practicable way of serving a party.

3.1.2 International Service and the Hague Convention

The trend toward service of summons via social media really got its kick-start in serving people outside the United States. For service on persons in a foreign country, Federal Rule of Civil Procedure 4(f)(3) is the subpart parties use to obtain a court order allowing service to defendants through a nontraditional method such as email—and yes, in some cases, through Facebook. Rule 4(f)(3) provides in pertinent part:

> Unless federal law provides otherwise, an individual—other than a minor, an incompetent person, or a person whose waiver has been filed—may be served at a place not within any judicial district of the United States:
>
> . . .
>
> (3) by other means not prohibited by international agreement [such as the Hague Convention on the Service Abroad of Judicial and Extrajudicial Documents], as the court orders.

When serving persons or businesses not located in the United States, service must comply with the Hague Convention on the Service Abroad of Judicial and

---

12. *Id.* at *4–5. Internal citations omitted.

13. As of this printing, these include Nationwide Affinity Ins. Co. of Am. v. Martinez, 2020 N.Y. Slip Op. 31187 (N.Y. Sup. Ct. 2020) (requiring plaintiff to seek alternate forms of service); Lcxag v. 1.274M U.S. Dollar Coin, 2022 N.Y. Slip Op. 32834 (N.Y. Sup. Ct. 2022) (approving service by Facebook messenger in divorce action); Searles v. Archangel, 60 Cal. App. 5th 43 (Cal. Ct. App. 2021).

Extra-Judicial Documents in Civil or Commercial Matters if the defendant resides in a country that is a party to the Hague Convention.[14] Interestingly enough, if a country is a party to the Hague Convention but has objected to Article 10 that allows service via mail (postal channels), this does not necessarily rule out getting a court order allowing service of the defendant through electronic means if the plaintiff does not have a physical address for the defendant in the country. Federal courts have reasoned that service by electronic means may be allowable because absent application of the Hague Convention (due to the signing country having objected to the service-of-summons provision), it's not apparent that there is any governing international agreement.[15]

- **Service via Facebook or Other Social Media**

Because of the challenges of serving a foreign national who does not live or work in the United States, courts are starting to allow electronic service via social media. It's important to note, however, that electronic service is viewed in the majority of cases as "supplemental" service used in combination with more accepted methods such as via mail. In other words, when seeking leave to serve a party through electronic service, include traditional methods for service as well, to bolster your chances that the court will grant your motion, or document why those methods are untenable.

- **Remove the Legal Hurdles in Your Way**

A plaintiff must clear a few legal hurdles before a federal district court can consider allowing service electronically via email or social media. First, the plaintiff must demonstrate that there is no international agreement barring service via email. If there is such a prohibition, then the plaintiff does not have a realistic chance of convincing a court to allow service via social media. Courts are likely to group social media as a less favored "stepchild" of email service. In addition, if the country the defendant lives in is a party to the Hague Convention, then the plaintiff must show that there is no physical address for the defendant in that country.[16] If there

---

14. https://www.hcch.net/en/instruments/conventions/full-text/?cid=17 (last visited Oct. 26, 2022).
15. D.Light Design, Inc. v. Boxin Solar Co., Ltd, 2015 U.S. Dist. LEXIS 14683 (N.D. Cal. Feb. 6, 2015), in which the court allowed service via email on two of the named defendants located in China because their physical addresses were unknown, and at least one of the businesses, Skone Lighting, listed the email address being used for service as its preferred method of contact. Skone Lighting also conducted its business online via email and provided no valid street address when registering its websites. The plaintiffs also showed that emails to the Skone Lighting email address were sent successfully. Similarly, the other defendant, Sailing Motor, listed the email address on its price sheet, and a man identifying himself as the owner of the company provided the email address as the company's contact information to the plaintiff's investigators.
16. Cf. RPost Holdings, Inc. v. Kagan, 2012 U.S. Dist. LEXIS 7566 (E.D. Tex. Jan. 23, 2012).

is a physical address, then the plaintiff must serve the defendant under the Hague Convention.

Next, the plaintiff must show that the social media account belongs to the defendant and that it is not a fake account created in the defendant's name. It helps considerably if the plaintiff can show that the defendant uses the social media account on a regular basis and will receive notice of the legal action through his regular use of Facebook (which is the most common social media account being used for service) or because the defendant has responded to messages sent through Facebook in the last few months.

In a patent and trademark infringement case, *RPost Holdings, Inc. v. Kagan*,[17] the court allowed service via email because the plaintiff RPost Holdings could not identify a physical address for the defendant Kagan, and Kagan's lawyer replied to service via email by refusing to accept service of the complaint on behalf of Kagan and further declined to provide a valid address through which Kagan could be served under the Hague Convention. The court was persuaded that constitutional notions of due process had been served because there was no real doubt that Kagan had been served. The court's order directed RPost Holdings to serve process on Kagan via email to the email address obtained from (Kagan's website) pointofmail.com's web host, by email to Kagan's counsel, and by international registered mail addressed to Kagan's lawyer at his law office in Israel.

- **Social Media Service as a Supplement**

Next, the party seeking relief from the court must show that traditional service methods will not work or, alternatively, that the party, in an overabundance of caution, wants to add service through social media but still plans to serve the other party through at least one traditional service method.

In a case in which the defendants were located in India, a federal district court allowed service of pleadings related to injunctive relief via email and Facebook. In *FTC v. PCCare*,[18] the plaintiff agency was allowed to serve via email and Facebook the individual and entity defendants in India who were accused of swindling United States citizens to "fix" nonexistent computer problems. Significantly, for the district court, the Federal Trade Commission (FTC) was seeking leave to serve pleadings other than the initial summons and complaint, which had been served by personal service on the defendants. Because the subject pleading was not the initial service of process, the Hague Convention did not apply.[19] Also, there was sufficient evidence showing that the defendants would receive the pleadings via email because they

17. *Id.*
18. FTC v. PCCare, 247 Inc., 2013 U.S. Dist. LEXIS 31969 (S.D.N.Y. Mar. 7, 2013).
19. *See* SEC v. Credit Bancorp, Ltd., 2011 U.S. Dist. LEXIS 14797 (S.D.N.Y. Feb. 14, 2011) (citing Volkswagenwerk Aktiengesellschaft v. Schlunk, 486 U.S. 694, 700 (1988)).

had communicated with the court using those very email addresses. Thus, service via email alone would satisfy due process.[20] In the case, defense counsel had withdrawn between the service of the complaint and the injunction related pleadings, so serving the defendants' now former counsel wasn't an option. The district court was reassured about allowing service on the Facebook account because the FTC had offered evidence demonstrating that the account used the same email address through which some of the defendants had previously communicated with the court.

- **Countries Allowing Service via Social Media**

Courts in other countries have used a similar approach before issuing an order allowing service of a party via social media. The party moving for an order to allow service via social media must show that 1) there is a reasonable likelihood that the other party will learn of the legal action and 2) through no fault of the moving party, there is no conventional method available for serving the party.

Discussed below are some of the countries allowing service via social media. These cases are helpful not only if you have a case in one of these countries, but also if you're trying to convince a U.S. court to issue an order allowing service on a party who resides in one of them. In other words, there is some legal precedence in the foreign jurisdiction for what you're asking the court to do.

- In Australia, a court allowed substituted service via Facebook of a default judgment. The creditor foreclosed on two borrowers who missed payments on their home loan and a default judgment was entered against them. The defendant debtors could not be served through personal service.[21]
- In Canada, a judge allowed "substitutional service" to occur with a three-pronged approach for ensuring that the defendant learned of the action: 1) service by publication with a notice in the newspaper, 2) forwarding a copy of the statement of claim to the human resources department where the defendant had previously worked, and 3) sending notice of the action to the defendant's Facebook account.[22]

---

20. *Id.* at *12–13. Service by email alone comports with due process where a plaintiff demonstrates that the email is likely to reach the defendant. Gurung v. Malhotra, 279 F.R.D. 215, 220 (S.D.N.Y. 2011); *see also* Philip Morris USA Inc, v. Veles, Ltd., 2007 U.S. Dist. LEXIS 19780, at *9 (S.D. N.Y. Mar. 13, 2007) (authorizing service by email where "defendants conduct business extensively . . . through their Internet websites and correspond regularly with customers via email" and rejecting "[d]efendants' objections about theoretical reliability of email service" where plaintiff "amply demonstrated the high likelihood that defendants would receive and respond to email communications"); Williams-Sonoma, Inc. v. Friendfinder Inc., No. C 06-06572 JSW, 2007 U.S. Dist. LEXIS 31299, at *5 (N.D. Cal. Apr. 17, 2007) (authorizing service by email where plaintiff "has established that the email accounts [it has] for defendants have been effective means of communicating with defendants").
21. MKM Capital Property Limited v. Corbo and Poyser, No. SC 608 of 2008 (Canada).
22. Knott v. Sutherland (Feb. 5, 2009) Edmonton 0803 002267 (Alta.Q.B.M.).

- In New Zealand, the High Court allowed service via Facebook in a commercial litigation concerning failed business transactions. Traditional methods of service were unsuccessful because the defendant could not be located, so the court allowed service through Facebook.[23]
- In South Africa, the court granted an application for substituted service of a notice of set down (a.k.a., trial notification) and pretrial directions on the respondent via Facebook message, in addition to published notice in a local newspaper.[24]
- In the United Kingdom, courts appreciate that plaintiffs should not be left without legal recourse when a defendant cannot be served through conventional means. In *AKO Capital LLP v. TFS Derivatives*,[25] the High Court allowed service of a commercial claim via Facebook in a case regarding an alleged business scam because it was difficult to locate one of the parties involved. The court ordered that the relevant documents could be sent as PDF attachments to a private message. Service was deemed to have occurred fourteen days after the message was sent. In *Blaney v. Persons Unknown*,[26] the United Kingdom High Court allowed an injunction against an anonymous blogger to be served via Twitter. The court allowed the service because the defendant was only known by his Twitter "handle" and could not be identified in another way.

3.1.3 What You Need to Show

Put simply, a party is expected to show the following:

1. The resident state law allows for alternative service methods when it's impracticable to serve a party through traditional methods.
2. The party trying to effect service has tried the traditional methods and been reasonably diligent in their efforts.
3. Due process interests will be met because the alternative method is expected to work—the person being served will actually receive the summons and complaint and have the opportunity to defend himself before a default judgment is entered against him (i.e., it was a recent method of communication between the parties).

---

23. Axe Market Gardens v. Craig Axe, CIV: 2008-485-2676 (New Zealand).
24. CMC Woodworking Machinery (Pty) Ltd v. Pieter Odendaal Kitchens (KwaZulu-Natal High Court, Durban, South Africa).
25. AKO Capital LLP v. TFS Derivatives (2012) (Feb. 17, 2012), United Kingdom and Wales, unreported (HCJ).
26. Blaney v. Persons Unknown (Sept. 2009), reported on by Bobbie Johnson, "High Court approves injunction via Twitter," The Guardian (Oct. 1, 2019), https://www.theguardian.com/technology/2009/oct/01/twitter-injunction (last visited Oct. 26, 2022).

When sending service via electronic means, research whether there's a feature that allows you to receive confirmation that your message was opened. For example, Microsoft Outlook allows you to attach a "Delivery" or "Read" receipt to emails, and Facebook messages have a date-stamped "Seen" feature.[27] In fact, this is a theme we'll revisit in this book: the importance of being able to connect the dots between a party and their social media accounts. There are ways to accomplish this, which will be discussed as they apply in respective chapters. For example, besides using the date-stamped "Seen" feature in Facebook, it's also helpful to demonstrate that the defendant has been using their Facebook account around the time of your service. This can be done if their page is public or if they post photos with visible date stamps or photos that show the approximate date they were posted (which you can also see by monitoring the page and taking screenshots when there is activity). If the page is private and you cannot see posts or photos, then ask the court to conduct an in camera review of the defendant's Facebook private page around the time you served them via Facebook before deciding the defendant's motion to set aside your default judgment (which is often when a defendant who has been evading service will make a special and limited appearance).

3.1.4 Mistakes to Avoid

Remember that electronic service is viewed by courts as a method of last resort. Here's what to avoid.

1. Not having your process server make sufficient attempts to serve someone at a residence or place of business. Put simply, if you have a physical address for a party, then find a way to serve them there. Courts are not going to set aside due process concerns just because it's expensive or time consuming to send your process server back again and again.[28]

2. The more complicated and elaborate your scheme to serve the defendant, the less likely a court will go along with it. Frustrated with being unable to serve a foreign defendant who had disabled its email accounts, the plaintiff in a 2012 trademark infringement case proposed setting up a website to

---

27. Some courts have actually required the plaintiff to set up some tracking method to establish that the summons and complaint would have been received via email.

28. *See* Joe Hand Promotions, Inc. v. Shepard, 2013 U.S. Dist. LEXIS 113578 (E.D. Mo. Aug. 12, 2013), in which the court held that service via Facebook was insufficient because the plaintiff had traced the defendant to a new eating establishment that the defendant opened and could have persevered to serve the defendant there. Instead, the process server made service attempts when the bar was closed and did not make any attempts when the bar was open and there was an actual chance of serving the defendant. The plaintiff's prior unsuccessful attempts to find the defendant at his old business address (which had been vacant for a while) or at a residence address that was now vacant did not excuse the plaintiff from not serving the defendant at his new restaurant business.

give defendants' notice of the lawsuit, arguing that the defendants were monitoring the legal action. The motion was denied.[29]

3. Don't let success in getting the motion for electronic service granted make you slack off on due diligence. If the defendant later comes forward and tries to set aside a judgment on the claim that they never received service, you want to have good records of the kind of documentation mentioned above: verification of receipt of an email or message; screenshots of concurrent activity on the defendant's social media site; or, if you really hit the jackpot, the defendant commenting on the fact that they have been summoned. It sounds like a crazy thing for someone to post, but remember back to the beginning of this book: people often say very foolish things on their social media sites.

3.2 Specific Personal Jurisdiction and Defendants with "Digital Footprints"

The question of whether a court has personal jurisdiction over a nonresident defendant would be much easier to answer if we could make the argument that anyone with a website is open for business wherever in the United States potential customers may be—or, alternatively, that there is personal jurisdiction when a business has an active social media presence with connections (Twitter followers or Facebook "likes") in the state in which the plaintiff has filed their action. However, this is not where courts have landed on this issue. Not surprisingly, courts draw upon well-established rules of civil procedure in deciding whether there is specific personal jurisdiction over a defendant who has a digital presence in the state through the internet but who doesn't have a brick-and-mortar store there.

These digital footprint cases are usually not cases where the court can exercise general personal jurisdiction over an out-of-state defendant. For general personal jurisdiction to apply, the out-of-state defendant must have engaged "in continuous and systematic general business contacts that approximate physical presence in the forum state."[30] This is not the typical case with a nonresident defendant who does business through a website or a social media account.

---

29. In Liberty Media Holdings, LLC v. Gan, 2012 U.S. Dist. LEXIS 18553 (D. Colo. Jan. 14, 2012), the court declined to allow service by publication on the internet even though the plaintiff argued that the defendant had disabled its website in this trademark infringement case around the same time that the court had granted a motion seeking early discovery in the case. The court held that there was still insufficient evidence to show that the defendant would learn of the legal action through the website, while recognizing that the defendant had seemingly cut off plaintiff from every means to serve him. The court also declined to order a nonparty website host provider to divert traffic from defendant's websites to the internet publication website that plaintiff proposed setting up in order to set up a more foolproof method of giving defendant notice of the legal action.

30. Mavrix Photo, Inc. v. Brand Technologies, Inc., 647 F.3d 1218, 1228 (9th Cir. 2011) (quotations omitted); Helicopteros Nacionales de Colombia, S.A. v. Hall, 466 U.S. 408, 414–16 (1984).

Accordingly, we will zero in on specific personal jurisdiction, which focuses on whether the nonresident defendant has numerous contacts with the forum state and whether these contacts include the acts that led to it being sued in the forum state. This is harder to show when the nonresident defendant has a passive website that is not targeting forum state residents or if the defendant has a social media site but the actions giving rise to the lawsuit don't concern his social media activity. For example, in *Woodhurst v. Manny's, Inc.*,[31] a bar in Illinois couldn't be sued after one of its patrons crossed a few miles over the border into Iowa and killed someone in a bar there. It didn't matter that the Illinois bar was using Facebook and MySpace because there was nothing on those pages to indicate that Manny's, the defendant bar, was advertising directly to Iowans. The *Woodhurst* court looked at whether "there was 'some act by which the defendant purposefully avail[ed] itself of the privilege of conducting activities within the forum State, thus invoking the benefits and protections of its laws.'"[32]

In *Facebook, Inc. v. Teachbook.com, LLC*,[33] the Ninth Circuit court applied a three-part test for deciding whether the court had specific personal jurisdiction over the defendant in a trademark infringement action. The court found that Teachbook having an internet presence was not enough for personal jurisdiction over the defendant because Teachbook was not looking to sign up users from California. The Ninth Circuit three-part test is similar to tests applied in other circuits:

1. The nonresident defendant must purposefully direct activities or consummate some transaction with the forum or resident thereof; or perform some act by which they purposefully avails themselves of the privilege of conducting activities in the forum, thereby invoking the benefits and protection of its laws;

2. the claim must be one which arises out of or is related to the defendant's forum-related activities; and

3. the exercise of jurisdiction must comport with fair play and substantial justice.[34]

---

31. Woodhurst v. Manny's, Inc., 832 N.W.2d 384 (Iowa Ct. App. 2013).
32. Goodyear Dunlop Tires Operations, S.A. v. Brown, 131 S. Ct. 2846, 2854 (2011) (quoting Hanson Denckla, 357 U.S. 235, 253 (1958)); *accord* Capital Promotions, L.L.C. v. Don King Prods., Inc., 756 N.W.2d 828, 833 (Iowa 2008) (stating a plaintiff must, as an initial matter, show that "'the defendant has purposefully directed his activities at residents of the forum and the litigation results from alleged injuries that arise out of or relate to those activities'") (quoting Burger King Corp. v. Rudzewicz, 471 U.S. 462, 472–73 (1985)).
33. Facebook, Inc. v. Teachbook.com, LLC, 2011 U.S. Dist. LEXIS 48590 (N.D. Cal. May 2, 2011).
34. *Id.* at *5; *see* Schwarzenegger v. Fred Martin Motor Co., 374 F.3d 797, 802 (9th Cir. 2004).

In *Facebook*, the court held that Teachbook was using essentially a passive internet advertisement through its website. While Teachbook was alleged to be competing against a California resident—Facebook—with its social and professional networking site for teachers, Teachbook was not competing in California because Teachbook had not registered any California users, nor was it trying to sign up California users. In fact, Teachbook offered evidence that it purposely avoided the California market. The court therefore found that none of the acts were "purposefully directed" at California.[35] It was not enough that Teachbook was competing with a California resident, as Facebook had argued. The case was dismissed for lack of personal jurisdiction and refiled by Facebook in Illinois, where Teachbook is a resident.[36]

3.2.1 "Zippo Sliding Scale" Test

Having a passive website—one in which the defendant has simply posted information that's accessible to online users and then does little more than make information available to anyone who expresses an interest in it—will not by itself result in personal jurisdiction. Courts look for 1) the interactivity of the defendant's website, 2) the geographic scope of the defendant's commercial ambitions, and 3) whether the defendant "individually targeted" a plaintiff known to be a forum resident.[37] These factors are gleaned from what is referred to as the "Zippo Sliding Scale" test:

> [O]ur review of the available cases and materials reveals that the likelihood that personal jurisdiction can be constitutionally exercised is directly proportionate to the nature and quality of commercial activity that an entity conducts over the internet. This sliding scale is consistent with well developed personal jurisdiction principles. At one end of the spectrum are situations where a defendant clearly does business over the internet. If the defendant enters into contracts with residents of a foreign jurisdiction that involves the knowing and repeated transmission of computer files over the internet, personal jurisdiction is proper. At the opposite end are situations where a defendant has simply posted information on an internet Web site which is accessible to users in foreign jurisdictions. A passive Web site that does little more than make information available to those who are interested in it is not grounds for the exercise [of] personal jurisdiction. The middle ground is occupied by interactive Web sites where a user can exchange information with the host computer. In these cases, the exercise of jurisdiction is

35. Facebook, Inc., 2011 U.S. Dist. LEXIS 48590, at *10.

36. *See* Facebook, Inc. v. Teachbook.com LLC, 819 F. Supp. 2d 764 (N.D. Ill. 2011), in which a federal district court in Illinois denied Teachbook's motion to dismiss for failure to state a claim.

37. Pooka Pooka LLC v. Safari Beach Club LLC, 2013 U.S. Dist. LEXIS 56900, at *13 (N.D. Cal. Apr. 17, 2013).

determined by examining the level of interactivity and commercial nature of the exchange of information that occurs on the Web site.[38]

- **Federal Cases with Specific Personal Jurisdiction**

In *Mighty Men of God, Inc. v. World Outreach Church of Murfreesboro, Tennessee*,[39] the plaintiff alleged injuries to its business in Florida from the defendants holding conferences, maintaining websites, and selling products incorporating the "Mighty Men" mark of the plaintiff. The defendants were individuals and non-profit corporations located in Tennessee. The defendants didn't dispute that they were competitors of the plaintiff and didn't rebut the allegations of the complaint with anything more than what the court described as self-serving conclusory declarations that they were not directing advertising into Florida or directly targeting Florida through their website, mightymenusa.org. The court denied the defendants' motion to dismiss for lack of personal jurisdiction and found that there was jurisdiction under Florida's long-arm statute.

In *Mrs. U.S. National Pageant, Inc. v. Miss U.S.A. Organization, LLC*,[40] a non-resident website located in South Carolina was subject to personal jurisdiction in New York State because its national marketing campaign seeking contestants from each respective state for its beauty talent competitions specifically sought a response from residents of all fifty states. According to the ruling, a website may be found to "target" a forum state for the purposes of personal jurisdiction merely by actively soliciting responses from residents of every state, and it is therefore unnecessary for the website to specifically single out the forum state as a particular focus of its commercial activity.

- **State Cases with Specific Personal Jurisdiction**

There are numerous cases in each jurisdiction that address service of process. Unfortunately, there is some divergence in how some states handle service and few reported state cases addressing service and social media. It is suggested that you research current case law in your particular state or jurisdiction to find updated case law or rules governing such.

In *Hale v. Richey*,[41] a Texas court held that there was specific personal jurisdiction through the Texas long-arm statute in a libel case over the defendant and appellant (Hale), a California resident who allegedly defamed the plaintiff (Richey),

---

38. Zippo Manufacturing Co. v. Zippo Dot Com, Inc., 952 F. Supp. 1119, 1124 (W.D. Pa. 1997).
39. Mighty Men of God, Inc. v. World Outreach Church of Murfreesboro, Tenn., 2015 U.S. Dist. LEXIS 44685 (M.D. Fla. Apr. 6, 2015).
40. Mrs. U.S. Nat'l Pageant, Inc. v. Miss U.S.A. Org., LLC, 875 F. Supp. 2d 211 (W.D.N.Y. 2012).
41. Hale v. Richey, 2012 Tex. App. LEXIS 261 (Tex. App. Jan. 11, 2012).

a Texas resident.[42] Personal jurisdiction was based on 1) the defendant allegedly sending messages through the internet, cellphone texting, and Facebook to people residing in Texas in which the defendant made false, negative statements about the plaintiff's involvement in a trust and the administration of the trust (in which the defendant was a beneficiary); 2) statements attributed to the defendant in national publications that attacked the plaintiff; and 3) the statements alleged to be libelous concerned a trust that was being administered in Texas.

- **Federal Cases Without Specific Personal Jurisdiction**

In *Ackourey v. Sonellas Custom Tailors*,[43] plaintiff Ackourey alleged that the defendant infringed his copyright by having images of Ackourey's fashion designs on the defendant's website. The court affirmed the district court's granting the defendant's motion to dismiss for lack of personal jurisdiction. Ackourey failed to show that Sonellas Custom Tailors, the Oregon defendant, had sufficient contacts with Pennsylvania, based on Sonellas's passive website. The website was set up to receive emails from customers requesting appointments for tailor services and to display a calendar showing Sonellas's availability for appointments throughout the United States. However, it didn't allow customers to place orders, make payments, or conduct other business on the website. Further, the court couldn't exercise jurisdiction over the defendant because it happened to order a stylebook with fashion designs that Ackourey shipped from Pennsylvania. Ordering something from another state wouldn't lead a reasonable person to anticipate he can be pulled into court there. There was no evidence that the defendant traveled to Pennsylvania for business appointments or that he had a customer base in Pennsylvania. It wasn't enough that the defendant may have satisfied the rare order from Pennsylvania customers referred to him by another tailor. In other words, under the Zippo Sliding Scale test, Sonellas did not have an active website on which he engaged in business with Pennsylvania residents. It wasn't enough that the defendant's website allegedly infringed Ackourey's copyright by having images of Ackourey's fashion designs on the Sonellas website.

In *Monkton Insurance Services v. Ritter*,[44] the court affirmed the district court's dismissal for lack of personal jurisdiction in a breach of contract action because there was not a sufficient showing that the third-party defendant, a Cayman Islands-based bank, had engaged in business in Texas. The bank's website confirmed that it was a Cayman Islands-based business and that while it conducted business with Texas, which the court noted was in response to actions taken by Ritter, it wasn't doing business in Texas. Further, the wire transfers from the Cayman bank to Texas residents were initiated by the third-party plaintiffs, not the Cayman bank.

---

42. This is an example of a case where personal jurisdiction was based in part on alleged acts that were made by an individual over the internet. It is not a case of applying the Zippo Sliding Scale test to a passive website.
43. Ackourey v. Sonellas Custom Tailors, 573 F. App'x 208 (3d Cir. Pa. 2014).
44. Monkton Ins. Servs. v. Ritter, 768 F.3d 429, 432 (5th Cir. Tex. 2014).

In *Best Odds Corp. v. iBus Media Ltd.*,[45] the court held in a trademark infringement case that it lacked personal jurisdiction over non-United States-based defendants that used the plaintiff's registered mark, MacPoker, on their global website. The plaintiff and defendants were competitors providing news about poker and the gaming industry on their respective websites. The plaintiff tried to use the defendants' media kits, which stated that the defendants had a "significant U.S. presence," to demonstrate that the court had personal jurisdiction. Looking to the actual links on the defendants' website to online poker rooms, however, the court found that it clearly stated that it was "Not Accepting US Players." Further, the court found that nothing on the defendants' interactive website indicated the defendants were targeting United States citizens, let alone Nevadans. Rather, the website's focus was on being a "global network."

- **State Cases Without Specific Personal Jurisdiction**

In *Wilkerson v. RSL Funding L.L.C.*,[46] Wilkerson, a California resident, successfully challenged the Texas court exercising jurisdiction over him in a libel suit for posts on websites concerning RSL Funding, a Texas business. RSL Funding had entered into an agreement with Wilkerson's daughter, a California state lottery winner, to pay her a lump sum for an interest in her future lottery payouts. Wilkerson, believing that RSL Funding was not making good on the lump-sum payment and was being unresponsive to calls about the dispute, posted negative reviews about RSL on websites he believed were operated by RSL. As it turned out, Wilkerson had posted his comments on Yahoo! And Yelp business review pages for RSL Funding. RSL Funding argued unsuccessfully that an individual posting on the internet should be subject to the Zippo Sliding Scale test, and because Wilkerson posted on interactive websites like Yahoo! And Yelp, Wilkerson stepped into their shoes, essentially, and was subject to specific personal jurisdiction. The court held that the interactive nature of the websites on which Wilkerson posted is not significant because Wilkerson is a third party using the sites, and there is no evidence showing that Wilkerson was targeting his comments about RSL Funding to people specifically in Texas (unlike the *Hale v. Richey* case described above in which Hale's statements over the internet and social media were directed to people residing in Texas). Significantly, the Texas court held that the Zippo Sliding Scale test for determining jurisdiction over websites does not apply to individuals who just happen to be posting on the websites but do not have an ownership interest in them:

> The dispute presents a question of when personal jurisdiction may be exercised over a defendant based solely upon his use of the internet. Both Wilkerson and RSL suggest that we should use the "sliding scale" analysis often used to evaluate whether jurisdiction may be exercised

---

45. Best Odds Corp. v. iBus Media Ltd., 2014 U.S. Dist. LEXIS 76096 (D. Nev. June 4, 2014).
46. Wilkerson v. RSL Funding L.L.C., 388 S.W.3d 668 (Tex. App. 2011).

> over a nonresident defendant based on the relative interactivity of its website. However, to the extent that the interactive features of Yahoo! And Yelp are the creations of the owners and operators of those websites, the interactive nature of a large-scale ubiquitous internet presence cannot be fully imputed to an individual user such as Wilkerson for the purpose of determining whether he established minimum contacts with Texas sufficient to justify exercising jurisdiction over him. Most Texas cases which apply the sliding-scale jurisdictional analysis to claims based upon internet usage arise from a nonresident defendant's ownership and operation of its own website. The analysis of a website's interactivity is not as useful when determining whether due process permits jurisdiction to be exercised over a third-party individual user of the website.[47]

Put another way, the sliding-scale jurisdictional analysis only applies to cases in which a nonresident defendant's ownership and operation of its own website is giving rise to the claims against the defendant and its website.

Key Points

Identify the forum state law and procedure for seeking a court order allowing service via social media.

Perform due diligence to seek the accepted substitute methods for serving a party: check public records, ask the party to be served, exhaust the party's former addresses, make several attempts to serve the party at what you believe to be its current address. Include with your motion a declaration setting forth how you have essentially left "no stone unturned."

Address why you believe the social media account belongs to the party to be served and propose combining service of summons on the account with established substitute service methods.

Assist the court by laying out how you will alert the party being served to check its social media account for the complaint and summons. In addition to giving notice, due process concerns include giving the party sufficient time to respond to the complaint and avoid a default judgment.

If you are suing a nonresident website and the people associated with it, be prepared to satisfy the Zippo Sliding Scale test: 1) the interactivity of the

47. *Id.* at 675–76.

defendant's website, 2) the geographic scope of the defendant's commercial ambitions, and 3) whether the defendant "knowingly targeted" a plaintiff known to be a forum resident.

Passive websites that are not directly advertising into the state or selling to state residents are likely to have their motion to dismiss for lack of jurisdiction granted, so you may want to sue the defendant where it's located and avoid wasting your client's time and money. As a practical matter, this may entail the additional cost of retaining local counsel or using a local firm, but in the end, it results in a happier client.

Chapter Four

Discovery, Ethics, and Motions to Compel

This chapter covers all aspects of discovering social media activity, from informal searches to formal discovery requests and motions to compel. Informal searches can lead to evidence that will help lay the foundation for getting discovery of private social media pages. Discovering someone's social media footprint and capturing screenshots of it can also help later if you become concerned that they are deleting their social media activity. These screenshots can be persuasive evidence in support of a motion to compel or motion for spoliation sanctions.

Equally important is making sure that the other side cannot make a case that the informal discovery was done improperly. "The best defense is a good offense" is played out in discovery disputes where a party tries to convince the court that the social media evidence being used against them was obtained through unlawful or unethical means. It is therefore important to know how a social media investigation can be conducted, and not to turn a blind eye to how people acting on your behalf are uncovering social media evidence. This is an area where counsel can unwittingly cross the line and open themselves and their clients up to sanctions.

Couple informal investigation with formal discovery requests to obtain copies of discoverable activity on the private pages of a party or witness. Because people tend to engage without filters on social media, there is often good impeachment evidence that the other side may simply object to and refuse to produce voluntarily. Accordingly, this discovery chapter includes legal arguments and authority for bringing and opposing motions to compel.

4.1 Step One: Informal Discovery

The suggestions contained in this chapter for conducting informal discovery of the social media accounts of parties also applies to other actors in a legal action, including without limitation nonparty witnesses, jurors, experts, arbitrators, and even judges. In other words, the usefulness of the information may vary depending on the role of the person in the legal action, but the tools for finding it are pretty much the same.

Because some courts may view discovery of social media activity as akin to a "fishing expedition," start early to discover what public information is out there. The public information can help demonstrate why the private social media activity of a party or witness is discoverable. Sometimes, the accounts can be found with a simple name search. Other times, additional information is needed to narrow the search results. For example, some people may use a fictitious name. In one case, a party was using a completely fictitious name on Facebook. Her Facebook account was found by happenstance when someone was looking at the co-plaintiff's "friends," and the plaintiff appeared as a friend under her fictitious name but with an actual picture of herself. In another case, the plaintiff had a very common name. His accounts were not discovered until he happened to mention in his deposition that he was passionate about bike riding. Googling his name and biking turned up various competitive rides he had done and links to some of his social media accounts. It's worth capturing screenshots of everything on the social media pages and checking back for updates. What may seem insignificant early on may later prove very helpful. As your case proceeds, what evidence is helpful becomes clearer.

In the case of the plaintiff who used a fictitious name, the plaintiff had responded to an interrogatory asking for a list of her social media accounts with an unequivocal statement that she had no social media accounts. A party who is willing to sign a declaration under penalty of perjury denying she has any accounts yet uses a fictitious name on a social media account is the rare case. However, with the suggestions below, you can find even that person on social media.

4.1.1 Search and Find

In many cases, if you know someone's name and the city or state where they live, just doing a simple Google search will help you find them and some of their social media accounts. Accounts on LinkedIn and Facebook appear near the top of search results due to the strong SEO (search engine optimization) of these sites. In addition to a Google search, perform direct searches on each social media site. For these searches, the more background information, the better:

- Name
- City/State
- Email address
- Phone number
- Photograph of the party or familiarity with their appearance

Basic searches are easy to run on social media sites. Most sites can be searched without having an account, but what you can view may be limited if you are not logged in as a user.

- **The Big Three: Twitter, LinkedIn, and Facebook**

To be sure, search each and every social media account that you know the target is, or may be, on. All platforms have some kind of search function, and the "big three" are no exception to the rule. The search box is usually near the top of the home page, near an image of a magnifying glass with the word "search" in the space provided. On Twitter, you can search people by entering their username or their actual name. Unlike on Facebook, Twitter users are authorized to use fictitious names as their username.

Their username will be preceded with the "@" symbol. The search results will show you tweets by that person, as well as tweets in which they are mentioned.

Search Boxes for LinkedIn, Facebook, and Twitter

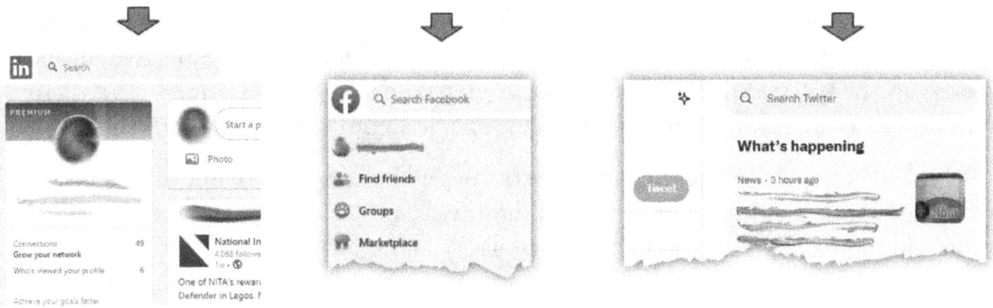

There is also the option of doing more advanced searches on some sites, although this often requires having an account on the site. For example, Twitter allows basic searches without being logged in as a user, but only logged-in users can access and use the Advanced Search feature[1] that helps narrow search results to particular words, persons, places, hashtags, time periods and more. There are three steps to doing an Advanced Search after you have logged in.

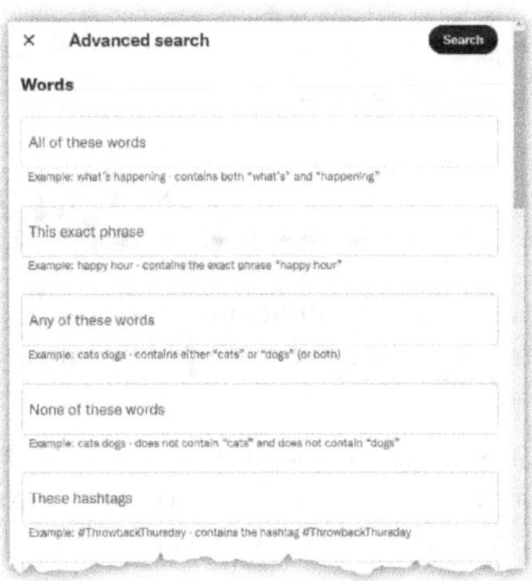

1. This Advanced Search feature is currently available on the desktop version of Twitter, but not the phone or tablet versions.

1. Enter your search term. Example: "Volleyball."

2. On the results page, click on the three dots "..." to the right of the search bar. Then select "Advanced Search." A pop-up box will provide numerous options for your search query.

3. Enter the words that should or should not be included in the results in the appropriate box.

Twitter users do not know who's looking at their account activity or tweets unless someone decides to "follow" them. There's no real reason to follow someone and reveal what you're doing. Further, in the case of actual or prospective jurors, there are state bar ethics opinions that understandably find that following them would be tantamount to an impermissible ex parte communication with them.[2]

LinkedIn requires a user to have an account and be logged in before allowing any searches. After logging in to LinkedIn, however, your searches can be narrowed if you add more details about the person you're looking for.

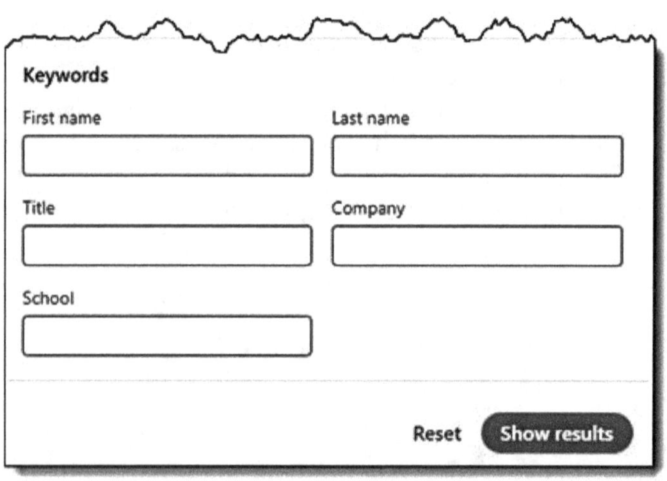

Additionally, the search feature will permit you to select a number of other options such as languages, what the person is "open to," their industry, connections, etc.

If you aren't finding someone through your informal searches, don't give up on asking them to list all their social media accounts through formal discovery requests. Users may have choices on who can search for their profile, how they can

2. New York State Bar Ass'n Social Media Ethics Guidelines, https://nysba.org/app/uploads/2020/02/NYSBA-Social-Media-Ethics-Guidelines-Final-6-20-19.pdf (last visited Oct. 26, 2022).

search for them, and how people can interact with them. These settings may skew your search results and give a false negative when the person actually does have an account on the site.

As social media sites become more robust, they also give the user much more control over what can be seen. For example, below is a screenshot of just a few of the many Facebook settings.

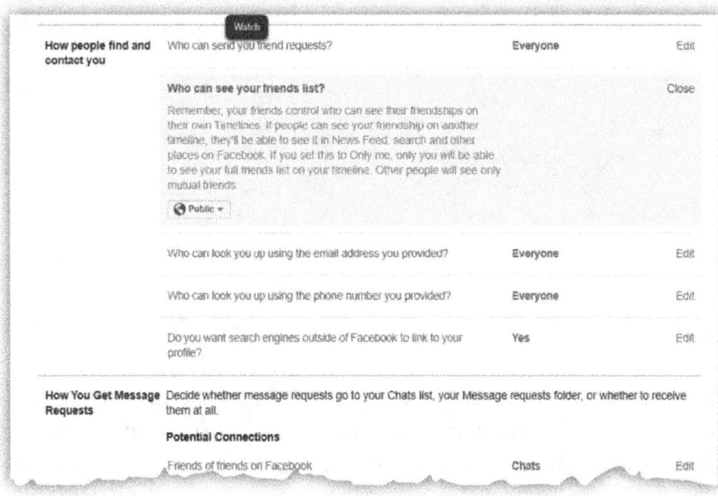

Over time, Facebook has given the user much more control over their privacy. However, by default, user information is fully searchable and viewable by other users. Many users fail to take advantage of the privacy features.

On Twitter, users choose whether they can be found by their email address and can make their tweets private, readable only by accepted followers.

LinkedIn allows users to block people from viewing their profile and to tailor the list of people who can find them through the telephone number listed on their account.

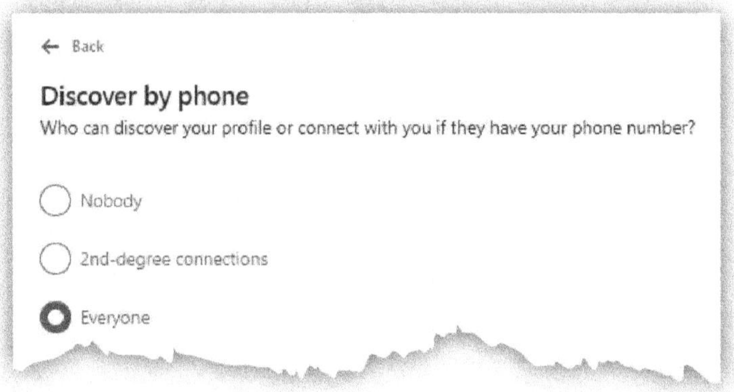

There are three steps to find this feature (and other features that people can use to restrict how searchable they are and how much information can be obtained by people who are not connected to them on LinkedIn):

1. Settings & Privacy
2. Visibility
3. Profile Discovery Phone Number

Under Visibility, there are two major areas with many settings enabling one to limit their visibility. The first is "Visibility of your profile & network":

The second is visibility of your LinkedIn activity:

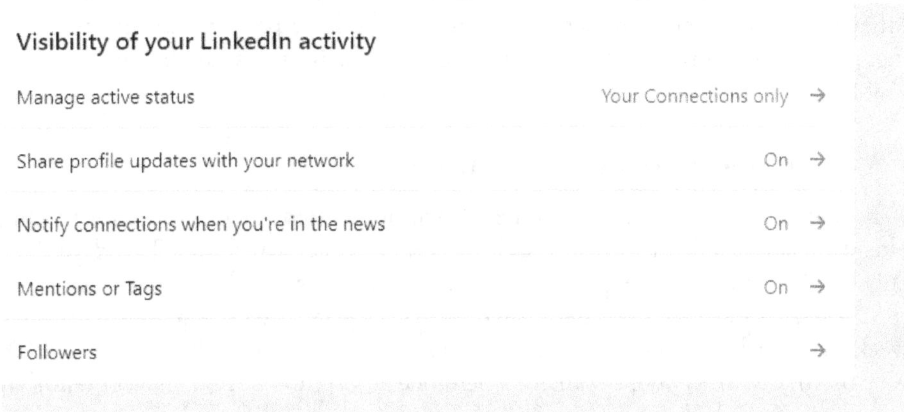

LinkedIn also allows people to restrict who can find their picture to your connections, your network, all LinkedIn members, and public. This feature is accessed through the following steps.

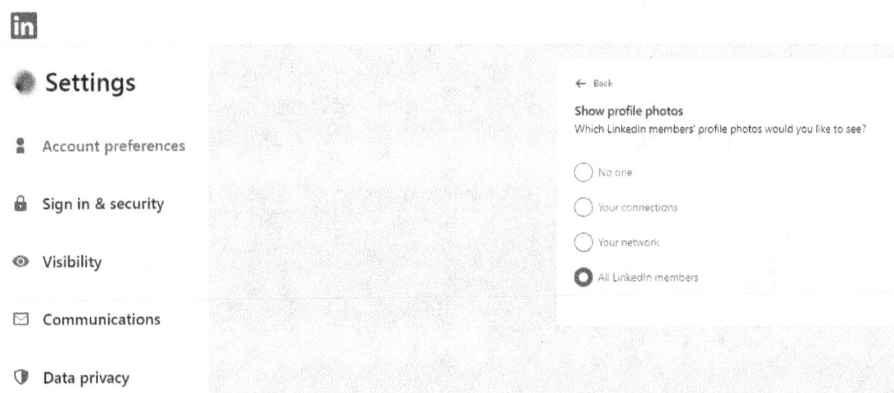

LinkedIn is the only one of the popular sites (Facebook, Twitter, Instagram, Pinterest, YouTube) that shows users who has viewed their profile.[3] Remember to adjust your privacy settings before doing searches if you want your profile to be "anonymous" so people can't see that you've viewed their profile (see Chapter I for instructions on making your LinkedIn profile anonymous).

3. In contrast, when researching someone on online dating sites, many of those sites show users who has looked at their profile. For dating sites, the "help" option may offer suggestions on how to remain anonymous. For example, Match reportedly does not tell users that someone has viewed their profile, provided the person doing the viewing has hidden their profile. However, once the profile is unhidden, then reportedly the person will show up for the user he was viewing.

And on the flip side, it is well within the e-discovery rules and professional codes of conduct for lawyers to recommend to their clients to adjust their LinkedIn or other social media account settings to higher levels of privacy during litigation. Content is not being deleted by adjusting these settings; it's just being made less visible.

- **The Wayback Machine: Website Archive**

Even when a website has been taken down or updated, there's a tool for finding old versions through the internet archive: The Wayback Machine.[4] This digital archive enables users to view previous versions of websites. Established around 1996, the Wayback Machine has archived pages of websites, revisiting sites every few weeks or months to archive a revised version when the content has changed. It's a very useful discovery tool because it's designed to capture and archive content that would otherwise be lost when a site is changed or taken offline.

It does have its limitations though. Some sites never get backed up here and those that do are backed up sporadically. Also, it cannot backup pages that are behind paywalls or that are restricted through security measures.

It may be found at: www.archive.org

4.1.2 Leaked Information

In August 2015, the dating site Ashley Madison was hacked and an estimated forty million account names were made public. Initially, the list of hacked names were only available if you ventured into the "dark web," which is comprised of intentionally "invisible" websites that virtually guarantee anonymity because the website owners' IP addresses are concealed, but the list of hacked names are now searchable on other websites.[5] As a site marketing directly to people who are married but looking to cheat on their spouses, Ashley Madison is worth a snoop to see

4. *See* https://archive.org/web/ (last visited Oct. 26, 2022).
5. For example, https://checkashleymadison.com/ (last visited Oct. 26, 2022).

if a party, witness, expert, or prospective juror appears on the hacked list of users. In some cases, being on Ashley Madison may be completely inconsistent with assertions being made by a party or witness. In other words, knowing the party appears as a user of the site may be a first step to getting a court to order that the party produce their account profile, what they were looking for in a match, and other information that could possibly make parts of their case implode. Not surprisingly, public figures whose names appeared on the list have insisted they didn't create the account. It's quite possible that someone appearing on Ashley Madison didn't create the account registered to their name, so you'll want to look for other indicia besides a name and email address to authenticate the account, such as credit card information and photos associated with the account. The information needed to set up an Ashley Madison profile is a useful guide for finding ways to authenticate the account. According to the Ashley Madison privacy policy in effect in September 2022:

> We collect and receive the following Personal Data and Non-Personal Data directly from you and automatically through your use of our Services:
>
> Data we will request from you
>
> - When you create a profile on our Platform(s), you will be required to provide the following data. Without this data, we will be unable to create an account for you or provide the Services:
>   - create a **username** (a unique name of your choice) and a **password**,
>   - **contact information** (for example, your email address),
>   - your **relationship status**, including what you are looking for from the Services (for example, if you are an attached male seeking females*); and
>   - **demographic information** (your city of residence, zip/postal code and date of birth for the purpose of determining your age).[6]

To address privacy objections that are likely to come up if you seek this information, you need look no further than the Ashley Madison privacy policy, which says Ashley Madison can sell information on its site and doesn't make any assurances that your information will be kept private:

> We may provide Personal Data to third parties in the following limited circumstances:

6. https://www.ashleymadison.com/app/public/privacy (last visited Oct. 26, 2022).

- To **trusted third parties**, to assist us in the provision of the Services and the operation of our business.
    - o We may share your Personal Data with third-party service providers that we have **engaged to perform services on our behalf**, based on our instructions, such as to our parent, subsidiary or sister companies, or to advertising agencies, marketing agents, credit card payment processors, data processing and storage companies or organizations which provide administrative and support services to us.
    - o We limit our disclosure of your Personal Data to such third parties to that which is **reasonably necessary for the purpose** or service for which the third-party service provider is engaged.
    - o We also use **contractual and other means** to provide a comparable level of protection while the data is being Processed by such third parties, including limiting such providers to using your Personal Data solely to provide us with the specific service for which those providers were engaged, and for no other purpose. You can obtain more information about our policies and practices with respect to the use of Personal Data by third-party service providers by contacting dpo@ashleymadison.com.
- To **courts, regulators and law enforcement** as required or permitted by law, including:

    to **government bodies and law enforcement agencies**, pursuant to warrant, order, subpoena or statutory requirement;

. . .

- In the event of a **sale or merger,** including:
    - o as required, in connection with the sale, assignment, bankruptcy proceeding or other transfer of the business or a portion of the business of our Platform(s), including a corporate merger, consolidation, restructuring, sale of assets or other corporate change of our direct or indirect parent companies that affects us, as well as the insurance or securitization of our assets. In any such case, the recipient parties will be required contractually to keep the information confidential and use it only for the purposes of the transaction, or proposed transaction, in question.[7]

7. *Id.* (emphasis in original).

In other words, the same arguments and case law support for why there is not a privacy privilege for social networking sites like Facebook should also apply to the Ashley Madison data. In fact, there is arguably less of a reasonable expectation of privacy because Ashley Madison users are sharing pictures of themselves, and perhaps more, with perfect strangers with whom they hope to have an affair. As Ashley Madison used to say in its tag line:

As we have seen in so many other cases of computer hacking, once information is plastered all over the internet, it is impossible to "put the genie back in the bottle." It would also cut against an attorney's ethical duty to zealously represent the client not to take advantage of this now public information as evidence in the client's case.

4.1.3 Digging in Public Pages

When you find someone's social media account, you may have the "keys to the kingdom" handed to you if they have a public site, meaning they haven't enabled the privacy settings on their account. What is more common these days is that "personal" sites (Facebook, Instagram) will have some level of privacy protection. For example, on Facebook, this looks like only "friends" or "friends of friends" can see their activity. This setting may apply to the entire account, with only the user's profile picture and bio information available, or a user may allow the public to see their list of friends on Facebook and some of their posted pictures and posts related to them. Facebook allows different privacy settings for the various ways in which someone is posting content. The following is an example of privacy settings.

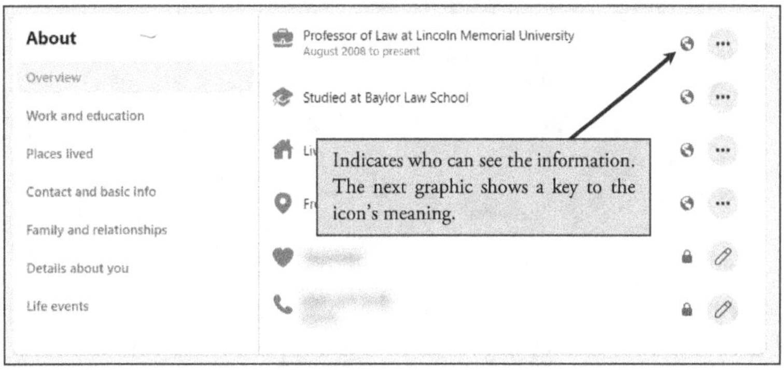

You can click on each icon and set the privacy setting for that particular information.

The look of how these options are presented may change, but the options themselves are, for the most part, the same.

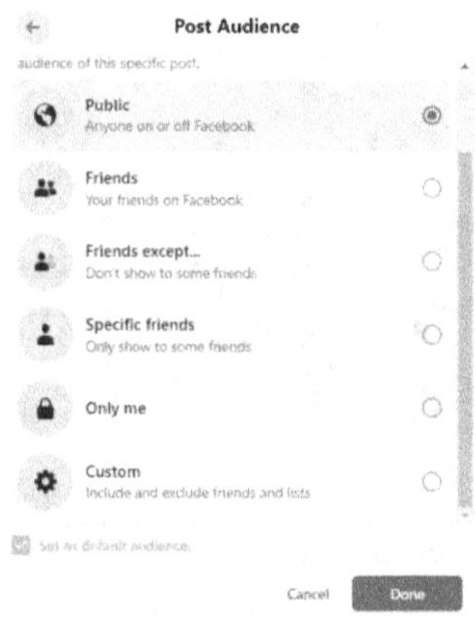

Assuming a semi-private page on Facebook, there's still useful information that can be obtained from profile pictures—current and former—and the list of friends. "More" is also a useful dropdown feature, with information such as videos, places, "likes," and events.

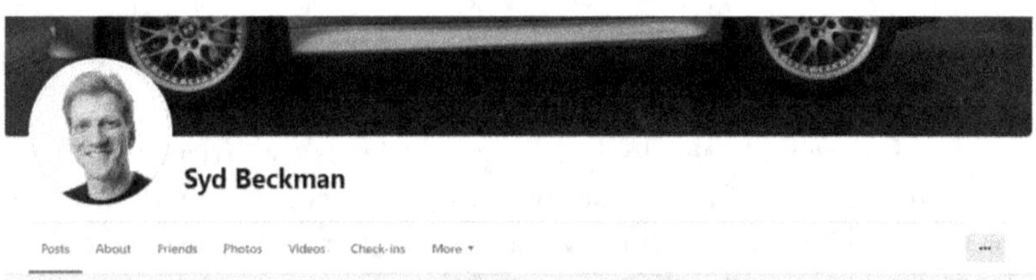

Selecting "More" gives you a popup box with a number of options:

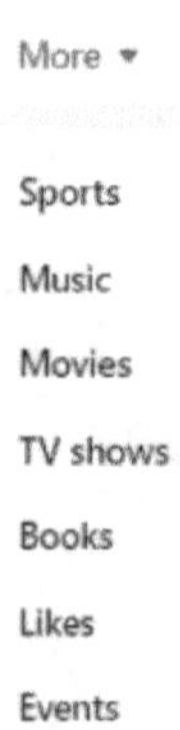

Pictures are often date stamped and may show the person engaged in an activity out of sync with what they're alleging in the litigation.

- **Accounts of Close Friends and Relatives**

The list of friends may also be useful because the names can be searched for relatives or known close friends of the social media user. Relatives and known close friends may have a more public page with posts by and between your target person, comments on their activity by your target person, or pictures that include the target person or even "tag" them, using a feature offered by Facebook and other social media sites.[8]

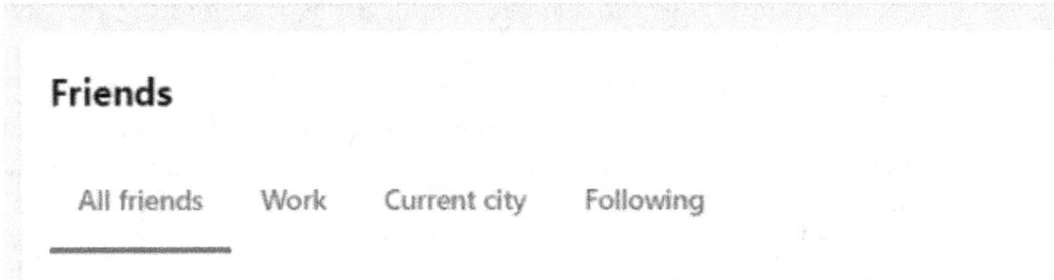

While there are outside vendors that will, for a fee, search the internet for social media accounts and websites belonging to a party or witness, it's useful to know of additional ways to mine their reports by digging deeper into, for example, the perhaps-public pages of their Facebook friends.[9]

Similarly, even if a user's account is private on Twitter, searches for their name will also pull up tweets by other people who have mentioned your target in their public accounts.

As social media usage grows, users often make posts to multiple platforms. Do not limit your searches to Facebook. Always search through platforms that you know are used by the person in question. Consider searching whatever the currently popular platforms are, such as TikTok and Instagram. A search of less popular platforms such as Pinterest may yield fruitful data too.

4.1.4 Making Connections

This is really an area in which to think creatively and outside the box. A list of friends on Facebook or connections on LinkedIn may help impeach a fact witness

---

8. When a Facebook user is "tagged" by a friend, the picture will also post on the user's page unless the user has their settings so they must approve the post in advance. Facebook also gives users the option to untag themselves from a photo.

9. Social Intelligence, www.socialintel.com (last visited Oct. 26, 2022), is one of these companies and has been in business for over ten years offering reports related to insurance claims investigation, employment, security clearance, and background investigations.

or expert because of an online relationship with a party or interested person. Seeing that a proposed arbitrator or assigned judge is connected on social media with a party, their counsel, or a key witness invites further questions about the nature of their relationship and the extent to which that party can be impartial (or at minimum have the appearance of impartiality) in your case.

In addition, think about whether any friendly witnesses in your case are connected on social media with the other side or a hostile witness in the case. Your friendly witness may be willing to print a copy of the entire social media account of the other side or hostile witness—including all the private pages that you wouldn't otherwise have access to. When asking a friendly witness to print these social media pages for you, be candid about who you represent in the legal action, and that you are making the request in order to obtain potentially relevant evidence for your client to use in the litigation. In other words, don't forget your ethical obligations as an attorney. In one case, the plaintiff in a hostile work environment case claimed in sworn discovery responses that her Facebook page was public, when, in fact, a friendly witness was able to provide hundreds of pages that were "private," and that the plaintiff was trying to keep from reviewing and producing in response to formal discovery requests.

4.1.5 Ethics Rules on Judges Using Social Media

A judge's use of social media may lead to them disqualifying themself. The American Bar Association (ABA) Standing Committee on Ethics and Professional Responsibility, in its Formal Opinion 462 (Judge's Use of Electronic Social Networking Media), cautioned judges on their use of social media. With the offline rules in mind, judges shall act at all times in a way "that promotes public confidence in the independence, integrity and impartiality of the judiciary," and avoids the "appearance of impropriety."[10]

The opinion also cautioned judges about the "sharing" nature of social media and that judges shouldn't presume that their posts will stay within their circle of friends and connections. "Comments, images or profile information—some of which might prove embarrassing if publicly revealed—may be electronically transmitted without the judge's knowledge or permission to persons unknown to the judge or to other unintended recipients. Such dissemination has the potential to compromise or appear to compromise the independence, integrity and impartiality of the judge, as well as to undermine public confidence in the judiciary," cautions the opinion. A good example of this is from 2008, when a well-respected Ninth Circuit judge suspended a criminal obscenity trial when sexually explicit

10. ABA Standing Comm. on Ethics & Prof'l Responsibility, Formal Op. 462 (2013) (discussing use of social networking sites by judges); accord Model Code of Judicial Conduct r.1.2 (Am. Bar Ass'n 2010).

content he posted on what he believed was a private website went public and was picked up by national media.[11] He later recused himself from the case and declared a mistrial.[12]

In 2019, the ABA issued Formal Opinion 488, which identified situations when judges must disqualify themselves because their impartiality might be questioned. Although not specifically incorporating the use of social media, the relationships identified in the opinion may be demonstrated by evidence of social media connections.

> [The] opinion identifies three categories of relationships between judges and lawyers or parties to assist judges in evaluating ethical obligations those relationships may create under Rule 2.11 [of the Model Code of Judicial Conduct]: (1) acquaintanceships; (2) friendships; and (3) close personal relationships. In short, judges need not disqualify themselves if a lawyer or party is an acquaintance, nor must they disclose acquaintanceships to the other lawyers or parties. Whether judges must disqualify themselves when a party or lawyer is a friend or shares a close personal relationship with the judge or should instead take the lesser step of disclosing the friendship or close personal relationship to the other lawyers and parties, depends on the circumstances. Judges' disqualification in any of these situations may be waived in accordance and compliance with Rule 2.11(C) of the Model Code.[13]

States have varying rules on whether judges can be "friends" with lawyers appearing before them, so consider researching those rules as well. For example, in *Chace v. Loisel,*[14] the plaintiff wife in a divorce case had her motion to disqualify the judge granted because there was evidence that the judge sent her a friend request on Facebook during the divorce proceedings, which, on the advice of her counsel, she ignored. Later in the case, most of the marital debt was allegedly assigned to the wife and she was ordered to pay what she alleged was an excessive amount of alimony to her ex-husband. The friend request was sufficient to disqualify the judge because it was an ex parte communication that put a party in an untenable position:

> It seems clear that a judge's ex parte communication with a party presents a legally sufficient claim for disqualification, particularly in the

---

11. Scott Glover, *9th Circuit's chief judge posted sexually explicit matter on his website*, L.A. Times (June 11, 2008), http://www.latimes.com/local/la-me-kozinski12-2008jun12-story.html (last visited Oct. 26, 2022).
12. Brief of Defendant–Appellant, United States v. Isaacs, No. 08-50423 (9th Cir. 2008), http://howappealing.abovethelaw.com/USAvIsaacs-oppcircuit.pdf (last visited Oct. 26, 2022).
13. ABA Standing Comm. on Ethics & Prof'l Responsibility, Formal Op. 488 (2019) (discussing relationships with lawyers or parties as grounds for disqualification or disclosure); accord Model Code of Judicial Conduct r.1.2 (Am. Bar Ass'n 2010).
14. Chace v. Loisel, 2014 Fla. App. LEXIS 750 (Fla. Dist. Ct. App. 5th Dist., Jan. 24, 2014).

> case where the party's failure to respond to a Facebook friend request creates a reasonable fear of offending the solicitor. The friend request placed the litigant between the proverbial rock and a hard place: either engage in improper ex parte communications with the judge presiding over the case or risk offending the judge by not accepting the friend request.[15]

Being friends on social media with a witness, however, will not necessarily lead to a judge being disqualified. In *State v. Madden,*[16] the court held that it was not an abuse of discretion to deny the defendant's motion to recuse the criminal court judge because there was no evidence that the defendant had been disadvantaged by any alleged trial court bias. It was not enough for the defendant to show that the judge was Facebook friends with an anticipated prosecution witness. Further, there was no evidence showing that the judge viewed Facebook posts by the prosecution witness concerning the victim, who was a college basketball team athlete who was allegedly killed by the defendant, her college roommate at Middle Tennessee State University.

Similarly, Oklahoma has concluded that it is okay for judges to be social media friends with lawyers who are unlikely to appear before them. Florida prohibits judges and lawyers from friending each other when the lawyers appear in the judge's courtroom. New York, Kentucky, South Carolina, and Ohio are a little more tolerant and allow these friendships on social media.[17] However, judges in these states are cautioned not to have what could be characterized as communications that would give the appearance of the lawyer having an undue influence over the judge. Judges in states allowing these social media friendships are probably well advised to "unfollow" Facebook friends affiliated with a case while it is pending or disconnect with the person if unfollowing is not an option provided by the site. Steps for unfollowing:

1. Click on "Friends" to get your friends list.
2. Next to the person's name you will see three dots.
3. Click on the three dots and you will get a popup box like this:

15. *Id.* at *3.
16. United States Supreme Court certiorari denied by Madden v. Tenn., 2015 U.S. LEXIS 1720 (U.S., Mar. 2, 2015).
17. 2011 Ok. Jud. Eth. 3 (Oklahoma ethics opinion in which other states' professional code of ethics on the "friending" issue are summarized), http://www.oscn.net/applications/oscn/DeliverDocument.asp?CiteID=464147 (last visited Oct. 26, 2022).

4. You can choose to follow or unfollow, friend or unfriend. The friend will not know that you've elected not to see their posts on your timeline.

Judges should avoid 1) posting comments that could be taken as an ex parte communication on a pending or impending matter in the judge's court (Rule 2.9(a) of the Model Code of Judicial Conduct), 2) using social media to obtain information about a pending matter (Rule 2.9(C)), 3) commenting on matters pending before any court (Rule 2.10), or 4) offering legal advice via social media accounts (Rule 3.10).

On the flip side of this are lawyers who make poor judgment calls to try to influence judges using social media and the internet. One Louisiana lawyer, wanting to help her friend who was in a bitter custody dispute with her ex-husband, went too far, according to the Louisiana Supreme Court. The lawyer allegedly launched a social media and internet campaign calling on the public to sign an online petition to judges presiding over related cases concerning custody of the girls and to directly contact the judges about the cases. She was disbarred for making false statements, having ex parte communications with the court by having members of the public contact the presiding judges, and for trying to influence and intimidate the judges with her internet campaign.[18]

4.1.6 Arbitrators and Social Media

Arbitrators are similarly bound to a code of ethics that usually includes avoiding the appearance of bias or partiality. Arbitration rules generally require arbitrators to disclose any relationships between them and parties appearing before them. The American Arbitration Association has a Statement of Ethical Principles[19] that includes a section on "Conflicts of Interest Avoidance," which addresses this disclosure, as well as a court possibly vacating an arbitration award if an arbitrator is found to be biased:

> When an arbitrator or mediator is selected from a list of potential neutrals, (s)he is required to disclose the existence of interests or relationships that are likely to affect impartiality or that might reasonably create an appearance that (s)he is biased against one party or favorable to another.

There is judicial oversight for arbitrator impartiality, as arbitrator bias is one of the grounds for vacating an award.

---

18. *Social Media Campaign Gets Lawyer Disbarred*, Jul. 14, 2015, https://news.bloomberglaw.com/us-law-week/social-media-campaign-gets-lawyer-disbarred?context=search&index=0 (last visited Oct. 26, 2022).

19. Am. Arb. Ass'n, *Statement of Ethical Principles*, at 2, https://www.adr.org/StatementofEthicalPrinciples (last visited Oct. 26, 2022).

Conflicts of interest can be the basis for vacating an arbitration award. In *Benjamin, Weill & Mazer v. Kors,*[20] a motion to vacate an arbitration award was granted because arbitrator Sean SeLegue allegedly did not disclose that his legal practice centered on representing law firms in disputes with their clients and that he was currently involved in representing a law firm in a fee dispute with its former client. The court held that California Code of Civil Procedure Section 1281.9 applied to the arbitration between the parties. Section 1281.9 sets forth the disclosure requirements for an arbitrator, and provides in pertinent part:

> (a) In any arbitration pursuant to an arbitration agreement, when a person is to serve as a neutral arbitrator, the proposed neutral arbitrator shall disclose all matters that could cause a person aware of the facts to reasonably entertain a doubt that the proposed neutral arbitrator would be able to be impartial, including all of the following:
> (1) The existence of any ground specified in Section 170.1 for disqualification of a judge. For purposes of paragraph (8) of subdivision (a) of Section 170.1, the proposed neutral arbitrator shall disclose whether or not he or she has a current arrangement concerning prospective employment or other compensated service as a dispute resolution neutral or is participating in, or, within the last two years, has participated in, discussions regarding such prospective employment or service with a party to the proceeding.
> (2) Any matters required to be disclosed by the ethics standards for neutral arbitrators adopted by the Judicial Council pursuant to this chapter.
> . . .
> (5) Any attorney-client relationship the proposed neutral arbitrator has or had with any party or lawyer for a party to the arbitration proceeding.
> (6) Any professional or significant personal relationship the proposed neutral arbitrator or his or her spouse or minor child living in the household has or has had with any party to the arbitration proceeding or lawyer for a party.

The perceived conflict could have been avoided if the arbitrator had disclosed the case. Alternatively, the arbitrator's conflict was reasonably discoverable, if the defendant in the fee dispute had researched the members of the arbitration panel. She would have found numerous Google hits showing the nature of the arbitrator's practice, including his profile on his law firm's website and his membership in the Association of Discipline Defense Counsel, an organization that describes itself as the "bar association for lawyers who represent lawyers and others in disciplinary,

20. Benjamin, Weill & Mazer v. Kors, 195 Cal. App. 4th 40 (Cal. App. 1st Dist. 2011).

admissions and regulatory proceedings before the State Bar of California and the California Supreme Court." Because Kors was in a fee dispute with her prior counsel, she probably could have asked SeLegue to withdraw as one of three arbitrators, had she known about his potential conflicts.

All of this is to say that arbitrators serve an important role in deciding cases and should look to the previous discussion on how judges should or should not use social media and adopt similar rules for themselves.

4.1.7 Ethical Constraints

If you cannot do it offline, you probably cannot do it online. This is a good way to think about social media and legal ethics. We know that lawyers are not allowed to communicate with a represented party on the other side of a legal action. That prohibition extends to communications over social media, even when such communications aren't direct.

Most states have an ethics rule similar to California Rule of Professional Conduct 2-100, which provides in pertinent part:

> (A) While representing a client, a member shall not communicate directly or indirectly about the subject of the representation with a party the member knows to be represented by another lawyer in the matter, unless the member has the consent of the other lawyer. (B) [A] "party" includes: (1) An officer, director, or managing agent of a corporation . . . or (2) an . . . employee of a . . . corporation . . . if the subject of the communication is any act or omission of such person in connection with the matter which may be binding upon or imputed to the organization for purposes of civil or criminal liability or whose statement may constitute an admission on the part of the organization.

"Rule 2-100 is intended to control communication between a member and persons the member knows to be represented by counsel unless a statutory scheme or case law will override the rule."[21]

Similarly, ABA Model Rule 4.2 provides: "In representing a client, a lawyer shall not communicate about the subject of the representation with a person the lawyer knows to be represented by another lawyer in the matter, unless the lawyer has the consent of the other lawyer or is authorized to do so by law or a court order." Comment 7 to ABA Model Rule 4.2 clarifies that in the case of a represented organization, a lawyer may not communicate with persons whose words or actions may be attributed to the organization:

21. Rule 2-100 Discussion Note.

> In the case of a represented organization, this Rule prohibits communications with a constituent of the organization who supervises, directs or regularly consults with the organization's lawyer concerning the matter or has authority to obligate the organization with respect to the matter or whose act or omission in connection with the matter may be imputed to the organization for purposes of civil or criminal liability.

It is, therefore, not a leap that communicating with represented parties through social media is prohibited. Lawyers may not directly friend a party on Facebook in order to see all of their Facebook activity. It's also unethical to direct someone to friend the other party or arguably to turn a blind eye to them doing it.

Some state bars have also extended this rule to unrepresented parties and witnesses. Namely, it is fine to look at their public social media presence, but lawyers cannot friend them or arrange for it to be done on their behalf. Attempts to friend parties or witnesses in this way usually involves some deception or lack of candor on the part of the lawyer, which is prohibited in many state codes of professional responsibility. ABA Model Rule 4.1 prohibits misleading statements to others: "In the course of representing a client a lawyer shall not knowingly: (a) make a false statement of material fact or law to a third person." ABA Model Rule 4.3 also prohibits lawyers from misleading unrepresented persons by omission or false statements:

> In dealing on behalf of a client with a person who is not represented by counsel, a lawyer shall not state or imply that the lawyer is disinterested. When the lawyer knows or reasonably should know that the unrepresented person misunderstands the lawyer's role in the matter, the lawyer shall make reasonable efforts to correct the misunderstanding.

ABA Model Rule 8.4(c) also applies here because advisory opinions have found that friending an unrepresented witness involves an act of deception. Rule 8.4(c) states: "It is professional misconduct for a lawyer to: (c) engage in conduct involving dishonesty, fraud, deceit or misrepresentation."

This rule is reflected in a number of other state bar rules of professional conduct and would limit lawyers from connecting with unrepresented persons on social media without identifying themselves as a lawyer in a case in which the person may be involved. For example, the Philadelphia Bar Association in Opinion 2009-02 dealt with the question of whether a lawyer could have a third person attempt to friend a witness on her social media accounts in order to gain access to the private parts of her accounts. The third person would use his real name, knowing that the witness would not recognize it in relation to the legal action, and taking advantage of the fact that the witness has a habit of accepting all friend requests. The Opinion concluded the proposed conduct would be deceptive in violation of Rule 8.4(c), and also be a false statement of material fact to a witness in violation of Rule 4.1(a).[22] It would be deceptive because the third person (aka the investigator) would be concealing a material fact that he intended to obtain the information and share it with a litigation attorney for the purpose of hopefully impeaching the testimony of the witness.

The level of disclosure that is required should put off most lawyers from trying to connect online with unrepresented persons. However, if a lawyer is still so inclined, then there probably needs to be enough of a disclosure so that the person receiving the friend request can make an informed decision about accepting, declining, or ignoring the friend request. As a practical matter, though, this may not be doable in combination with the request to connect. Most social media sites are not set up to allow for a message to be sent with the request to connect. This is still uncharted and risky territory because it has not been tested in the courts. The more prudent course of action for lawyers is not to try and connect with unrepresented persons on social media.

These guidelines, however, don't preclude lawyers from observing what's publicly available on social media. It's also permissible for a lawyer to access a social media account using their client's login and password (with the client's consent) and passively view the activity on their client's account without active participation such as commenting on or liking a post. More than passively observing activity on the social media account would give friends of the client the false impression that they were having an online conversation with the client.

These various state bar opinions highlight the importance of knowing how to effectively data mine information on the public pages of social media sites, and then know how to use that information to persuade a court to compel discovery of private social media pages, if necessary.

4.1.8 Sanctions for Unauthorized Discovery Efforts

Taking shortcuts to get to social media activity on the private pages of someone's account without a formal discovery request may lead to sanctions. A very good example of this is the sixteen year royalty dispute between the family that held the lucrative merchandising rights to Winnie the Pooh and the licensee Walt Disney Company. The plaintiff licensor was seeking hundreds of millions of dollars in royalties for Winnie the Pooh-related merchandise, computer software, and videocassettes, only to lose the right to pursue its action as a result of terminating sanctions issued by the trial court and sustained by the court of appeal. The trial court terminated the action after finding that the plaintiff had used unlawful self-help to

22. Philadelphia Bar Ass'n, Prof'l Guidance Comm., Op. 2009-02 (2009), https://philadelphiabar.org/?pg=Opinions20052009. Click on 2009-2 to access the opinion (last visited Oct. 26, 2022).

obtain confidential and privileged documents belonging to the Walt Disney Company, then doctored the documents to conceal what it had done.

In *Stephen Slesinger, Inc. v. Walt Disney Company*,[23] the court of appeal sustained the dismissal and found that the trial court has the inherent power to issue the ultimate sanction based in part on evidence showing that the plaintiff's investigator obtained pages of privileged and confidential documents by trespassing on Disney premises and those of a private disposal site that Disney used—to dig through Disney's trash. At the sanctions hearing, the plaintiff argued unsuccessfully that the Disney office trash receptacles from which they took documents were accessible to the public and, therefore, the taking of the documents was lawful. This case provides a nice analogy for parties who believe that the other side has used deception or unethical means to access the private pages of a party's or witness's social media activity. It's a virtual form of trespass and may result in sanctions.

4.2 Step Two: The Litigation Hold Letter

A litigation hold letter puts the opposing party on notice. Such notice is particularly important given the potential for sanctions in the event discoverable information is lost. Rule 37(e) of the Federal Rules of Civil Procedure sets out potential sanctions:

> **Failure to Preserve Electronically Stored Information.** If electronically stored information that should have been preserved in the anticipation or conduct of litigation is lost because a party failed to take reasonable steps to preserve it, and it cannot be restored or replaced through additional discovery, the court:
> (1) upon finding prejudice to another party from loss of the information, may order measures no greater than necessary to cure the prejudice; or
> (2) only upon finding that the party acted with the intent to deprive another party of the information's use in the litigation may:
> (A) presume that the lost information was unfavorable to the party;
> (B) instruct the jury that it may or must presume the information was unfavorable to the party; or
> (C) dismiss the action or enter a default judgment.[24]

Send the litigation hold letter early as possible. Failure to do so may result in not only lost evidence but also the inability to obtain court intervention or appropriate sanctions under the Rule. A checklist for the contents of a litigation hold letter may be found in the Appendix.

---

23. Stephen Slesinger, Inc. v. Walt Disney Co., 155 Cal. App. 4th 736 (Cal. App. 2d Dist. 2007).
24. Fed. R. Civ. P. 37(e) (2022).

4.2.1 Lay the Groundwork for Spoliation Claims

There are several reasons to send a litigation hold letter to the other side early in the litigation. First, some lawyers still naïvely forget or don't understand that social media activity is discoverable and therefore fail to take steps to preserve it. Second, social media activity can be very helpful in a case, so why risk the other party deleting its content? Third, sending a litigation hold letter lays a nice foundation for obtaining sanctions or other relief from the court.

To support a motion for spoliation sanctions, the moving party must show that the other side knew the evidence was discoverable when it was destroyed:

> Spoliation of evidence is defined as "the destruction or significant alteration of evidence, or the failure to preserve property for another's use as evidence in pending or reasonably foreseeable litigation." "[Parties] engage in spoliation of documents as a matter of law only if they had 'some notice that the documents were potentially relevant' to the litigation before they were destroyed." Therefore, the duty to preserve begins when a party reasonably should have known that the evidence is relevant to anticipated litigation. Moreover, a spoliation remedy requires some degree of culpability. Specifically, prior to imposing sanctions, the court must first make a finding of fault. Then, the court should fashion a remedy which serves "the prophylactic, punitive, and remedial rationales underlying the spoliation doctrine."[25]

Sending a litigation hold letter that sets forth the need to preserve social media evidence and gives examples of how social media content is discoverable in the current case will be very persuasive evidence if the party ignores the letter and deletes social media activity.

A 2010 study found that courts impose strong sanctions against lawyers and their clients for failing to comply with the e-discovery rules.[26] In a study of 401 cases before 2010 in which sanctions were sought, sanctions were awarded in over half of them. Some sanctions were especially severe and included case dismissals, adverse jury instructions, and large monetary sanctions. $5 million in sanctions were ordered in five cases, and $1 million or more in four others. Defendants were sanctioned for e-discovery violations nearly three times as often than plaintiffs, and the number one reason for imposing sanctions was failure to preserve electronic evidence.

25. Painter v. Atwood, 2014 U.S. Dist. LEXIS 35060, at *10 (D. Nev. Mar. 18, 2014) (internal citations omitted).

26. Dan H. Willoughby, Jr., Rose Hunter Jones, Gregory R. Antine, *Sanctions for E-Discovery Violations: By the Numbers*, 60 Duke L.J. 789 (2010), http://scholarship.law.duke.edu/cgi/viewcontent.cgi?article=1487&context=dlj (last visited Oct. 26, 2022).

4.2.2 Recommended Content for Litigation Hold Letter

There's no magical language for a litigation hold letter. However, the letter puts the other side on notice that social media and internet activity, including without limitation Facebook, Twitter, YouTube, LinkedIn, listserv accounts, blogs, and websites, are discoverable and treated the same as other electronically stored information.

- **List social media sites by name.** The letter should specifically highlight sites that an informal investigation has uncovered belonging to the other party and remind the other side (through its legal counsel) that deleting, deactivating, or failing to preserve these accounts may lead to discovery sanctions. If there are multiple parties on the other side who are represented by the same counsel, list all parties in the letter and ask that their counsel individually notify each party of the letter and its discovery obligations.
- **List known usernames for each social media site.** Litigation hold letters should be specific enough to require the preservation of information for both known and unknown sites. Therefore, if you are aware of usernames for particular sites, list those in the letter. If an identical username is used for two or more sites, list those for each site as well.
- **Include generic requests for unknown sites.** It is highly likely that your client will not be aware of each site, app, or platform that the opposing party uses. Because of this, the litigation hold letter should include a generic reference to all social media sites used (both currently and in the past) by the opposing party or parties. Such requests should also reference any and all usernames used (both currently and in the past) by the opposing party or parties. Many people use multiple usernames on various platforms.
- **Cite cases in which a party was sanctioned for not preserving social media activity.** A cite to one or two cases in which discovery sanctions were awarded is suggested; ideally, include one cite that's controlling state or federal case law. In addition to the wrongful death case, *Lester v. Allied Concrete Company*, which we discussed in detail in section 2.1.5 concerning the serious downside of deleting or altering social media activity,[27] here are some other cases in which courts issued sanctions for the spoliation of social media evidence.
- In *Painter v. Atwood*,[28] the plaintiff was a former employee suing her employer—a dentist—for emotional distress damages suffered as a result of the defendant allegedly sexually assaulting her at work. The defendant claimed the sexual nature of their relationship was consensual and that he

27. Lester v. Allied Concrete Co., No. CL08-150 (Va. Cir. Ct. Sept. 1, 2011) *aff'd*, No. 120074 (Va. Ct. App. Jan. 10, 2013).
28. Painter v. Atwood, 2014 U.S. Dist. LEXIS 35060 (D. Nev. Mar. 18, 2014).

was only trying to tickle the plaintiff during the incident in question. The defendant filed a motion for spoliation sanctions after it was discovered that the plaintiff had deleted from Facebook both pictures from a cruise she took with the dentist and his family and posts in which she talked about how much she enjoyed her job in the dentist's office, how he was a great boss, and how much she enjoyed working with him. The defendant asserted that he knew of these posts because his wife had been Facebook friends with the plaintiff when she posted them. The defendant also alleged the plaintiff and two of her key witnesses deleted texts that contradicted her deposition testimony. The trial court declined to terminate the action but granted the relief the defendant requested in the alternative. The trial court held that the jurors would receive adverse inference instructions concerning the Facebook posts that the plaintiff could not retrieve, with jurors being instructed to draw the inference as described in the declaration of the defendant's wife about the plaintiff enjoying her job and working with the defendant.[29] The court was unsympathetic to the plaintiff's claims that she was young and naïve about litigation:

> [A]s the Court stated at the hearing, it is of no consequence that Plaintiff is young or that she is female and, therefore, according to her counsel, would not have known better than to delete her Facebook comments. Once Plaintiff retained counsel, her counsel should have informed her of her duty to preserve evidence and, further, explained to Plaintiff the full extent of that obligation.[30]

- In *Hosch v. Bae Systems Information Solutions, Inc.*,[31] the defendant's motion for sanctions based on discovery abuses and spoliation was granted and the plaintiff's case was dismissed. The plaintiff filed an action for retaliation against his former employer, an aerospace and defense contractor. He claimed he was terminated from his position as the manager of the Eastern-Afghanistan Counter-Intelligence team because he was blowing the whistle about allegedly fraudulent billing practices. The court found that the plaintiff wiped his cellphone and Blackberry clean and deleted pictures, emails, texts, and social media. Most egregious, the defendant demonstrated that the plaintiff started deleting content after he'd already decided to bring his legal action and continued deleting even after he received litigation hold and document preservation letters and discovery for which the ESI would have been responsive. The court found that the plaintiff deleted

29. In *Painter*, the Court set forth the tests that courts in the Ninth Circuit apply in deciding whether terminating sanctions or adverse sanctions are warranted. *Id.* at *22–24.
30. *Id.* at *18.
31. Hosch v. Bae Sys. Info. Solutions, Inc., 2014 U.S. Dist. LEXIS 57398 (E.D. Va. Apr. 24, 2014).

some content after he was warned by the court that he'd be sanctioned if he didn't comply with the court's discovery order. Much of the content wasn't recoverable, and the court saw through the plaintiff's claims that the cellphone content was inadvertently lost when he damaged his SIM card.

- In *Federico v. Lincoln Military Housing, LLC*,[32] military families sued a government contractor for mold conditions in their military housing. The court declined to issue severe discovery sanctions but held that the plaintiffs would be solely responsible for the approximately $29,000 in consultant costs they incurred to have a third party review their numerous emails and social media activity for documents responsive to discovery requests instead of doing it themselves or taking advantage of the "Accessing Your Facebook Data" feature on Facebook. The court noted that the plaintiffs should have expected the discovery requests early in the case because the defendant had sent a litigation hold letter to plaintiffs' counsel outlining the electronically stored information that should be preserved.

- **Briefly summarize the anticipated discovery requests.** Summarize the type of content that needs to be preserved with general and specific descriptions (such as pictures, videos, posts, and other activity relating to the subject matter of the litigation); relating to the party who is serving the discovery request (and any of its employees, customers, vendors, or people acting on its behalf); the nature of the relationship between parties (for example, responding party's employment with the defendant); the damages the party is seeking; the claims and defenses being asserted in the case; and activities, hobbies, trips, and other life events relating to the physical and emotional health of the responding party. Be comprehensive and don't worry about being over-inclusive. Write the letter as much with the court in mind as the party receiving it. Be guided by the document requests you anticipate serving on the other side; ask that the same areas of information on the party's social media accounts be retained. Include instructions for downloading account activity from social media sites that provide a tool for it, such as Facebook.[33]

- **Request written confirmation that the other party will comply.** And, finally, ask for written confirmation that the other side has received the letter, that they understand the obligations being imposed, and that they're taking adequate steps to preserve the electronically stored information in accordance with the discovery rules. Regardless of whether they comply,

32. Federico v. Lincoln Military Hous., LLC, 2014 U.S. Dist. LEXIS 178943 (E.D. Va. Dec. 31, 2014).
33. Facebook instructions on "Accessing Your Facebook Data," https://www.facebook.com/help/405183566203254/ (last visited Oct. 26, 2022).

it may be helpful to have made this request when filing a motion for sanctions.

4.3 Step Three: Formal Discovery Requests

4.3.1 Document Subpoenas for Social Media and Internet Activity

Serving a civil subpoena on a social media site (as opposed to the individual user) for a user's nonpublic content will draw objections that a court should sustain. Social media sites are internet service providers (ISPs) covered under the Stored Communications Act (SCA), 18 U.S.C. §§ 2701, et seq.[34] The SCA limits the government's ability to compel ISPs to disclose information in their possession about their customers and subscribers. Section 2702 provides in pertinent part:

> (a) Prohibitions. Except as provided in subsection (b) or (c)—
>
> (1) a person or entity providing an electronic communication service to the public shall not knowingly divulge to any person or entity the contents of a communication while in electronic storage by that service; and
>
> (2) a person or entity providing remote computing service to the public shall not knowingly divulge to any person or entity the contents of any communication which is carried or maintained on that service . . . .

In the seminal case applying the SCA to social media sites, *Crispin v. Christian Audigier, Inc.*,[35] the plaintiff artist alleged that the clothing brand Christian Audigier, Inc., violated an oral license for the use of his art on garments manufactured by the defendant. The defendant attempted to subpoena Crispin's Facebook and MySpace communications, stating that the communications demonstrate the "nature and terms of the agreement, if any, into which Crispin and Audigier entered." The court held that Crispin had standing to challenge the third-party subpoenas because his private communications are analogous to other personal information like bank records. The court held that Facebook and MySpace are electronic communication service (ECS) providers under the SCA and that the SCA protects any unopened private messages sent via an ECS provider as "temporary" storage.[36] A private and undeleted message that a user opens "renders that communication stored for backup purposes as defined in the statute." Because the SCA applied to the private messages, subpoenas could only be issued under its terms and the magistrate's subpoena failed to meet the stringent standards. The court also held

34. Crispin v. Christian Audigier, Inc., 717 F. Supp. 2d 965 (C.D. Cal. 2010).
35. *Id.*
36. 18 U.S.C. § 2510(17)(A).

that private wall postings and comments are protected under the SCA either as restricted access electronic bulletin boards or because Facebook and MySpace are remote computing service (RCS) providers that provide storage of the comments for the limited use of a few users. In light of *Crispin*, it's more expeditious to serve discovery requests and subpoenas on the person who has the social media account.[37] The subpoena will be served pursuant to Federal Rule of Civil Procedure Rule 45.

Parties in state courts may also run into problems enforcing document subpoenas against social networking sites, many of which are located in California, because their respective state laws may not be empowered to enforce a subpoena duces tecum against a nonparty, nonresident witness. For example, in *Yelp, Inc. v. Hadeed Carpet Cleaning, Inc.*,[38] the Virginia Supreme Court reversed a court of appeal decision affirming a district court order of contempt against a nonparty social networking site that refused to comply with a subpoena duces tecum served on it by the respondent carpet cleaning company. The Virginia Supreme Court held that the district court was not empowered to enforce the subpoena seeking the names of Doe defendants who'd posted Yelp reviews the respondent claimed were defamatory. Yelp was outside the court's subpoena reach because it was a nonparty, nonresident corporation.[39]

4.3.2 Document Discovery and Requests

- **Federal Rule of Civil Procedure 26(a)—Initial Disclosures**

Rule 26(a)(1)(A)(ii) of the Federal Rules of Civil Procedure requires a party to produce "a copy—or a description by category and location—of all documents, electronically stored information, and tangible things that the disclosing party has in its possession, custody, or control and may use to support its claims or defenses, unless the use would be solely for impeachment." Because social media and internet activity are "electronically stored information," a party should include these documents in its initial disclosure to the other party. Because social media is often overlooked by parties and their legal counsel, bring it up in the Rule 26(f) early meeting of counsel.

---

37. *See, e.g.*, In re Subpoena Duces Tecum to AOL, LLC, 550 F. Supp. 2d 606, 609 (E.D.V.A. 2008) (upholding a magistrate judge's order quashing a subpoena requesting a nonparty's emails from AOL because there is no exception in the SCA for such disclosure).
38. Yelp, Inc. v. Hadeed Carpet Cleaning, Inc., 770 S.E.2d 440, 443 (Va. 2015).
39. *Id.* at 446 ("subpoena power was not conferred upon the circuit court by Yelp's act in registering to conduct business in Virginia or designating a registered agent for service of process in the Commonwealth").

- **Federal Rule of Civil Procedure 34—Document Requests**

When requesting social media and internet activity through a discovery request, first update the definition of "documents" so there's no argument later that social media is electronically stored information that should have been produced:

Include social media in the definition section for writings and documents:

> "WRITINGS" or "DOCUMENT(s)" means all documents or electronically stored information pursuant to Fed. R. Civ. Proc. 34(a)(1)(A) including, but not limited to, any written, printed, recorded, graphic or photographic matters of any kind or description, however produced or reproduced, or stored, including, without limitation, any tapes, mechanical recordings, or transcriptions of such recordings or any oral material or other sound or visual reproductions; and drawings, sketches, schematics, blueprints, or any other descriptive materials; any memoranda, logs, notes, calendar schedules; emails, posts and comments on social media sites including without limitation Facebook, Twitter, Instagram, TikTok, LinkedIn, websites and blogs, and other computerized material . . .

Tailor the document requests so they aren't overbroad on their face. True, a document request can be narrowed through the "meet and confer" process. However, taking a little time to craft a document request that reflects discoverable issues in the case will make it harder for the other side to stonewall and refuse to produce any documents. It will also have better optics with a court if a motion to compel is needed. Here are some suggested requests to choose from and modify as needed:

> For each social media account maintained by you at any time since [date], including but not limited to accounts with Facebook, Twitter, Instagram, YouTube, or LinkedIn, produce a copy of all activity for the period from [date] through the present that concerns, relates to, or reflects any of the following: 1) the subject matter of this legal action; 2) your [employment/dealings with] [the party propounding the discovery]; 3) your managers, supervisors, co-workers, or customers of [the party propounding the discovery]; 4) the damages you are seeking in this legal action; 5) your present job or other sources of income; 6) any emotion, feeling, or mental state, as well as communications that reveal, refer, or relate to events that could reasonably be expected to produce a significant emotion, feeling, or mental state [and add specific examples if you have reasonable knowledge of them by way of example].
>
> You may download and print your Facebook data by logging onto your Facebook account, selecting the "Settings and Privacy" from your homepage, clicking on the "Your Facebook Information" link

and then selecting "Download Your Information", and following the directions on the "Download Your Information" page.[40]

Any and all posts on social media accounts, blogs, or websites maintained by you from [year] through the present that reflect, relate to, or refer to any claim or defense at issue in this Action, including, without limitation, your Facebook and LinkedIn accounts.

For employment-related actions:

Each and every document which in any manner evidences, constitutes, reflects, discusses, mentions, comments upon, or refers to you posting on social media sites, blogs, or websites concerning [defendant employer], your [symptoms of disability, *e.g.* headaches], [list managers and supervisors], YOUR emotional state, your mental state, or your efforts to find a new job after being terminated by [defendant].

Here is a screenshot of where Facebook provides this easy production tool for users.

Step One—Select "Settings and Privacy":

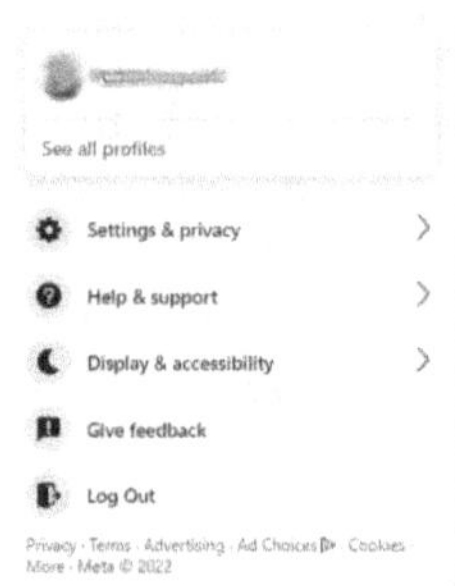

Step Two—Select "Your Facebook Information":

40. Facebook periodically changes how it refers to this feature, so verify and update these instructions as needed when serving a document request.

Step Three—Select "Download Your Information":

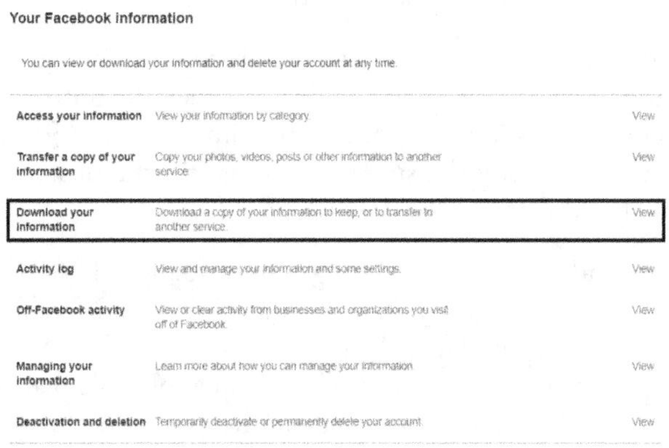

In addition, there's no real downside to throwing in a general request because some responding parties will not object and may just give complete access to the social media accounts:

> For each social media account maintained by you at any time since [date], including but not limited to accounts with Facebook, Twitter, Instagram, YouTube, or LinkedIn [include all applicable platforms], produce a copy of all activity for the period from [date] through the present. You may download and print your Facebook data by logging onto your Facebook account, selecting the "Settings and Privacy" from your homepage, clicking on the "Your Facebook Information" link, and then selecting "Download Your Information" and following the directions on the "Download Your Information" page.

This has happened before: a party has responded by providing the login and password for their Facebook account. Note, this is not a recommended way of responding. The only person who ends up being happy in the long run is the party who was given complete access.

- **Federal Rule of Civil Procedure 33—Interrogatories**

Serve interrogatories that complement your informal investigation of social media sites. Don't assume that you're working from a complete set of sites, even if you obtained a report through a social media research service. Here are some suggested interrogatories:

- For each and every one of your social media accounts (including without limitation Facebook, Twitter, Pinterest, Vine, Tumblr, YouTube, Instagram, LinkedIn and Snapchat), identify the social media account, your username, the email address you used for the account, and the start and end dates for which you have had the account.

- For each and every internet site on which you have posted a review of a restaurant, hotel, or other service provider (including without limitation Yelp and TripAdvisor), during the time period of [date range relevant to the case], identify the site, your username, the businesses that you reviewed, and the date of your review.

- For each and every online dating service for which you have created an account or a profile (including without limitation Match, Tinder, OkCupid, eHarmony, OurTime, PlentyofFish, Zoosk, ChristianSingles, JDate, Grindr, Adam4Adam, and Growlr [list all applicable platforms]), identify the site, your username, the email address you used for the account, and the start and end dates for which you have had the account.

The responses to these interrogatories can be used to supplement your informal discovery of social media accounts and activity. In addition, refer back to your social media-related discovery requests and any documents you received from the other side, and fill in any holes in the requests or production as needed through supplemental discovery requests or a "meet and confer" letter.

- **Federal Rule of Civil Procedure 36—Requests for Admission**

Looking ahead to a motion for summary judgment or trial, use requests for admission to have the other side admit that printed screenshots of their social media accounts (from the informal discovery efforts) are true and correct copies of posts made by them. Further, if there's any concern that the producing party will dispute the authenticity of social media activity they produced, serve requests for admission directed to these documents. Rule 36 expressly provides for requests for admission directed to having a party admitting the genuineness of documents:

> (1) Scope. A party may serve on any other party a written request to admit, for purposes of the pending action only, the truth of any matters within the scope of Rule 26(b)(1) relating to:
>
> (A) facts, the application of law to fact, or opinions about either; and
>
> (B) the genuineness of any described documents.
>
> (2) Form; Copy of a Document. Each matter must be separately stated. A request to admit the genuineness of a document must be accompanied by a copy of the document unless it is, or has been, otherwise furnished or made available for inspection and copying.

Couple this request with an interrogatory in which the party is asked to explain all reasons for denying the genuineness of any screenshots in response to requests for admission.[41]

4.3.3 Online Privilege Waivers

Unless a party has had a lawyer with the foresight to caution them about the use of social media during the litigation (and unless the party was smart enough to follow that advice), the party may find themselves in the position of having waived some privileged conversations. In one case, a mother was suing over a takedown notice that was sent to YouTube for a video she posted of her young child dancing to a song by the artist Prince. The mother, Stephanie Lenz, filed a lawsuit against Universal Music in which she claimed that this media company knowingly filed a false claim and undermined her First Amendment rights. Lenz was represented by legal counsel from the Electronic Frontier Foundation (EFF). When the case had been litigated for over three years and was near the summary judgment stage, Universal obtained a court order requiring Lenz to produce over eighty documents of communications with her lawyers.[42]

Universal was able to show that Lenz had been discussing the substance of what she and her lawyers discussed in emails to friends and family, Gmail chats, and on her personal blog. The areas of disclosure ranged from the motivations behind her lawsuit; the extent to which she had been damaged by the brief takedown of her video,[43] which was reposted and left on YouTube for millions to view; and the legal merits of her case. As set forth in the court's opinion:

> In an email to a friend, Lenz stated that EFF was "very, very interested in the case," and that "EFF is pretty well salivating over getting their teeth into [Universal Music Group] yet again." [Internal citations omitted.] Lenz also sent an email to her mother stating that she could not "say much," but that EFF was planning a "publicity blitz and/or a lawsuit against Universal."
>
> [I]n an electronic chat with a friend, Lenz stated that "I told [EFF counsel] Corynne [McSherry] that since pursuing the federal portion of the case achieves the ends I have in mind, that's [*sic*] fine to drop the state portion (that they filed a false DMCA notice, tha[t] they're

---

41. Sample interrogatory: "For any requests for admission for which you did not admit unequivocally the genuineness of the document(s) attached and included by reference in the request of admission, state in detail the reasons for your denial or admission with qualifications."
42. Lenz v. Universal Music Corp., 2010 U.S. Dist. LEXIS 125874 (N.D. Cal. Nov. 17, 2010). *See also* Greg Sandoval, Strange Turn in Dancing Baby vs. Prince Case, c|net (Feb. 14, 2011), https://www.cnet.com/culture/strange-turn-in-dancing-baby-vs-prince-case/ (last visited Oct. 26, 2022).
43. YouTube video at issue in *Lenz*, https://www.youtube.com/watch?v=N1KfJHFWlhQ (last visited Oct. 26, 2022).

accusing me of copyright infringement and that a ruling in your case could clarify a cloudy decision known as 'Rossi')."

Lenz told a friend that her lawyer was hinting in her second amended complaint that "Prince bullied" Universal into going after Lenz and that "there has been ample public proof that he wants everyone targeted, no matter whether they're actually guilty of anything." Second, Lenz told a friend in a separate chat that her attorney thought Prince was forcing Universal to fight the suit rather than settle. Third, Lenz indicated to a reporter for Zerogossip.com that she had contacted EFF on the recommendation of a lawyer friend from Canada, and that "[i]n discussing the situation with one of the EFF lawyers, we came to the conclusion that I did not infringe the copyright and eventually we decided to file this lawsuit." . . . Finally, in a response to a reader comment on her blog about a fair use defense, Lenz wrote "You're right Richard. Mine's not a 'fair use' case at all. It's something different. I've never heard of anything like it, which is why I contacted EFF." [Excerpts taken from the court's opinion. *Id.* at *5–10.]

The production of some attorney-client communications was not fatal to Lenz and her case, but having to turn over otherwise privileged documents and answer deposition questions concerning them is something no party wants to be in the position of having to do. Alternatively, legal counsel should be on the watch for social media and internet waivers of privileges including without limitation attorney-client, marital, and psychotherapist (all of which are communications that are areas ripe for people to want to share with their "friends" on social media).

4.4 Motions to Compel

The most common objection lawyers raise to serving discovery requests for social media activity seems to be that a court will not order the discovery. To be fair, there are a number of cases where courts have held that the request was overly broad, a fishing expedition, or likely to include sensitive, privacy-protected information concerning health that's irrelevant to the action. However, there are also several cases with courts ordering the discovery. Pushing for this discovery should be part of any discovery plan because it has the potential of winning and settling cases. There are a number of reported accounts of smart, successful people posting content that blows up for them personally and professionally. Here are a few.

- In March 2011, a social media marketing agency reportedly lost Chrysler as a client when one of its employees used the F-bomb in a tweet on the Chrysler social media account (which he mistakenly thought was his Twitter account): "@ChryslerAutos account: "I find it ironic that Detroit is known as the #motorcity and yet no one here knows how to fucking drive."[44]

- In December 2013, the senior director of corporate communications for a large media company posted a tweet that was viewed as racist and insensitive to millions suffering from AIDs, while en route from New York to South Africa, only to land and find that it had gone viral and that it would lead to her employer terminating her.[45]
- In May 2014, a PayPal executive stepped down after posting obscene tweets while he was reportedly drinking and enjoying Jazz Fest.[46]
- In May 2015, a Michigan prosecutor posted on Facebook that people rioting in Baltimore over incidents of police abuse directed against blacks should be shot: "So I am watching the news in Baltimore and see large swarms of people throwing bricks, etc [sic] at police who are fleeing from their assaults," the prosecutor posted. "15 in the hospital already. Solution. Simple. Shoot em. Period. End of discussion. I don't care what causes the protestors to turn violent . . . what the 'they did it because' reason is . . . no way is this acceptable. Flipping disgusting."[47]
- In June 2015, the prosecutor in the Aurora movie shooting case drew the ire of the criminal court judge when he reportedly forgot the court's admonition for lawyers not to tweet during court sessions and was accused by the defense lawyer of not paying attention in court: "A day earlier, while the defense cross-examined a key mental health expert, a message went out from Arapahoe County District Attorney[]'s Twitter account referencing the 22 hours of video-recorded interviews that Dr. William Reid conducted with James Holmes and that jurors in the trial watched this week and last. 'I agree on the video,' the message read. 'I hope the jury thinks so, too.'"[48]

---

44. David Kiley, *Chrysler Splits With New Media Strategies Over F-Bomb Tweet*, Advertising Age (March 10, 2011), http://adage.com/article/digital/chrysler-splits-media-strategies-f-bomb-tweet/149335/ (last visited Oct. 26, 2022).
45. Jon Ronson, *How One Stupid Tweet Blew Up Justine Sacco's Life*, New York Times (Feb. 12, 2015), http://www.nytimes.com/2015/02/15/magazine/how-one-stupid-tweet-ruined-justine-saccos-life.html?_r=0 (last visited Oct. 26, 2022).
46. Sophia Rosenbaum, *PayPal Executive Leaves Company After Obscene Twitter Meltdown*, New York Post (May 5, 2014), http://nypost.com/2014/05/05/now-former-paypal-executive-continues-his-epic-twitter-rant/ (last visited Oct. 26, 2022).
47. Noah Rayman, *This Facebook Post About Baltimore Cost a Prosecutor Her Job*, Time Magazine (May 1, 2015), https://time.com/3844061/baltimore-facebook-post-prosecutor-michigan/ (last visited Oct. 26, 2022).
48. John Ingold and Jordan Steffen, *Prosecutor's Social Media Gaffe Annoys Theater Shooting Trial Judge*, Denver Post (June 5, 2015), http://www.denverpost.com/theater-shooting-trial/ci_28257953/defense-questions-psychiatrist-aurora-theater-trial/ (last visited Oct. 26, 2022).

4.4.1 Scope of Discovery

Rule 26(b)(1) of the Federal Rules of Civil Procedure sets forth the parameters for discovery in a case:

> (b) Discovery Scope and Limits. (1) Scope in General. Unless otherwise limited by court order, the scope of discovery is as follows: Parties may obtain discovery regarding any nonprivileged matter that is relevant to any party's claim or defense and proportional to the needs of the case, considering the importance of the issues at stake in the action, the amount in controversy, the parties' relative access to relevant information, the parties' resources, the importance of the discovery in resolving the issues, and whether the burden or expense of the proposed discovery outweighs its likely benefit. Information within this scope of discovery need not be admissible in evidence to be discoverable.

In addition, Rule 26(b)(2)(B) sets some additional limitations on electronically stored information:

> (B) Specific Limitations on Electronically Stored Information. A party need not provide discovery of electronically stored information from sources that the party identifies as not reasonably accessible because of undue burden or cost. On motion to compel discovery or for a protective order, the party from whom discovery is sought must show that the information is not reasonably accessible because of undue burden or cost. If that showing is made, the court may nonetheless order discovery from such sources if the requesting party shows good cause, considering the limitations of Rule 26(b)(2)(C). The court may specify conditions for the discovery.

These rules will guide what a court will allow for social media discovery.[49]

4.4.2 How Hyperbole Helps

Parties tend to be dramatic in their complaints and early summaries of their case. These assertions can be used to open up social media discovery. For example, many employment and personal injury actions include allegations about how much the events in question have been emotionally disturbing to the injured party and have disturbed the peace and enjoyment of their life in some way. These allegations of emotional distress or negative affect will usually open up some of their

49. Glazer v. Fireman's Fund Insurance Co., 2012 U.S. Dist. LEXIS 51658, at *8 (S.D.N.Y. Apr. 4, 2012) (plaintiff in race discrimination action could be ordered to give consent to production of her posts on a social media site if they are "likely to contain information relevant to [the] case").

private social media activity because the other side is entitled to test their claims.[50] In *Robinson v. Jones Lang LaSalle Americas., Inc.*, the defendant had been seeking all pictures, videos, blogs, and social media activity on Facebook, LinkedIn, and MySpace that revealed or related to the plaintiff's "emotion, feeling, or mental state," or to "events that could be reasonably expected to produce a significant emotion, feeling, or mental state."[51]

The *Robinson* court relied on *E.E.O.C. v. Simply Storage Management, LLC*,[52] which it described as the benchmark case in this area, and the case that legal professionals can use to drill down and find cases in their jurisdiction. In *Simply Storage*, a sexual harassment case, the court allowed discovery of social media communications beyond the events described in the plaintiff's complaint. The court found that:

> It is reasonable to expect severe emotional or mental injury to manifest itself in some [social media] content, and an examination of that content might reveal whether onset occurred, when, and the degree of distress. Further, information that evidences other stressors that could have produced the alleged emotional distress is also relevant.[53]

The *Simply Storage* court recognized that social media can provide information that offers possible explanations for the plaintiff's emotional distress other than his allegation that the defendant caused it. Alternatively, the social media may also undermine his allegations of the severity of that distress. Accordingly, the court allowed discovery of:

> [A]ny profiles, postings, or messages (including status updates, wall comments, causes joined, groups joined, activity streams, blog entries) and [social media] applications for [plaintiffs] for the [relevant period] that reveal, refer, or relate to any emotion, feeling, or mental state, as well as communications that reveal, refer, or relate to events that could reasonably be expected to produce a significant emotion, feeling, or mental state. . . . Third-party communications to [plaintiffs] . . . if they place these [plaintiffs'] own communications in context.[54]

In *Caputi v. Topper Realty Corporation*,[55] a wage-hour employment action, the court ordered limited discovery of the plaintiff's Facebook account and declined to give unlimited access to the defendant:

---

50. *See* Robinson v. Jones Lang LaSalle Ams., Inc., 2012 U.S. Dist. LEXIS 123883 (D. Or. Aug. 29, 2012) (court allowed discovery of posts on social media sites relating to emotional distress in a race discrimination and retaliation case).

51. *Id.* at *5–7.

52. E.E.O.C. v. Simply Storage Mgmt., LLC, 270 F.R.D. 430, 432 (S.D. Ind. 2010).

53. *Id.* at 435.

54. *Id.* at 436.

55. Caputi v. Topper Realty Corp., 2015 U.S. Dist. LEXIS 24969 (E.D.N.Y. Feb. 25, 2015).

> Defendants are entitled to a sampling of Plaintiff's Facebook activity for the period November 2011 to November 2013, limited to any "specific references to the emotional distress [Plaintiff] claims she suffered" in the Complaint, and any "treatment she received in connection [there]with." *Id.* at *116. Defendants may renew their application for the balance of Plaintiff's Facebook account information upon probative evidence uncovered from the sampling, if any. In addition, in mounting a defense, Defendants are entitled to any Facebook activity, for the same time period, that refers to an alternative source or cause of Plaintiff's alleged distress. *See id.* Accordingly, the motion is granted, in part, as to Plaintiff's Facebook account information to substantiate her claims of emotional distress. Plaintiff is also directed to preserve all of her Facebook activity for the duration of this litigation.[56]

4.4.3 Competing Interests: Discovery versus Privacy

Courts are understandably concerned about ordering the production of all social media activity and will rarely issue such a broad order. On the other hand, courts also appreciate that a third-party review of the social media activity in camera may strike the right balance between the parties' competing interests. In *EEOC v. Original Honeybaked Ham Company*,[57] a class action for alleged sex harassment and retaliation with about twenty-two putative class members, the court assigned a forensic expert as a special master to manage the collection of the class members' social media activity. The defendant demonstrated that the class members had been using social media to communicate with each other and others about the case, their employment and termination from Honeybaked Ham, and other topics that the defendant argued may be admissible evidence. In deciding to use a special master to be paid for by both parties, the court was influenced by the amount at stake in the litigation—plaintiffs were seeking damages in the low- to mid-seven figure range—and also that there was some evidence already that the social media content may contain admissible evidence based on content from one class member:

> There is no question the Defendant has established that the documents it seeks contain discoverable information. Defendant has shown, for example, that Plaintiff-Intervenor Cabrera posted on her Facebook account statements that discuss her financial expectations in this lawsuit; a photograph of herself wearing a shirt with the word "CUNT" in large letters written across the front (a term that she alleges was used pejoratively against her, also alleging that such use offended her) [citation omitted]; musings about her emotional state in having lost

56. *Id.* at *19–20 (*quoting* Giacchetto v. Patchogue-Medford Union Free Sch. Dist., 293 F.R.D. 112 (E.D.N.Y. 2013)).
57. EEOC v. Original Honeybaked Ham Co., 2012 U.S. Dist. LEXIS 160285 (D. Colo. Nov. 7, 2012).

> a beloved pet as well as having suffered a broken relationship; other writings addressing her positive outlook on how her life was post-termination; her self-described sexual aggressiveness; statements about actions she engaged in as a supervisor with Defendant (including terminating a woman who is a class member in this case); sexually amorous communications with other class members; her post-termination employment and income opportunities and financial condition; and other information.[58]

In other words, the defendant persuaded the court that it was not "the proverbial fishing expedition; these waters have already been tested, and they show that further effort will likely be fruitful."[59]

The court outlined a process for the parties to follow:

1. the claimants give the special master the login and password information he needs to access their text messages, social media accounts, and email or web blog account that they used to communicate with one another during a set period of time;[60]
2. the parties work jointly on parameters for the special master to use for his collection of information;
3. the court reviews in camera all of the information collected by the special master;
4. the court will deliver the information that is found to be discoverable to the EEOC to conduct a privilege review, and then generate a privilege log for any documents withheld under the protective order and produce the unprivileged documents to the defendant; and
5. the irrelevant documents will be returned to the EEOC.

This decision highlights the usefulness of having done an informal investigation to identify admissible evidence on the public pages of social media.[61]

A special master is neither necessary nor required in all cases in which a party is moving to compel the production of social media discovery. Parties should not

58. *Id.* at *4–5.
59. *Id.* at *7.
60. The parties were also tasked with creating a questionnaire, with assistance as needed from the court, for the claimants to complete in order to make sure that all sources of possible information were identified and then made available to the special master to access.
61. *See also* Richards v. Hertz Corp., 100 A.D.3d 728 (N.Y. App. Div. 2d Dep't 2012) (in a personal injury action arising from an automobile accident, the court ordered an in camera review of the social media activity for one plaintiff, because the defendant was able to demonstrate that there was a reasonable likelihood of discoverable documents based on a picture of the plaintiff skiing following the accident taken from the plaintiff's Facebook public profile).

forego trying to get social media evidence for fear that it will get expensive. It doesn't have to be. Here are some more cases in which courts ordered the production of social media evidence without the parties having to use a special master or forensic professional to download the social media activity.

In one benchmark case for discovering social media activity when a party alleges severe emotional distress as the result of the other party's acts, the court held that social media activity with substance or content relating to the emotional state of the claimant was discoverable. This discovery also included social media activity concerning other stressors that may have produced the party's alleged emotional distress. The plaintiff EEOC had tried unsuccessfully to limit the discovery to social media activity that directly comments on or addresses allegations in the complaint. The defendant's discovery requests had called for the production of all social media activity—profiles, status updates, comments, posts, "likes," videos, etc.[62] In narrowing the requests, the *Simply Storage* court was still very inclusive about what social media activity needed to be produced:

> any profiles, postings, or messages (including status updates, wall comments, causes joined, groups joined, activity streams, blog entries) and SNS [social networking site] applications for claimants . . . that *reveal, refer, or relate to any emotion, feeling, or mental state, as well as communications that reveal, refer, or relate to events that could reasonably be expected to produce a significant emotion, feeling, or mental state.*[63]

The court held that videos or photographs posted on a party's social media account are generally discoverable using the highlighted test above, and less so if the party was "tagged" in a picture posted by someone else on social media.[64] The highlighted language is written nicely for putting into a discovery request and having the case ready to cite in any "meet and confer" letter. A party opposing discovery, and trying to distinguish *Simply Storage*, will need to argue that they're only asserting "garden variety emotional distress claims," which seems against their interest if they are trying to recover damages for emotional distress. In other words, it may make more sense to produce the responsive social media activity.

In a personal injury action, the defendant was able to get even broader discovery of the plaintiffs' social media activity when the court ordered the production of social media activity relating to the plaintiffs' enjoyment of life. The plaintiffs had alleged that exposure to chemicals had left them with breathing disorders that

---

62. Equal Employment Opportunity Commission v. Simply Storage Management, LLC, 270 F.R.D. 430 (D. Ind. 2010).

63. *Id.* at 436 (emphasis added).

64. "Tagging" is a process by which the person posting the picture can link the picture to the profiles of their various friends or connections, and have the picture appear on the pages of those tagged friends (unless the person tagged has set up their privacy protections so that content is not added to their profile without their approval).

kept them from swimming, jogging, and enjoying other physical activities they had engaged in before.

> Koch claims that Rachel and Sarah's Facebook content may reveal relevant information as to the extent their injuries have impacted their "enjoyment of life, ability to engage in outdoor activities, and employment," along with their "claims regarding permanent injuries, lack of pre-existing symptoms, and impairment of future earnings capacity." Since the extent of Rachel and Sarah's losses in these areas directly impacts the appropriate damages award, the court finds this information relevant.[65]

Further, the court held that photos posted by other people on Facebook in which they tagged the plaintiffs were also discoverable and that those nonparties did not have a right of privacy interest in them because the pictures were in the "possession, custody, or control" of the plaintiffs.[66] The court noted that it's consistent with Facebook's privacy policy that all posting is done at one's own risk.

Consider, too, *Ogden v. All-State Career School,*[67] a gender discrimination and retaliation case in which the court ordered the plaintiff to produce social media activity relating to his emotional state during the relevant period of time or, alternatively, provide the defendant with access to his accounts and a summary of what he believes is within the scope of the authorized discovery. The *Ogden* court denied, however, the defendant's discovery of social media activity showing that the plaintiff conversed with others on his Facebook account in ways similar to what he alleged created a hostile work environment for him in the office from his female colleagues. The court held that Federal Rule of Evidence 412 is a bar to offering evidence of sexually related conduct outside the workplace to suggest that the behavior in the workplace would not have been offensive to the complaining witness, or that the complaining witness has engaged in or has a predisposition for sexual-in-nature conduct.

Another teaching point from these cases is that going into a motion to compel with a discovery request for all social media activity is an uphill challenge. Courts will either narrow what the party has to produce or deny the motion in its entirety. For example, in *Smith v. Hillshire Brands,*[68] the defendant employer was trying to get access to all of the plaintiff's social media accounts in an FMLA (Family and Medical Leave Act) and Title VII case. The defendant argued the request was justified because it provided an online diary of the plaintiff's activities that would be relevant to his emotional distress claim and, further, that it may show

---

65. Higgins v. Koch Development Corp., 2013 U.S. Dist. LEXIS 94139, at *6 (S.D. Ind. July 5, 2013).
66. *Id.* at *8.
67. Ogden v. All-State Career Sch., 299 F.R.D. 446 (W.D. Pa. 2014).
68. Smith v. Hillshire Brands, 2014 U.S. Dist. LEXIS 83953 (D. Kan. June 20, 2014).

that he was violating his FMLA leave with some of his activities. The court noted that the defendant may not appreciate the ramifications of its arguments, because it could potentially open up the personal social media accounts of the Hillshire Brands' managers and supervisors involved in the termination decision because the accounts might show discriminatory pretext.[69] The court took what it described as the intermediate approach being used by courts (the *Simply Storage* court approach) and allowed discovery of "any content that reveals plaintiff's emotions or mental state, or content that refers to events that could reasonably be expected to produce in plaintiff a significant emotion or mental state."[70]

At the far end of the spectrum for not allowing discovery of social media accounts is a case from the United States District Court for the Central District of California, *Mailhoit v. Home Depot U.S.A., Inc.*[71] The *Mailhoit* court criticized the intermediate approach taken in *Simply Storage* (and the discovery requests suggested by the court) and held that asking for social media activity that relates to an emotional state or is likely to produce a strong emotional reaction does not describe the responsive documents with "reasonable particularity" as required by Federal Rule of Civil Procedure Rule 34(b)(1)(A) and, therefore, the request is not likely to lead to the discovery of admissible evidence. If you find yourself in a district that follows *Mailhoit*, use the results of your informal investigation and add the types of life events you know the responding party has been facing, and for which a reasonable person would experience strong emotional distress, to your request (e.g., a divorce, serious illness or chronic pain, death of a family member or friend, family issues). In other words, clearly spell out that something's been going on in this person's life, it's likely to be on social media, and it's likely to lead to the discovery of admissible evidence.

4.5 Motion for Spoliation Sanctions

Because many people overshare on social media, your social media activity discovery requests may be met with outright objections or a social media account that's been cleaned up (when the party would have been subject to a litigation hold). Therefore, do your advance work: send a litigation hold letter and capture screenshots from the public social media pages.

Courts define "spoliation of evidence" as the destruction or significant alteration of evidence when litigation is pending or reasonably foreseeable.[72] "[Parties] engage in spoliation of documents as a matter of law only if they had 'some notice that the documents were potentially relevant' to the litigation before they were destroyed."[73]

---

69. *Id.* at *13.
70. *Id.* at *19–20.
71. Mailhoit v. Home Depot U.S.A., Inc., 285 F.R.D. 566 (C.D. Cal. 2012).
72. United States v. Kitsap Physicians Serv., 314 F.3d 995, 1001 (9th Cir. 2002).
73. *Id.*

This is why sending a litigation hold letter can help set up a motion for discovery sanctions.

Courts have broad discretion in deciding what sanctions to impose for spoliation of evidence.[74] This may include adverse inverse instructions (instructing jurors to infer that the destroyed evidence would have been unfavorable to the responsible party) to outright dismissal of the action. Because these sanctions circumvent a trial on the merits, courts will hold off on ordering sanctions except when there's a showing that the missing evidence was critical to the case of the moving party.[75] In *Painter v. Atwood*,[76] the court set forth the tests used in the Ninth Circuit.

4.5.1 Standards Applied by the Ninth Circuit

Federal Rule of Civil Procedure 37(c) sets the bar for a party seeking sanctions for spoliation of electronically stored information (including social media and internet evidence). This rule now requires the moving party to show that the ESI is lost and cannot be recovered or obtained from another source. Rule 37(e) also requires that the irretrievable ESI should have been preserved in the anticipation of or conduct of litigation and the party failed to take reasonable steps to preserve it and that there has been prejudice to another party from the loss of the ESI. While this rule is relatively new, older case law and guidance from the Ninth Circuit retain some persuasive value in arguing prejudice to your client and that some form of sanctions should be imposed for the deletion of social media activity (that cannot be restored or replaced through additional discovery).

- **Terminating Sanctions**

Even though discovery sanctions for spoliation are within the discretion of the district court, courts will consider certain objective factors before terminating a case in favor of the party moving for sanctions: "(1) the public's interest in expeditious resolution of litigation; (2) the court's need to manage its dockets; (3) the risk of prejudice to the party seeking sanctions; (4) the public policy favoring disposition of cases on their merits; and (5) the availability of less drastic sanctions."[77]

- **Adverse Inference Instructions**

The party seeking an adverse inference instruction must establish that 1) the spoliating party had an obligation to preserve the evidence, 2) the evidence was

---

74. Chambers v. NASCO, Inc., 501 U.S. 32, 45 (1991).
75. Ingham v. United States, 167 F.3d 1240, 1246 (9th Cir. 1999).
76. Painter v. Atwood, 2014 U.S. Dist. LEXIS 35060 (D. Nev. Mar. 18, 2014).
77. Leon v. IDX Sys. Corp., 464 F.3d 951, 958 (9th Cir. 2006) (citing Anheuser-Busch, Inc. v. Natural Beverage Distributors, 69 F.3d 337, 348 (9th Cir. 1995)).

destroyed or significantly altered with a culpable state of mind, and 3) the evidence was relevant to the moving party's claim in that a reasonable trier of fact could find that it would support that claim.[78] A similar test is used in other circuits for determining appropriate sanctions in spoliation cases.[79]

- **Defeating a Motion for Sanctions**

If a client has unfortunately deleted relevant social media content before retaining counsel, or in spite of your advice, argue why sanctions are not warranted. First, and most effective, is arguing that there's no prejudice to the other side because the deleted documents are not irretrievably lost. This can be demonstrated by recovering and producing the social media content that was deleted or, alternatively, locating and producing other copies of the deleted pictures or posts. For example, Facebook makes it hard for users to permanently delete their activity. Content or photos deleted from a timeline are still available and can be accessed through a user's "Activity Log" or the "download a copy" application.

It also helps to argue that social media accounts by their nature are not static (unlike an email or letter that has been sent), and, therefore, the party moving for sanctions should have sent a litigation hold letter. In other words, the party with the social media accounts had no "bad intent" to destroy or alter discoverable documents, but, rather, was clueless that the moving party considered them to be relevant. It helps your case for opposing sanctions if you can list other categories of documents already produced such as emails, correspondence, and other hard copy documents. Social media evidence is still enough outside the traditional discovery process that some courts may find this is a legitimate excuse. This excuse probably has an expiration date, however, because social media discovery is quickly becoming mainstream.

When responding to a motion for discovery sanctions, highlight the social media activity that your client has been able to produce, including posts that are not necessarily helpful to the client's case. It also helps to demonstrate that it was the normal practice of the client to periodically delete content on their social media accounts so it looks less like obstruction of the discovery process. It's very helpful if

---

78. *See* LaJocies v. City of North Las Vegas, 2011 U.S. Dist. LEXIS 49046 (D. Nev.) (*citing* In re Napster, 462 F. Supp. 2d 1060, 1072 (N.D. Cal. 2006)).

79. These other circuits include, without being exhaustive, the Second Circuit (Residential Funding Corp. v. DeGeorge Fin. Corp., 306 F.3d 99, 107 (2d Cir. 2002)); Fourth Circuit (Federico v. Lincoln Military Hous., LLC, 2014 U.S. Dist. LEXIS 178943 (E.D. Va. Dec. 31, 2014)); and Eleventh Circuit (Managed Care Solutions, Inc. v. Essent Healthcare, Inc., 736 F. Supp. 2d 1317, 1323–24 (S.D. Fla. 2010)).

your client can show that the party moving for sanctions is speculating that the deleted content would have been prejudicial to the client and that there is no evidence to support this wild allegation.[80]

Key Points

Conduct informal discovery of social media activity and capture screenshots.

Expand your search, as needed, to include close friends and family members.

Know ethics lines and stay within them.

Send a litigation hold letter with broad and specific descriptions of what social media should be preserved.

Serve written discovery, avoiding overly broad requests unless you're in a district court that allows it.

Expect resistance. Push for social media discovery.

80. *See* Osburn v. Hagel, 2013 U.S. Dist. LEXIS 164574 (M.D. Ala. Nov. 13, 2013), in which the court declined to order terminating sanctions in a sex discrimination and retaliation case. The court held that it was too severe a penalty to impose just because the plaintiff's husband testified that he learned of his wife allegedly being raped by a former supervisor over Facebook, but none of the Facebook pages produced by the plaintiff referred to the incidents in the complaint. The court declined to base sanctions on the defendant's speculation that the Facebook content the plaintiff deleted as part of her normal practice would have been relevant to the action and in addition to what the husband already testified about in his deposition.

Chapter Five

Experts and Their Digital Footprints

People often brand themselves as knowledge leaders through their blog and social media posts. The same will be true for many expert witnesses. What they're saying on topics relevant to your case may help you turn them into an expert who has 1) written in support of your client's position in a case; 2) questioned the various approaches for measuring damages or analyzing an issue on which they are testifying in your case, thereby possibly opening up areas for impeachment; or 3) praised your designated expert by relying on their professional writings or by referring to your expert as a respected authority.

In their professional writings, paid consultants/experts are pretty mindful about not expressing views that are inconsistent with the positions they typically take in litigation matters. However, as we have seen in previous chapters, people don't always self-edit or exercise good judgment when they post to social media and the internet. Embarrassing revelations unrelated to professional inconsistencies can still undercut them professionally.

- In December 2008, a White House speechwriter was forced to explain pictures of him acting out with a life-size cutout picture of Hillary Clinton, the incoming Secretary of State.[1]
- In October 2010, a Republican congressional candidate from Ohio was shown in a photo dressed up as a Nazi for a World War II re-enactment.[2]
- In November 2010, a Democratic congressional candidate from Virginia was forced to address six-year-old pictures of her wearing a Santa cap and sexy hosiery while holding and putting her mouth around a sex toy.[3]

---

1. Al Kamen, *One More Question*, Wash. Post (Dec. 4, 2008), http://voices.washingtonpost.com/44/2008/12/one-more-question.html (last visited Oct. 26, 2022).
2. Evan McMorris Santoro, *Ohio Tea Partier Spent Weekends Playing Nazi Games* (VIDEO), TPM DC (Oct. 9, 2010), http://talkingpointsmemo.com/dc/ohio-tea-partier-spent-weekends-playing-nazi-games-video (last visited Oct. 26, 2022).
3. *Krystal Ball on Sexy Photos Scandal: 'It Was Devastating'* (VIDEO), Huffington Post (Nov. 29, 2012), http://www.huffingtonpost.com/2012/11/29/krystal-ball-photos_n_2212963.html (last visited Oct. 26, 2022).

- In December 2011, Charlie Sheen, intending to send a direct message to Justin Bieber, accidentally tweeted his phone number to all of his 5.5 million followers.[4]
- In May 2011, a New York congressman with a very promising political future arguably derailed his career when a sexually suggestive photo of himself went viral on social media after he mistakenly tweeted the picture instead of sending it as a direct message to the intended recipient on Twitter.[5]
- In June 2015, Kim Kardashian was embarrassed by Armani when she incorrectly spelled Giorgio Armani's first name "Georgio."[6]
- In May 2017, hip-hop artist Bow Wow announced on social media he was traveling by private jet to New York City. Alert readers, on traveling on the same commercial flight as Bow Wow, posted that Bow Wow used a stock photo.[7]
- In January 2022, a member of the House of Representatives was permanently banned from Twitter for posting misinformation concerning COVID-19.[8]

Consequently, this is an area ripe for discovery for you of the other side's experts—and while you're at it, making sure there aren't any social media minefields awaiting your own experts.

5.1 Social Media Due Diligence

5.1.1 Your Expert's Digital Footprint

Before designating your own experts, perform your due diligence on what they have written in the past on social media and the internet in connection with your client, its industry, and also the issues for which the witness is being asked to testify. If there are any red flags, you need to know sooner rather than later.

---

4. https://www.glamour.com/story/charlie-sheen-accidentally-twe (last visited Oct. 26, 2022).
5. Juli Weiner, *Anthony Weiner's Twitter Scandal: New York Congressman Claims Account was Hacked,* Vanity Fair (May 11, 2011), https://www.vanityfair.com/news/2011/05/anthony-weiners-twitter-scandal-new-york-congressman-claims-account-was-hacked (last visited Oct. 26, 2022).
6. Mindaugas Balčiauskas and Rokas Laurinavičius, *35 Celebrity Social Media Screw-Ups That Will Forever Haunt Them On The Internet,* Bored Panda, https://www.boredpanda.com/celebrity-social-media-fails/?utm_source=google&utm_medium=organic&utm_campaign=organic (last visited Oct. 26, 2022).
7. *Id.*
8. *Elected officials suspended or banned from social media platforms,* Ballotpedia, https://ballotpedia.org/Elected_officials_suspended_or_banned_from_social_media_platforms (last visited Oct. 26, 2022).

In 2012, Oprah Winfrey set out to promote the Microsoft Surface by tweeting that she loved it and already had purchased 12 as Christmas gifts. The problem? She sent the tweet from her Apple iPad.[9]

In 2013, a publicist made an inappropriate joke about AIDS before leaving on a leg of her flight originally from New York destined for South Africa. During the 11-hour flight, her tweet went viral. That tweet ultimately led to her termination from employment.[10]

In 2016, a police officer jokingly posted that he stole cocaine from the evidence room. He was subsequently suspended without pay.[11]

One presidential candidate, known for carefully vetting staff, was embarrassed when a foreign policy aide with impressive credentials drew political fire, in part, for Twitter posts that were seen as cutting and unprofessional, and which were missed during a screening process that apparently skipped over social media activity:

> [Mitt Romney's] aides called around to Mr. Grenell's colleagues, seeking references, but as the warm reviews flowed in, a campaign known for its no-stone-unturned meticulousness overlooked his electronic footprints: namely, dozens of cutting Twitter postings. One swipe at Newt Gingrich's weight, for example, went like this: "I wonder if [N]ewt has investments in Lipitor."
>
> . . .
>
> Within days, stories about Mr. Grenell's Twitter feed surfaced, prompting him to delete more than 800 posts. Mr. Grenell apologized for what he called "hurtful" comments.[12]

In 2022, a contract employee working with Apple was non-renewed after posting a seemingly tame day-in-the-life video of her working at the tech company.[13] While little was shown about Apple, the tech giant is known for its strict non-disclosure

9. Brandon Griggs, *Oprah plugs Surface tablet—from her iPad*, CNN (Nov. 21, 2012) https://www.cnn.com/2012/11/20/tech/social-media/oprah-surface-tweet#:~:text=On%20Sunday%2C%20she%20went%20a,the%20tweet%20from%20an%20iPad (last visited Oct. 26, 2022).

10. Jon Ronson, *How One Stupid Tweet Blew Up Justine Sacco's Life*, New York Times (Feb. 12, 2015), https://www.nytimes.com/2015/02/15/magazine/how-one-stupid-tweet-ruined-justine-saccos-life.html (last visited Oct. 26, 2022).

11. Carolyn Sun, *These Social Media Fails Got People Fired*, Entepreneur (Mar. 18, 2016), https://www.entrepreneur.com/science-technology/these-social-media-fails-got-people-fired/271823 (last visited October 23, 2022).

12. Michael Barbaro, Helene Cooper, Ashley Parker, *Romney Camp Stirred Storm Over Gay Aide*, New York Times (May 2, 2012), http://www.nytimes.com/2012/05/03/us/politics/richard-grenell-resigns-from-mitt-romneys-foreign-policy-team.html (last visited Oct. 26, 2022).

13. Kyra Alessandrini, *This Apple Employee's Contract Wasn't Renewed After 'Day In The Life' TikTok Goes Viral*, Girls United (Oct. 19, 2022) https://girlsunited.essence.com/article/tiktok-viral-apple-contractor/ (last visited on Oct. 23, 2022).

policies, having fired many employees in the past for seemingly non-descript videos posted on social media.

Also in 2022, a senior executive at Apple was fired after he appeared on a post of a popular TikTok creator making inappropriate and crude jokes. The high-ranking executive had been with the company for 22 years.[14]

5.1.2 Engagement Letter

Knowing that professionals use the internet to market themselves, act proactively to ensure their digital marketing doesn't compromise your case or reflect poorly on your client. When engaging an expert, spell out when and how (if at all) they can talk about the case. You may have a client that wants to manage all communications about litigation matters through its public relations team. This should be clearly stated in the engagement letter so that your expert agrees not to write about the case even when it's over. At a minimum, the engagement letter should spell out that your expert will not discuss the case on social media and the internet (or in any other forum) until it is fully completed through any appeal process and that anything discussed with the party client or its counsel that did not come out through discovery or trial is confidential and should never be disclosed.

5.1.3 Opposing Expert Witnesses

Informal and formal discovery of fact witnesses using social media and the internet applies as well to expert witnesses. Through pretrial discovery (subpoena duces tecum and deposition), ask the other side's expert to identify the social media platforms on which they have posted and to produce screenshots of their profile pages (or the username and email address they use) for each site so they can be located. Use the standard document requests for offline discovery of experts as a guide and be clear that the definition of "documents" or "writings" includes LinkedIn activity (group discussions, status updates, profile, and articles posted by the expert); electronic email lists (i.e., listservs[15]), blogs, websites, and social media accounts including, without limitation, Facebook, Twitter, and YouTube:

---

14. Andrew Orr, *Apple procurement VP fired over TikTok breast joke*, APPLE INSIDER (Sep. 29, 2022), https://appleinsider.com/articles/22/09/29/vulgar-remark-in-tiktok-gets-apples-procurement-vp-fired (last visited Oct. 23, 2022).

15. A listserv is a particular application, but it is used generically to refer to all electronic email lists. Subscribers to a listserv can easily send emails to subscribers and solicit responses to a particular topic. Listservs are sometimes closed groups, giving subscribers the false impression that there is some level of confidential protection for their communications. Because this is a common misapprehension, subscribers sometimes find that their communications are shared outside of the listserv or are discoverable, assuming they are within the scope of discovery. *Cf.* Muniz v. UPS, 2011 U.S. Dist. LEXIS 11219 (N.D. Cal. Jan. 28, 2011), in which the court granted the motion to quash and struck the listserv documents from the record that the defendant UPS filed in support of its opposition to the motion to quash filed by plaintiff's counsel, and held that the requested listserv

> "Documents" or "Writings" include electronic communications through email distribution lists or groups (including but not limited to any distribution lists or groups for professional organizations or associations such as [LIST SPECIFIC LISTSERVS USED BY PROFESSIONALS SUCH AS THE DESIGNATED EXPERT], websites and/or blogs. . . MySpace, Facebook, Twitter, LinkedIn, and/or any other internet service provider.

It is also worth highlighting in specific document requests whether the expert has considered or relied on any blogs or other online sources for their opinion.

The Federal Rules of Civil Procedure allow for this discovery. The only question is whether lawyers will remember to ask for social media and online documents. Do not assume opposing counsel or its expert will think to look for and produce online, discoverable documents. Rule 26(a)(2) identifies the documents that should be produced without a deposition subpoena by experts: "the facts or data considered by [the expert] in forming [all of their opinions]" ((B)(ii)) and a "list of all publications authored in the previous 10 years" ((B)(iv)). Blog articles are a form of publication and should be produced. Listservs, the blogs of others in the field, Twitter links that may have been considered and "favorited" so they could easily be found again, and LinkedIn group discussions are possible online sources of documents *considered by the expert in forming their opinion* and should be asked for in the other side's Rule 26(a)(2) disclosure.

Federal Rule of Evidence 702 sets forth the type of testimony that can be offered via expert testimony and applies to assessing the admissibility of scientific and non-scientific expert testimony:

> A witness who is qualified as an expert by knowledge, skill, experience, training, or education may testify in the form of an opinion or otherwise if:
>
> (a) the expert's scientific, technical, or other specialized knowledge will help the trier of fact to understand the evidence or to determine a fact in issue;
>
> (b) the testimony is based on sufficient facts or data;
>
> (c) the testimony is the product of reliable principles and methods; and
>
> (d) the expert has reliably applied the principles and methods to the facts of the case.

---

and Facebook documents (not already available to defendant) were irrelevant. Significantly, the court did not find that the listserv communications were privileged. In Muniz, defendant UPS had served a subpoena to get documents showing the conversations that plaintiff's counsel was having on Facebook and various plaintiffs' bar association listservs about the "'work' and 'efforts' of Plaintiff's counsel in this case and/or case 'events.'" UPS was seeking the discovery in order to respond to a motion for attorney fees filed by plaintiff and her counsel. *Id.* at *22.

The Advisory Committee Notes explain further that Rule 702 is intended to give courts the latitude to exclude opinion evidence that is unreliable.[16]

Rule 45 of the Federal Rules of Civil Procedure provides for the depositions of nonparty witnesses, including designated experts. Subsection 45(c)(2)(A) provides that a witness may be required to produce documents at her deposition: "A subpoena may command: (A) production of documents, electronically stored information, or tangible things at a place within 100 miles of where the person resides, is employed, or regularly transacts business in person." As covered in Chapter IV, ESI includes posts and activity on social media and websites. Accordingly, you are entitled to ask for these documents in your Rule 45 deposition subpoena to the other side's expert.

5.1.4 Potential Biases of Expert Witnesses

Just as experts are asked how many times they have been retained or testified for the plaintiff versus defendant in a case, or whether they have worked with a particular client or law firm before, this line of questioning should include an informal and formal inquiry of their social media relationships with a party or legal counsel. Does the expert follow or "like" on Facebook the party or law firm that's retained them in the case? This is easier to discover than one would think, because the websites of law firms and companies have the social media icons with direct links on the home pages of their websites inviting people to follow them on social media. In other words, their social media sites and links to them are readily available, so there is no guesswork involved in determining what social media sites they're on. Businesses are so much easier to find on social media than individuals because they *want* to be found and have signposts on their websites making it easy to find them. This block, for example, appears at the bottom of the Best Buy website.

16. Fed. R. Evid. 702 was amended to incorporate holdings in Daubert v. Merrell Dow Pharmaceuticals, Inc., 509 U.S. 579 (1993) (setting forth nonexclusive checklist for courts in assessing the reliability of scientific expert testimony); and Kumho Tire Co. v. Carmichael, 119 S. Ct. 1167 (1999) (extending the concept of Daubert-like factors to assessing the reliability of nonscientific expert testimony). *See* Fed. R. Evid. 702 advisory committee's note to 2000 amendment.

Similarly, near the bottom of its website home page, Skadden, Arps, Slate, Meagher & Flom LLP, a law firm with offices throughout the United States and in a number of other countries, asks website visitors to connect with it on Facebook, Twitter, and LinkedIn.

The draw to follow businesses and law firms is fairly strong as can be seen by the number of businesses and people following Skadden Arps: 11,500 plus followers on Twitter and over 75,700 people on LinkedIn.

Skadden Arps on Twitter

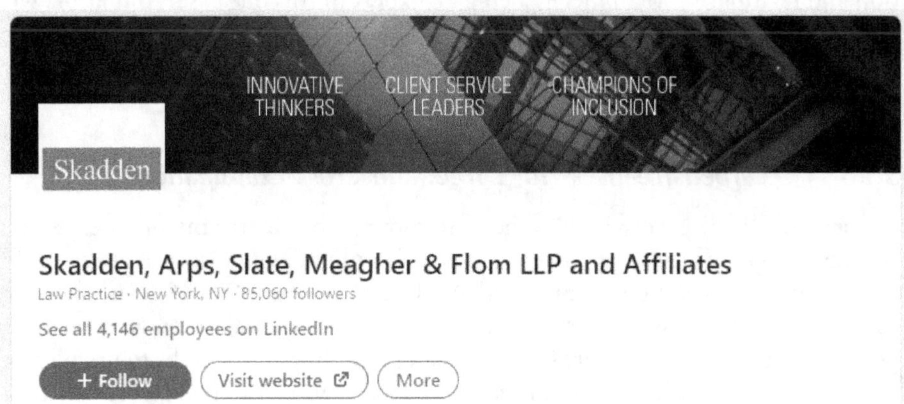

Skadden Arps on LinkedIn

It is almost certain that Skadden Arps is being followed by persons or businesses who they do business with on a regular basis.

Knowing the social media sites used by a business party or its legal counsel also makes it easier to do a "reverse lookup" by looking for these businesses on the social media sites used by their expert. Look at the "likes" on a designated expert's Facebook page to see if it includes the law firm, and check out which companies they follow on LinkedIn and Twitter. On Facebook, a user's activity has privacy settings and page's administrators and users can manage who sees their activity. Here's a screen view from a user's page.

Your Activity	Who can see your future posts?	**Public**	Edit
	Review all your posts and things you're tagged in		Use Activity Log
	Limit the audience for posts you've shared with friends of friends or Public?		Limit Past Posts
	Who can see the people, Pages and lists you follow?	**Public**	Edit

Managing Your Activity on Facebook

Because of privacy settings and other factors, your search of an expert's social media activity may not lead to anything, so it's worth following up on these issues during the expert's deposition.

While people are very freewheeling about who they "like" or follow, on social media a skilled trial lawyer can still plant doubt in the minds of the jurors as to how professional and objective an expert really is when they are connecting with the party and/or law firm via social media. It suggests a more permanent connection and relationship than merely being an expert in this one case. And jurors who themselves are reserved about whom they follow or like on social media (or accept as friends) may view the expert as being less objective and unbiased if the expert follows a party or legal counsel in the case.

5.1.5 "Learned Treatises" for Direct and Cross-Examination

Social media discovery is also a helpful resource for identifying other experts in the area who may have blog posts that counsel could offer as a "learned treatise" for impeaching the expert pursuant to Federal Rule of Evidence 803(18). You can make this argument based on, among other things, the fact that courts now cite to blog posts in their opinions.[17] There's an increasing trend for court clerks to use blogs as a research source for legal issues, in much the same way they used law review comments in the past. In a speech on August 19, 2010, Justice Anthony Kennedy made a passing remark that law review case comments usually come out too late to be of

17. *See, e.g.*, United States v. Everett III, 601 F.3d 484, 493 (6th Cir. 2010).

use to the Court, so he finds his clerks are reading blogs in interesting cases. In an expert's deposition, try to have them validate other blog sites as accepted authorities in their field of expertise.

With respect to the expert's social media posts, the foundation should be easily established for authenticating and using the evidence at trial for impeachment purposes. If it's an embarrassing post that the expert denies authoring, the discussion in Chapter Nine will be useful.

You also may be able to use blogs by other people in the same field to corroborate a theory being offered by your expert. This information can be introduced through direct examination on how they reached their opinion in the case. Federal Rule of Evidence 703 provides for the witness to testify about facts "perceived by or made known to the expert at or before the hearing . . . if of a type reasonably relied upon by experts in the particular field in forming opinions or inferences upon the subject," even if the facts would not otherwise be admissible.

Key Points

When vetting potential experts, ask about their digital footprint.

Ask your expert to refrain from discussing your case on social media and the internet.

Check online relationships when researching the potential biases of the other side's experts.

Use informal discovery tools to investigate the other side's expert: blogs, listservs, social media, etc.

Highlight in formal discovery that social media and Internet activity are covered by Rule 26(a) discovery and document subpoena.

Closed group (listserv) discussions are discoverable and include subject matter topics.

Remember that some online sources can be used as "learned treatises."

Part Two

Trial

Trial creates many challenges when dealing with social media. Whether the goal is to have social media and related evidence admitted or excluded, a thorough understanding of how the rules of evidence apply is paramount. When presenting a case to jurors, it's ideal to have direct evidence of whatever you're trying to prove. More often, though, we are trying to satisfy our burden of proof with circumstantial evidence that's indirect proof of an event, occurrence, or proposition in a case. It is often the sum of circumstantial evidence that persuades jurors. However, there's always the risk that a trier of fact will not agree with us that, taken together, the circumstantial evidence actually *is* what you're trying to establish. In other words, for some triers of fact, 1 + 1 will not always = 2. This is why we're always looking for direct evidence to make our case.

In this part of the book, we will examine how to monitor social media during a trial, how to use social media to aid in the jury selection process, considerations for evidentiary foundations, and take a deeper dive into authentication and hearsay.

CHAPTER SIX

MONITORING SOCIAL MEDIA AT TRIAL

Once trial begins, or is about to, shift your social media and internet discovery into a monitoring mode, with someone on your staff periodically checking the social media sites of parties, witnesses, the other side's legal counsel, and your trial judge to pick up any posts that are relevant to the claims or defenses or that border on conduct that may be grounds for a sanctions order (e.g., counsel that ignores a court's gag order) or asking a judge to recuse herself (e.g., a judge posting about an ongoing case or exchanging posts with a party witness or legal counsel about the case). The importance of monitoring jurors is covered in Chapter Seven, with a discussion of how to monitor without running afoul of the ethics rules prohibiting ex parte communications.

6.1 Trial Counsel

Sometimes a picture is worth a thousand words. In the middle of a murder trial that drew nationwide attention, the defense attorney took a selfie with his daughters eating ice cream, which one daughter then posted on Instagram, along with her thoughts on how her father (counsel for the defense) did in the first few days of the trial.

Controversial Instagram Post

Because her father, Don West, was defending George Zimmerman, on trial for second-degree murder and manslaughter of an unarmed black teenager, Trayvon Martin, in a hotly debated case, the response to her Instagram post was negative.

> The post drew an immediate and harsh reaction online. It had attracted over 2,200 comments on Instagram as of Friday evening [two days after her Wednesday post], most of them negative, even vulgar. On Twitter, a #mollywest hashtag attracted a slew of outraged responses, many connecting the tweet to Don West's relentless questioning, over two days, of Rachel Jeantel, the nineteen-year-old friend of Martin's who was on the phone with him until just moments before he was killed.

Sharon @LAwomanSharon · Jun 28, 2013
I can't believe that an attorney's daughter would be ignorant enough to post that photo. Well played, #mollywest Who is stupid now, cupcake?
1 12 4

DIB Turner @dibcupcake · Jun 28, 2013
IGNORANCE at the highest level! A child is dead and #DonWest daughters joke about it? WTF #standmyground #mollywest
6 2

K I N G @TAMYINTHISBITCH · Jun 28, 2013
How ironic the caption is "we beat stupidity..." With her stupidity so clearly on display. #mollywest
1 1

Just Sunny @SunnyDayze · Jun 29, 2013
Hey #MollyWest @Mollywesttttt u didn't beat stupidity, you just displayed you & your Dad's stupidity by posting that stupid & insensitive pic
1 21 10

Response on Twitter: swift and scathing.

Following this post, it was reported in the same article[1] that two more posts were made on Instagram while the Zimmerman trial was still ongoing:

1. Joy Ann Reid, *Zimmerman Lawyer's Daughters Spark Outrage With Instagram Posts—"We Beat Stupidity Celebration,"* The Grio (June 29, 2013), https://thegrio.com/2013/06/29/zimmerman-lawyers-daughters-instagram-post-we-beat-stupidity-celebration/ (last visited Oct. 26, 2022).

> Two new photos surfaced Saturday, apparently uploaded by Rachel West to her Instagram account this week (the account has since been closed). In one of them, Rachel and Molly West are pictured together, with the caption: "rachelkwest Zimmerman trial defense room" and it is directed at @mollywesttt, Molly West's screen name. The picture was shared with several online friends, most of whose Instagram accounts have been made private.[2]

Zimmerman's defense counsel apologized for the Instagram post by his daughter(s) and stated that he had not authorized the publication of the picture he took of him and his daughters having ice cream in what was reported to be a family tradition to mark when he starts a new trial.

In the Aurora, Colorado, movie theater shooting case, both the court's public information officer and the prosecutor came under fire for their social media activity. The defense complained to the court about Twitter posts between the public information officer and one of the prosecutors, arguing that they violated the court's gag order. The court found there was no violation of the gag order, but the tone of the Twitter posts raised complaints about the information officer following on Twitter the district attorney's office and the district attorney himself, not to mention the "jovial tone" of their tweets.[3]

However, the Aurora theater shooting court was less forgiving when a defense attorney brought to the court's attention that a different prosecutor in the case was tweeting during the defense's cross-examination of a mental health expert. Reportedly, his tweet (which the prosecutor said he meant as a direct message but tweeted by mistake) commented on twenty-two hours of videorecorded interviews that the testifying mental health expert conducted with defendant James Holmes, which jurors had viewed. "I agree on the video," the prosecutor tweeted. "I hope the jury thinks so, too." The prosecutor was verbally reprimanded for disregarding the court's instruction for legal counsel not to use social media during court proceedings:

> [Judge] Samour was less than pleased by Brauchler's apology Friday, and he warned attorneys on both sides not to send social media or text messages during court again. "If you're bored and don't want to pay attention to the proceedings, then you can leave," he said.[4]

---

2. *Id.*
3. Melanie Asmar, *Aurora Theater Shooting: Court Spokesman's Tweets Didn't Violate Gag Order, Judge Says*, Westword (Mar. 20, 2014), http://www.westword.com/news/aurora-theater-shooting-court-spokes-mans-tweets-didnt-violate-gag-order-judge-says-5847290 (last visited Oct. 26, 2022).
4. John Ingold and Jordan Steffen, *Prosecutor's social media gaffe annoys theater shooting trial judge*, Denver Post (June 5, 2015), http://www.denverpost.com/theater-shooting-trial/ci_28257953/defense-questions-psychiatrist-aurora-theater-trial (last visited Oct. 26, 2022).

6.2 Judges

Presiding judges also make social media missteps. In Texas, a state court judge was reprimanded by the State Commission on Judicial Conduct for posting on Facebook about her cases.[5] The judge appealed the reprimand, and a special court of review set aside the reprimand, finding that the Commission failed to meet its burden of proving by a preponderance of the evidence that the judge violated the Canons of Judicial Conduct or Article V, Section 1-a(6)(A) of the Texas Constitution, when an unsolicited comment was posted on her social media account.[6] Among other things, the Texas judge argued that the judicial canons of conduct, as applied to her social media activity, were an unconstitutional violation of her First Amendment rights.

The social media posts at the center involved a pending criminal case about a father who was accused of keeping his nine-year-old son in a 6-foot x 8-foot box. The judge posted about the "Boy in the Box" case on her judicial Facebook page (as opposed to her personal page). The judge made the following post even though the box had not yet been introduced as evidence: "After we finished Day 1 of the case called the 'Boy in the Box' case, trustees from the jail came in and assembled the actual 6x8 'box' inside the courtroom!" The judge also posted a link to a Reuters article about the boy in the box. She later defended the post by saying it was an objective story about the case. Her posts resulted in a mistrial and she was removed from the case.

The judge also posted the year before about a "difficult" child pornography case pending before her:

> "We have a jury deliberating on punishment for two counts of possession of child pornography," she wrote. "It is probably one of the most difficult types of cases for jurors (and the judge and anyone else) to sit through because of the evidence they have to see. Bless the jury for their service and especially bless the poor child victims."[7]

Even though the judge was successful in having the Judicial Commission's admonition set aside, her social media activity led to a mistrial. The case was retried—at the taxpayers' expense.

The Special Court of Review noted that while not rising to the level of violating judicial codes of ethics, the social media activity was troublesome:

---

5. Texas State Comm'n on Judicial Conduct, *Public Admonition and Order of Additional Educ.* (Apr. 20, 2015), https://judicialethics.files.wordpress.com/2015/04/jef_michelle-slaughter-public-admonition-for-facebook-posts.pdf (last visited Oct. 26, 2022).
6. In re Honorable Michelle Slaughter, Presiding Judge of the 405th Judicial District Court, Galveston County, Texas, Docket No. 15-0001 (Special Court of Review of Texas, Sept. 30, 2015), https://caselaw.findlaw.com/tx-special-court-of-review-sct/1719821.html (last visited Oct. 26, 2022).
7. Texas State Comm'n on Judicial Conduct, *supra* n. 5, at 4.

> While we have held that such communications did not rise to the level of communicating to others how the judge might have ruled in the case, the timing of the posts is troublesome for the judiciary. A judge should never reveal his or her thought processes in making any judgment. Even calling attention to certain facts or evidence found significant enough for the judge to comment on in a pending matter before any decision has been rendered may tend to give the public the impression that they are seeing into the deliberation process of the judge.
>
> Additionally, extrajudicial comments made by a judge about a pending proceeding will likely invite scrutiny, as it did in this case. While the Respondent's comments were ultimately proven to not be suggestive of her probable decision on any particular case, the process for reaching this conclusion required the expenditure of a great deal of time, energy, and expense. And as this case illustrates, comments made by judges about pending proceedings create the very real possibility of a recusal (or even a mistrial) and may detract from the public trust and confidence in the administration of justice.[8]

This Texas judge is not alone in having her social media activities come under attack. A senior judge of the U.S. District Court of Appeals for the Eastern District of California has a Twitter account in which he tweets about more than "Returning to the Thrilling Days of Yesteryear" under his Twitter moniker @Nostalgist1. In his previously public Twitter account, Judge William B. Shubb tweeted about a case in which he had just denied a motion to terminate a settlement between the federal government and a lumber producer, Sierra Pacific Industries. Sierra Pacific Industries had settled the action without admitting liability concerning a 2007 wildfire that scorched almost 65,000 acres in Northern California. Sierra Pacific argued that the settlement was based in part on what is now described as an improper government investigation of the fire, which the government blamed on Sierra Pacific for the alleged negligent hiring and supervision of a logging contractor. Sierra Pacific Industries moved to vacate the settlement, arguing that it was reached as the result of a fraud on the court. Judge Shubb denied the motion—and that's when the questionable Twitter activity started. In its opening brief to the Ninth Circuit, Sierra Pacific raised ethical concerns about the online relationship between Judge Shubb and the U.S. Attorney's Office:

> Judge Shubb issued his order denying Defendants' motion on April 17, 2015, at 2:45 p.m. Over the next two hours, the Sacramento AUSA's used their "@EDCAnews" Twitter account to broadcast eight congratulatory Tweets concerning Judge Shubb's order and the case's merits to their office's Twitter followers. Defendants have since confirmed

8. *Id.* at 19–20.

> that, through his then-public Twitter account, titled "@notstalgist1," Judge Shubb "followed" @EDCAnews and thus received these Tweets. The mere existence of social network relationships between a judge and one of the parties appearing before him creates an appearance of bias and raises "significant concern" regarding the risk of ex parte communications. California Judges Association, Formal Opinion No. 66-Online Social Networking § III (C)(3)–(D) (2011). Those concerns materialize when a "followed" party posts Tweets regarding the case's merits and the judge's reasoning, which are then directed to the judge in his capacity as a follower.[9]

Perhaps even more worrisome, however, is how Judge Shubb described his decision in *Sierra Pacific* on his Twitter account, according to the Sierra Pacific Opening Brief:

> Additionally, that evening at 9:51 p.m., Judge Shubb completed the feedback loop by posting on his @nostalgist1 public Twitter account: "Sierra Pacific still liable for Moonlight Fire damages." Just beneath this post, Judge Shubb linked to an article with the same title from the Central Valley Business Times. Contrary to Judge Shubb's imprimatur, the title was false. Sierra Pacific was never found liable and has paid no damages. Indeed, Judge Nichols, the only neutral to evaluate the merits of this joint prosecution, found the government's partner unable to make a prima facie case against Defendants. In the federal settlement, Defendants expressly disclaimed liability and have never paid a cent in damages.
>
> Judge Shubb's inaccurate public post violates Canon of Judicial Conduct 3(A)(6) and only increases the appearance of bias. It also prejudices Sierra Pacific and all Defendants in the pending state court appeal regarding the Moonlight Fire. When a judge selectively posts third-party communications pertaining to his or her cases, it necessarily creates the appearance of bias, especially with respect to articles that are inaccurate and prejudicial. The act of picking and choosing one article of many reveals a willingness to step out of the role of a neutral. By assenting to and posting a particular article, the court entangles itself with the message and slant of that article, thereby creating the appearance of having picked sides or of favoring one spin over another.[10]

What is also significant and worth highlighting is that Judge Shubb is an experienced jurist and a highly trained and educated legal professional. He was a former

9. Brief of Petitioner-Appellant at 80–81, United States of America v. Sierra Pacific Industries, No. 15-15799 (9th Cir. Nov. 6, 2015) (internal cites and footnotes omitted).
10. *Id.* at 81–82 (internal cites and footnotes omitted).

U.S. Attorney and is also an alumnus of one of the top law schools in the country, Boalt Hall School of Law. Born in 1938, he is outside the age demographic that most people believe is part of the social media age.

The social media activity of these two judges highlights how important it is not to dismiss social media accounts as a resource for researching judges, opposing counsel, experts, and witnesses, no matter their age or professional pedigree. Though neither judge was punished for their social media activity, that activity resulted in at least one costly mistrial and damaged the credibility of the judicial process.

6.3 "Big Picture" Concerns

To put these social media posts by trial lawyers and judges in the proper context, these posts are being made in cases where the jurors had been admonished not to talk about the case to anyone, and certainly not to post about it on social media. Further, as the Texas State Commission on Judicial Conduct noted in its order, judges tell jurors that they are not allowed make any independent investigation of the case and that this admonishment applies to the court as well.

Put simply, how can courts expect jurors to respect the instructions of the court when the same rules are not being applied to officers of the court? What is being said on social media by prosecutors and defense counsel about the cases being presented may border on ex parte communications to sitting jurors about the case unless courts are going to try to keep jurors off of social media sites while a case is pending. This seems like a much harder hurdle to meet than directing court officers not to post about cases that are in trial before a jury.

In addition, these examples are meant to underscore how naïve it is to expect jurors to respect admonitions by the court about social media. Accordingly, as discussed in the next chapter, the burden falls on trial counsel to monitor the social media activity of jurors and to raise any grounds for replacing a juror with an alternate (or excusing them with cause from the jury pool) early in the case.

Key Points

Remember, monitoring social media doesn't stop with opening statements.

Witnesses, parties, lawyers, and judges all have the potential to slip up and cross a line. Don't miss it. It may help your case.

Social media posts about the case by your family or employees can reflect poorly on you and your professionalism. "I didn't know it would be public" is not a good excuse.

Be prompt in bringing issues to the court's attention.

Chapter Seven

Selecting and Monitoring Jurors

While there's little doubt social media has forever changed litigation and trial practice, the good news is that stories of "jurors gone wild" appear to be exaggerated, based on a 2013 survey of federal court judges.[1] Of the 494 judges responding to the survey, only thirty-three reported knowing of jurors using social media, and even then it only occurred in one or two of their cases. While this report is encouraging, read it with caution. First, the report is based on a survey to which slightly less than half the federal judges responded, which means more than 500 judges did not respond. Second, as the report's authors recognized, the results were based on anecdotal experience, not actual empirical evidence of how much jurors are following (or not following) the court's instructions about social media usage.[2]

According to the report, jurors who break the court's social media rules are most likely to divulge confidential information about the case on social media. The next common transgression was jurors trying to communicate with someone involved in the case: a party, witness, legal counsel, or judge.

The report also found that judges have made a difference by talking about social media use, rather than assuming jurors will understand that the standard admonitions (i.e., not to discuss the case or do independent research) include social media and internet usage. Judges have employed the following techniques, with some apparent success:

- **Be clear.** Say what you mean. Mean what you say. Explain the reason for the social media ban in plain, nonlegal language.
- **Say it, and say it again.** Instruct the jurors at multiple points during the trial.
- **Start early.** Remind jurors at voir dire to refrain from using social media.
- **Before trial.** Use use the Judicial Conference Committee's model jury instructions, or some form of jury instruction, on the use of social media and

1. United States Courts, *Survey Finds Infrequent Use of Social Media by Jurors* (July 29, 2014), https://www.uscourts.gov/news/2014/07/29/survey-finds-infrequent-social-media-use-jurors (last visited Mar. 28, 2022).
2. *Id.* at 3.

electronic communications. The prohibition on social media and electronic communications deserves its own jury instruction.

- **Remove temptation.** Confiscate phones and electronic devices during deliberations.
- **Alert jurors to the possible personal consequences,** such as being held in civil or criminal contempt, if they use social media or the internet to discuss the trial. Scare tactics can be useful.

You may be thinking now that judges have social media use under control, and you can focus on your case. Not so fast. Judges rely on you and others to detect and report violations:

> Judges acknowledge that it is difficult to detect jurors' inappropriate use of social media, and that judges rely on others to bring it to their attention. Of the 27 judges [in the 2013 survey] who indicated how they learned of the incident, 12 judges said another juror had reported it. Eight judges said an attorney had reported it, and seven said it was reported by court staff or by one of the parties. Three judges said a juror's use of social media came up in post-trial motions. Only one judge reported observing jurors using electronic devices in the courtroom.[3]

Think about it. Who has the biggest investment in making sure that your jurors aren't turning to the internet and their social media connections to decide the case instead of relying on the case that you have worked so hard to present? You and your client do. Jurors and social media are not the Wild West; there are actions you can take from the very start of your case.

Before you do anything, though, check to see if your court has any standing orders about researching and monitoring jurors using the internet. If the court prohibits researching and monitoring jurors, you may either ask the judge to lift the prohibition or you must comply with it. The discussion that follows will assume there is no local court rule or standing order that prohibits researching jurors on social media and the internet.

7.1 Jury Selection

Some cases have enough at stake that your client is willing to pay for a mock trial and a jury consultant to recommend the ideal jury composition for the case—unfortunately, the ideal jury is never reflected in the actual jury pool for your particular judicial district. Moreover, people aren't always as they appear in the artificial setting of the courtroom. Yet even with these factors, you are trying to decide who to excuse based on the answers they've given during voir dire. Depending on the

3. *Id.* at 6.

judge, you may be allowed to question the prospective jurors yourself, or the judge may do all of the questioning, with input from you and other counsel in the case.

Fortunately, you have another tool available to you in cases where jurors are identified by their full name rather than juror number. Online research and access to social media have the potential for opening up a whole new avenue to excuse a juror for cause. Remember, this research can be farmed out to a vendor, such as Social Intelligence,[4] while you focus on preparing for trial. Coordinate with the vendor in advance, so it's prepared to do the research on a rush basis.

Social media activity may show that despite jurors' responses to questions, they aren't being candid or truthful. In *State v. Dellinger*,[5] the court held that a juror lacked complete candor in her responses to voir dire questions. She didn't disclose that she knew the defendant or that she'd sent him a message between receiving her jury summons and appearing for jury duty. Juror Amber Hyre sent the following message to the defendant and appellant via MySpace, a social networking site (with her misspellings left uncorrected here):

> Hey, I dont know you very well But I think you could use some advice! I havent been in your shoes for a long time but I can tell ya that God has a plan for you and your life. You might not understand why you are hurting right now but when you look back on it, it will make perfect sence. I know it hard but just remember that God is perfect and has the most perfect plan for your life. Talk soon![6]

On appeal, Dellinger argued that Juror Hyre's lack of candor on voir dire should have been grounds for a new trial. The *Dellinger* court reversed the trial court and ordered a new trial: "[T]he totality of Juror Hyre's responses during the June 11, 2008, coupled with her repeated silence during voir dire, leads this Court to conclude that she had such connection with Appellant and witnesses Frame and Slaughter that bias must be presumed."[7]

As trial lawyers, we sometimes experience a gut feeling that a juror is holding back on strong biases against a particular case in order to exercise vigilante justice through the jury process. Researching the juror on social media may reveal a blog site or posts that we can use to support a request to the court that the juror be excused for cause.

Here are some stories, ripped from the headlines, about jurors trying to game the voir dire selection process:

4. www.socialintel.com (Last visited Sep. 7, 2022).
5. State v. Dellinger, 696 S.E.2d 38, 225 W. Va. 736 (2010).
6. *Id.* at 738.
7. *Id.* at 741.

- A juror concealed the fact that she had gone to law school and practiced law until her license was suspended. On voir dire, she only shared that she had a BA in English literature and classics.[8] The conviction in the tax fraud case she was a juror on was overturned because of the various lies she told in order to make herself "marketable" as a juror.[9] Her lies came to light when defense counsel scoured public records about her *after* the juror sent a letter post-conviction, congratulating the prosecutors on the excellent job they did during the tax fraud case.[10]
- A juror in a murder trial failed to disclose that she was ineligible to serve because she was a convicted felon. This material omission was discovered when an investigator for the district attorney's office happened to come into the courtroom when the jury was returning its verdict in the first-degree murder trial—and the investigator recognized the juror. The juror mistakenly believed her conviction had been expunged, so she did not disclose it to the court.

There are hundreds of online websites for searching whether someone has been convicted of a crime. All it takes is a quick Google search with "conviction report searches" as the search terms.

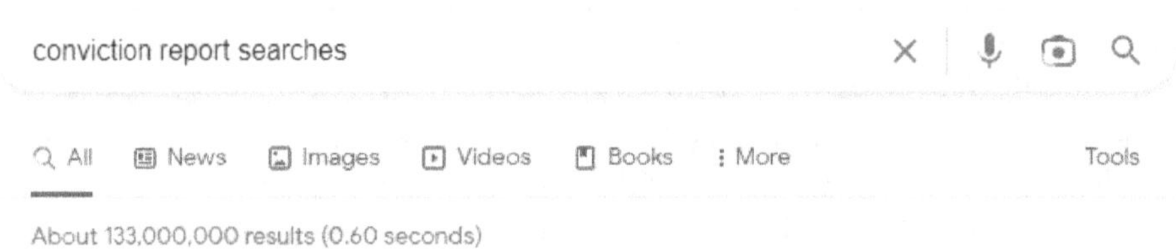

- A jury foreperson failed to disclose that she thought of some of the victims' families as her friends and clients. As a result, the murder conviction and death penalty sentence was appealed and subject to further court review.[11] A search of the foreperson's social media could have revealed early on in the trial that she was Facebook "friends" with some of the victims' families, thereby disqualifying her from serving as a juror in the first place.

8. United States v. Parse, 789 F.3d 83, 88 (2d Cir. N.Y. 2015).
9. *Id.*; Josh Saul, Fraud conviction tossed over alcoholic, shrimp-stealing juror: docs, New York Post (June 8, 2015), http://nypost.com/2015/06/08/lying-juror-gets-ex-deutsche-bank-tax-fraud-case-tossed/ (last visited Oct. 26, 2022).
10. Richard F. Albert, Jurors Behaving Badly, Forbes (May 2, 2012), https://www.forbes.com/sites/insider/2012/05/02/jurors-behaving-badly/?sh=153a9df97873 (last visited Oct. 26, 2022).
11. Cunningham v. Hudson, 756 F.3d 477, 487 (6th Cir. Ohio 2014).

7.2 Monitoring Jurors through Social Media

Using social media to get more information on your jurors should not end once jurors have been selected. Always ask the court to have the jurors list blogs or websites to which they regularly post, then check those sites both during and after the trial to ensure none of the jurors have breached the legal obligations they have as jurors.[12] In one widely reported case, a criminal defense attorney's son was researching the jurors in a resisting arrest case and found a juror's troubling Facebook post: "gonna be fun to tell the defendant they're GUILTY." The juror didn't wait until jury deliberations to make this post; she posted it before the defendant put on her case. The juror was removed from the jury, fined $250, and ordered to write an essay on the Sixth Amendment of the Constitution.[13]

Alas, this Facebook-posting juror was not an isolated case. There are a number of other known examples—and likely many others that are never discovered at all. In a murder case in Ventura, California, a juror blogged about the case during trial. In his blog, "The Misanthrope," the juror posted photographs of the fifteen-inch, double-edged, saw-toothed knife that was used as a murder weapon. The juror also set up a "chat room" so that blog visitors could ask him questions about the trial. The defense attorneys learned of the blog and informed the judge. The defense also moved for a new trial during the sentencing phase, based on juror misconduct. The court denied the motion, and the defendant's twenty-seven-year sentence was not overturned on appeal notwithstanding the online posting by the juror.[14]

While not all jurors are trying to be the next *Drudge Report*[15] from the jury box, the number of jurors who talk about being on jury duty is still quite alarming. A Reuters Legal study, using data from Westlaw online, found that tweets from people describing themselves as prospective or sitting jurors appeared at the rate of one nearly every three minutes.[16]

7.2.1 Jury Instructions

Fortunately, courts are responding appropriately to the pervasive use of social media at trials and often include social media in their jury instructions both before

12. A legal blog directly on point for examples of jurors not following the rules, aptly titled, "Jurors Behaving Badly," written and edited by Judge Stephen M. Falsey, Wright County District Court, http://jurorsbehavingbadly.blogspot.com/ (last visited Oct. 26, 2022).
13. Tanya Roth, Esq., *Juror Expelled for Posting Verdict on Facebook*, Findlaw Blotter (Aug. 31, 2010), http://blogs.findlaw.com/blotter/2010/08/juror-expelled-for-posting-verdict-on-facebook.html (last visited Oct. 26, 2022).
14. People v. Ortiz, 2009 Cal. App. Unpub. LEXIS 8061 (Cal. App. 2d Dist. Oct. 8, 2009).
15. *See* https://en.wikipedia.org/wiki/Drudge_Report (last visited Oct. 26, 2022).
16. Brian Grow, *As jurors go online, U.S. trials go off-track*, Reuters (Aug. 8, 2010), https://www.reuters.com/article/us-internet-jurors/as-jurors-go-online-u-s-trials-go-off-track-idUSTRE6B74Z820101208 (last visited Oct. 26, 2022).

the trial begins and prior to jury deliberations. Below are jury instruction samples that a court may consider using:

Before Trial

> You, as jurors, must decide this case based solely on the evidence presented here within the four walls of this courtroom. This means that during the trial, you must not conduct any independent research about this case, the matters in the case, and the individuals or corporations involved in the case. In other words, you should not consult dictionaries or reference materials; search the internet, websites, or blogs; or use any other electronic tools to obtain information about this case or to help you decide the case. Please do not try to find out information from any source outside the confines of this courtroom. Until you retire to deliberate, you may not discuss this case with anyone, even your fellow jurors. After you retire to deliberate, you may begin discussing the case with your fellow jurors, but you cannot discuss the case with anyone else until you have returned a verdict and the case is at an end. I know that many of you use cellphones, tablets, the internet, and other tools of technology. You also must not talk to anyone at any time about this case or use these tools to communicate electronically with anyone about the case. This includes your family and friends. You may not communicate with anyone about the case on your cellphone, tablet, iPhone, through text messaging, email, or on Twitter, through any blog or website, including Facebook, Google+, Instagram, LinkedIn, or YouTube. You may not use any similar technology or social media, even if I have not specifically mentioned it here. I expect you will inform me as soon as you become aware of another juror's violation of these instructions.[17]

The last sentence of this proposed instruction reflects the fact that juror misconduct involving social media comes frequently to the court's attention only as a result of jurors reporting on violations by a fellow juror.

At the Close of the Case

> During your deliberations, you must not communicate with or provide any information to anyone by any means about this case. You may not use any electronic device or media, such as the telephone, a cellphone, smartphone, iPhone, tablet, or computer, the internet, any

17. Links to California civil and criminal jury instructions concerning electronic communications, Judicial Council of California Civil Jury Instructions, https://www.courts.ca.gov/partners/documents/Judicial_Council_of_California_Civil_Jury_Instructions.pdf; Judicial Council of California Criminal Jury Instructions (*see* Instrs. 101 and 116) (last visited Oct. 26, 2022).

> internet service, any text or instant messaging service, any internet chat room, blog, or website such as Facebook, Instagram, LinkedIn, YouTube, or Twitter, to communicate to anyone any information about this case or to conduct any research about this case until I accept your verdict. In other words, you cannot talk to anyone on the phone, correspond with anyone, or electronically communicate with anyone about this case. You can only discuss the case in the jury room with your fellow jurors during deliberations. I expect you will inform me as soon as you become aware of another juror's violation of these instructions. You may not use these electronic means to investigate or communicate about the case because it is important that you decide this case based solely on the evidence presented in this courtroom. Information on the internet or available through social media might be wrong, incomplete, or inaccurate. You are only permitted to discuss the case with your fellow jurors during deliberations because they have seen and heard the same evidence you have. In our judicial system, it is important that you are not influenced by anything or anyone outside of this courtroom. Otherwise, your decision may be based on information known only by you and not your fellow jurors or the parties in the case. This would unfairly and adversely impact the judicial process.[18]

Counsel for the parties should make a point of asking the court to instruct jurors not to discuss the case on Facebook, Twitter, LinkedIn, blogs, or any social media. Even vague references to the case should not be permitted. It's hard to predict if an appellate court will order a new trial based on juror misconduct. The courts seem reluctant to do so unless there is some showing that the social media misconduct prevented the jury from rendering a fair verdict based on the evidence introduced at trial. However, if jurors are specifically instructed not to discuss the case on social media and ignore this instruction, then the facts may be stronger for the court granting a motion for new trial.

7.2.2 Consequences to Jurors

Courts also hold jurors in contempt for ignoring jury instructions that direct them not to discuss the case or research it using electronic communication such as social media. Courts have been unreceptive to jurors trying to withhold their social media activity when it's the subject of a motion for a new trial by a criminal defendant. For example, a California court of appeals held that the criminal defendant's

18. *Proposed Model Jury Instructions, The Use of Electronic Technology to Conduct Research on or Communicate about a Case,* Prepared by the Judicial Conference Committee on Court Administration and Case Management (June 2020), https://www.uscourts.gov/sites/default/files/proposed_model_jury_instructions.pdf (last visited Oct. 26, 2022).

interest in being able to show that there was reversible prejudice trumped the juror's unsubstantiated privilege against self-incrimination and privacy concerns:

> The present matter no longer involves a claim of potential misconduct. Misconduct has been established without question. The only remaining issue is whether the misconduct was prejudicial. This cannot be determined without looking at the Facebook posts. Yet Juror Number One would bar the trial court from examining the posts to determine if there was prejudice because there has been no showing of prejudice. In summary, in the present matter, Juror Number One does not claim respondent court exceeded its inherent authority to inquire into juror misconduct. Just as the court may examine jurors under oath, it may also examine other evidence of misconduct. In this instance, the court seeks to review in camera the very items—the Facebook posts—that constitute the misconduct.[19] Juror Number One contends such disclosure violates the SCA [Stored Communications Act], but it does not. Even assuming the Facebook posts are protected by the SCA, the SCA protects against disclosure by third parties, not the posting party. Juror Number One also contends the order is not authorized, because the court has completed its investigation of misconduct. But such investigation obviously has not been completed. Juror Number One also contends the compelled disclosure violates his Fourth and Fifth Amendment rights. However, beyond asserting this to be so, he provides no argument or citation to authority. Thus, those arguments are forfeited. Finally, Juror Number One argues forced disclosure of his Facebook posts violates his privacy rights. However, Juror Number One has not shown he has any expectation of privacy in the posts and, in any event, those privacy rights do not trump real parties in interest's right to a fair trial free from juror misconduct. The trial court has the power and the duty to inquire into whether the confirmed misconduct was prejudicial.[20]

7.2.3 Federal Court Survey

If you have a case that is especially salacious or newsworthy, you might ask the court to be even more proactive about keeping jurors off of social media. The 2013 survey of the federal judges cited at the beginning of this chapter is an excellent resource for actions a court may wish to take. Because jurors running amok on social media are a nuisance to both sides, consider making your request to the court in the form of a joint stipulation or unopposed motion.

---

19. People v. Hedgecock, 51 Cal. 3d 395, 417–418 (1990).
20. Juror Number One v. Superior Court, 206 Cal. App. 4th 854, 868 (Cal. Ct. App. 2012).

7.2.4 Juror Pledges

Some judges have had jurors pledge in writing that they will refrain from conducting outside research or communicating about the case, and made jurors subject to perjury charges if they violate the pledge they made under oath. In one federal district court case in Manhattan, the judge had prospective jurors sign the pledges during voir dire and excused a prospective juror who refused to sign it. The judge was particularly sensitive about jurors using the internet because the criminal case was high profile, with a defendant who was a Russian businessman accused of trying to sell guns to Colombian rebels. The judge was concerned that if jurors researched the defendant, they'd find stories describing him as a notorious arms dealer.[21] In a state court case in California, the judge required potential jurors to sign a pledge stating they would not communicate electronically about the case. The case involved an unusual set of facts where the plaintiff was suing a radio station over the death of his wife, who had participated in a contest in which participants drank excessive amounts of water every fifteen minutes without going to the restroom. His wife died from water intoxication five hours after finishing second in the contest. One issue in the case was whether the radio station was negligent in not having researched the risks of water intoxication before it hosted the contest, so there was some concern that jurors would go online to research water intoxication during the trial.[22]

7.3 Bright-Line Rules to Remember

Researching and monitoring jurors during your case come with some bright-line rules to remember. The same offline ethics rules apply to your online reconnaissance.

7.3.1 Do Not "Friend" Your Jurors

Offline rules provide a bright line for social media contact with jurors. Looking at the public sites of jurors without having any direct or indirect contact with them is allowed by state bars and the American Bar Association (ABA).[23] Gaining access to jurors' private pages by "friending" them, however, is not.

---

21. Colin Moynihan, *Judge Considers Pledge for Jurors on Internet Use*, New York Times (Sept. 18, 2011), http://www.nytimes.com/2011/09/19/nyregion/us-judge-considers-making-jurors-vow-not-to-use-web.html?_r=0 (last visited Oct. 26, 2022).
22. Strange v. Entercom Sacramento LLC, No. 07AS00377 (Cal. Super. Ct. Sacramento Cnty., Jan. 25, 2007); Greg Moran, *Revised jury instructions: Do not use the Internet*, San Diego Union-Tribune (Sept. 13, 2009), https://www.sandiegouniontribune.com/sdut-revised-jury-instructions-do-not-use-internet-2009sep13-story.html (last visited Oct. 26, 2022).
23. Or. State Bar Ass'n, Formal Op. 2013 189 ("Lawyer may access publicly available information [about juror, witness, and opposing party] on social networking website"); N.Y. Cnty. Lawyers Ass'n, Formal Op. 743 (2011) (lawyer may search juror's "publicly available" webpages and ESM); Ass'n of the Bar of the City of N.Y. Comm. on Prof'l Ethics, supra n. 3 (lawyer may use social media websites to research jurors); Ky. Bar Ass'n, Op. E-434 (2012) ("If the site is 'public,' and accessible to all,

Ethics committees from the ABA and state bars agree that direct contact with jurors via social media is prohibited. Direct contact includes trying to friend them on Facebook, subscribing to the RSS feed of their blog, asking them to connect with you on LinkedIn, or asking to follow their private Instagram account. However, there is a split among the ABA and some state bars as to whether lawyers can be faulted for indirect (and unintended) contact with jurors via social media. In other words, what burden are we willing to impose on lawyers to understand the operations of the social media sites that they are using to monitor jurors? Should a lawyer research and know beforehand that the social media site automatically alerts users that someone has viewed their public social media account? As discussed in chapters one and four, social media sites such as LinkedIn tell users who has reviewed their profile (unless the viewer has adjusted their privacy settings to make their profile anonymous when they look at other people's profiles), and Twitter and Instagram automatically alert users when they gain a new follower.

For now, lawyers are mostly off the hook, ethically, for these indirect contacts. In Formal Opinion 466, the ABA Standing Committee on Ethics and Professional Responsibility provides that a lawyer monitoring social media must do so without contacting the juror, but then splits with some state bars as to whether it is an "indirect" contact if that social media platform sends an automated notification to the juror that the lawyer has reviewed his account. The state bars of California and New York indicate that lawyers are responsible for knowing how a site works and to avoid following a juror's Twitter account.[24]

The ABA Formal Opinion is somewhat ambiguous in this regard, because while it says that this passive following is not a prohibited ex parte communication, the Opinion also states that lawyers should familiarize themselves with the workings of the social media site they are using as a research tool:

> While this Committee concludes that ESM-generated notice to a juror that a lawyer has reviewed the juror's information is not communication from the lawyer to the juror, the Committee does make two additional recommendations to lawyers who decide to review juror social media. First, the Committee suggests that lawyers be aware of these automatic, subscriber-notification features. By accepting the terms of use, the subscriber-notification feature is not secret. As indicated by Rule 1.1, Comment 8, it is important for a lawyer to be current with technology. While many people simply click their agreement to the

---

then there does not appear to be any ethics issue."). *See also* N.Y. State Bar Ass'n, Advisory Op. 843 (2010) ("A lawyer representing a client in pending litigation may access the public pages of another party's social networking website (such as Facebook or MySpace) for the purpose of obtaining possible impeachment material for use in the litigation.").

24. N.Y. Cnty. Lawyers Ass'n, supra n. 5 ("Significant ethical concerns would be raised by sending a 'friend request,' attempting to connect via LinkedIn.com, signing up for an RSS feed for a juror's blog, or 'following' a juror's Twitter account.").

> terms and conditions for use of an ESM network, a lawyer who uses an ESM network in his practice should review the terms and conditions, including privacy features—which change frequently—prior to using such a network. And, as noted above, jurisdictions differ on issues that arise when a lawyer uses social media in his practice.
>
> Second, Rule 4.4(a) prohibits lawyers from actions "that have no substantial purpose other than to embarrass, delay, or burden a third person." Lawyers who review juror social media should ensure that their review is purposeful and not crafted to embarrass, delay, or burden the juror or the proceeding.

It's important to know the state and federal ethics rules on this issue because this is an area where they are not consistent.

The recommended practice is to research jurors without engaging in a way that the automated notification system would detect monitoring and alert the juror. Aside from the ethical considerations, most jurors will not take kindly to the idea that a party to a case and its counsel are spying on them. It feels like cyberstalking, which few people will tolerate and accept as one of the costs of taking time to serve as a juror.

7.3.2 Bring Juror Misconduct to the Court's Attention

In a hypothetical situation, let's assume the plaintiff's lawyer learns from social media that a juror intentionally failed to disclose she was prejudiced against the defendant manufacturer in the case because the juror herself was once a victim of a similar industrial accident. The lawyer thought this particular juror was sympathetic to his client's case, so the last thing he wants to do is lose her. This is an ethical question that's likely to come up for lawyers, and the answer is the same as with other offline misconduct of jurors: as an officer of the court, the lawyer is required to bring the alleged misconduct to the court's attention.[25] ABA Model Rule of Professional Conduct 3.3(b) imposes this duty on lawyers:

> A lawyer who represents a client in an adjudicative proceeding and who knows that a person intends to engage, is engaging or has engaged in criminal or fraudulent conduct related to the proceeding shall take reasonable remedial measures, including, if necessary, disclosure to the tribunal.

---

25. ABA Standing Committee on Ethics and Professional Conduct, Formal Op. 466, *Lawyer Reviewing Jurors' Internet Presence* (Apr. 24, 2014), https://www.americanbar.org/content/dam/aba/administrative/professional_responsibility/formal_opinion_466_final_04_23_14.pdf (last visited Oct. 26, 2022).

Key Points

The burden is on the parties to ensure jurors do not use the internet and social media to discuss or research the case.

Judges are receptive to adding jury instructions directed at social media usage.

Ask the court to highlight the importance of jurors not using the internet in relation to the case and that violating this rule can lead a juror to being held in contempt of court.

Monitor your jurors but stay below the radar. Do not have ex parte communications with jurors by making a social media connection with them—directly or indirectly.

Chapter Eight

Laying Foundations

Hopefully, by now, you are comfortable with how to find and gather relevant social media evidence in your case. Good for you, because discomfort is one of the reasons why lawyers resist seeing the utility of social media and dismiss it as frivolous online conversations they can ignore. Second to discovering social media activity, lawyers seem equally confounded by how to get it admitted into evidence. This is the hurdle we tackle in the next few chapters. Just as we've done previously in this book, we'll start with some fundamental rules, then see how they apply with equal effect to social media and internet evidence.

As you know, there are three hurdles to getting something admitted into evidence: relevance, authentication, and trustworthiness (i.e., it's not hearsay—or if it is, it's admissible under one of the hearsay exceptions).

8.1 Hurdle One: What Is Relevant Evidence?

It's evidence that makes a disputed fact either more or less likely. According to Federal Rule of Evidence 401:

> Evidence is relevant if:
>
> (a) it has any tendency to make a fact more or less probable than it would be without the evidence; and
>
> (b) the fact is of consequence in determining the action.

For example, an online video of the other side's economic damages expert doing the chicken dance[1] is not going to come into evidence just for the sake of trying to embarrass the expert. However, a similar online video of the plaintiff doing the chicken dance at a wedding may be relevant to show that she didn't suffer crippling back injuries sustained in the automobile accident that's the subject of a personal injury lawsuit against the other driver.

---

1. *See, e.g.*, Jennifer Parker, How to Do the Chicken Dance, https://www.youtube.com/watch?v=4BdltUczNIQ (last visited Oct. 26, 2022).

8.2 Hurdle Two: What Does It Mean to Authenticate Evidence?

The party offering the evidence needs to show that it actually *is* what it's being offered to be. Rule 901 of the Federal Rules of Evidence provides in pertinent part:

> (a) In General. To satisfy the requirement of authenticating or identifying an item of evidence, the proponent must produce evidence sufficient to support a finding that the item is what the proponent claims it is.
>
> (b) Examples. The following are examples only—not a complete list—of evidence that satisfies the requirement:
>
> (1) Testimony of a Witness with Knowledge. Testimony that an item is what it is claimed to be.
>
> . . .
>
> (3) Comparison by an Expert Witness or the Trier of Fact. A comparison with an authenticated specimen by an expert witness or the trier of fact.
>
> (4) Distinctive Characteristics and the Like. The appearance, contents, substance, internal patterns, or other distinctive characteristics of the item, taken together with all the circumstances.

Put simply, you must show that the social media evidence actually *is* what you claim it to be. It actually *is* a Facebook or Twitter post by the witness or party; it actually *is* a LinkedIn profile created by the witness (as opposed to someone else without the knowledge or consent of the witness).

Former Congressional Representative Anthony Weiner (D-NY) was caught up in a Twitter scandal that torpedoed his promising political career in 2011 (and again in 2013). Much like Charlie Sheen's debacle with his phone number, Weiner, intending to send a direct message (DM) to a twenty-one-year-old woman on Twitter, accidentally tweeted a photo of his crotch as a very public post to his followers and anyone else on Twitter who happened to come across the post. It's a very easy mistake to make and not that uncommon:

> To send a DM to a Twitter follower using TweetDeck, the Twitter application Weiner was reportedly using when he sent the fateful photo, a user prefaces a tweet with the letter D, followed by the Twitter username of the person he or she wants to communicate with privately (e.g. "@bbosker"). To send an @ mention, a user would preface a tweet with the @ symbol followed by the Twitter username of the person he or she wants to converse with in a targeted, but public, way (e.g. "@bbosker").[2]

---

2. Bianca Bosker, *The Twitter Typo That Exposed Anthony Weiner*, Huffington Post (Aug. 7, 2011), http://www.huffingtonpost.com/2011/06/07/anthony-weiner-twitter-dm_n_872590.html (last visited Oct. 26, 2022).

Initially, Weiner tried to avoid fallout from his sexting incident by claiming his Twitter account had been hacked. However (and more significantly, for our purposes), Weiner ultimately had to admit that *he* posted the photo after he was bombarded with questions from the press as to whether the photo depicted him and why, if his account had been hacked, he hadn't demanded an investigation into finding the alleged hacker. If Weiner's post were being offered at trial, foundation could be established by Weiner's press conference in which he admitted posting the photo, or alternatively, by comparing the tweeted photo to other undisputed photos of Weiner.[3]

Key Points

Remember the three basics of getting evidence admitted and be prepared to satisfy each of them for social media evidence: relevance, authentication, and laying a foundation to address any hearsay objections.

Try to get the declarant to authenticate the social media in the discovery process.

Use the "selfie era" to your advantage and get social media posts in as exceptions to the hearsay rule, or nonhearsay statements by a party.

---

3. Fed. R. Evid. 901(b)(1) or (3).

Chapter Nine

Authentication

In an ideal world, a witness with social media activity has produced something on social media and "owned it" as something they generated, or alternatively, through the discovery process (i.e., requests for admission or depositions), has admitted they generated the content. This chapter is not for those easy cases. Instead, it's about social media evidence for which you must lay a foundation that the evidence is what it purports to be.

9.1 Fundamentals

Authenticating traditional evidence such as documents, video recordings, audio recordings, and the like is not particularly difficult. As one court put it, "a failure to authenticate [evidence] almost always is a self-inflicted injury which can be avoided by thoughtful advance preparation."[1] As technology has progressed and "digital" evidence has become more common, the challenges associated with authentication have increased as courts will often give greater scrutiny to such evidence. One reason for the added scrutiny is that fabrication and alteration of such evidence is easier than ever. Additionally, it is easier for individuals to pretend to be someone they are not.

9.2 Drawing a Straight Line between Social Media and the Witness

The foundational requirement of authentication may be the greatest challenge because people can use pseudonyms on social media. It can be hard to show a clear path from the person to the social media post and, thereby, demonstrate the preliminary fact that the witness made the statement. Information found on social media sites is susceptible to fraud and manipulation. Sometimes there is a problem with viruses and spam messages from "friends" due to online hacking. For example, there was a widely reported criminal and civil case against Sanford Wallace, who was nicknamed the "Spam King" for the phishing and spamming operation that he openly ran from the early 1990s, at first sending junk faxes

1. Lorraine v. Markel American Ins. Co., 241 F.R.D. 534 (D. Md. 2007).

and flooding inboxes with unsolicited emails, then embracing the internet. He was convicted for operating his business from 2008 to 2009. Wallace opened a Facebook account using a pseudonym, then messaged Facebook users with a website link they were invited to click. Those who were unfortunate enough to click the link were tricked into revealing their Facebook login information to Wallace. Wallace reportedly obtained access to approximately 500,000 Facebook accounts, and then posted over 27 million unauthorized posts on the Facebook pages of friends of the hacked users. Wallace made money from this scam by driving traffic to affiliate marketing companies that pay per click on their websites. These clicks came from the Facebook friends of the hacked users, who would click on the website links in the spam messages not knowing that the messages were being generated by Wallace, not the hacked users. This criminal enterprise resulted in a $711 million judgment entered against Wallace in the civil action filed by Facebook and to a plea bargain for criminal charges that can result in a sentence as long as three years, according to reports in Bloomberg and the Associated Press.[2]

Perhaps scarier for someone trying to authenticate social media evidence are the sites with tutorials on how to create fake social media accounts and fake tweets that appear to be coming from a public figure.[3] In other words, fake tweets could be generated for anyone, not just the public figures. There are an increasing number of people who take the quickest path to creating a fake celebrity account by just opening an account that claims to be a celebrity's authentic account and quickly attract followers that way.[4]

Then there's the problem of "bots" activity on social media. Bots (short for "robots") are algorithm-generated programs that walk, talk, and look like flesh-and-blood users on social media. One such bot, "Lajello,"[5] became the second most popular poster in his online book group. Lajello was so friendly! How could you not like him? He would, for example, recommend books to the members of the group, just like the Amazon "Featured Recommendations" system. Bots have also been used as fake followers on social media accounts and have been known to skew

---

2. *See, e.g.*, Facebook, Inc. v. Wallace, 2009 U.S. Dist. LEXIS 107771 (N.D. Cal. Oct. 29, 2009); *"Spam King" Pleads Guilty to Sending 27 Million Messages to Facebook Users*, CBS/AP (Aug. 24, 2015), http://sanfrancisco.cbslocal.com/2015/08/24/spam-king-pleads-guilty-facebook-messages-sanford-wallace/ (last visited Oct. 26, 2022).

3. *How to Create a Fake Twitter Account: Author Hoaxes and Microblogging*, Huff. Post (Jan. 2, 2013), http://www.huffingtonpost.com/2013/01/02/how-to-create-a-fake-twitter-author-hoax_n_2391525.html (last visited Oct. 26, 2022).

4. Alexis Sobel Fitts, *It's Easier Than Ever to Impersonate a Celebrity Online—And We've All Been Duped*, Huff Post Tech & Science (Aug. 4, 2015), http://www.huffingtonpost.com/entry/instagram-celebrity-impersonators_55bbc26be4b0d4f33a02c3d7 (last visited Oct. 26, 2022).

5. *See* https://www.technologyreview.com/s/529696/how-a-simple-spambot-became-the-second-most-powerful-member-of-an-italian-social-network/ (last visited Oct. 26, 2016).

public opinion by posting "likes" or tweets that don't reflect actual public opinion.[6] Thus, there is good cause to be skeptical of content posted on social media, so it's best to be prepared to lay a foundation that a post truly was posted by a witness in your case.

Social media accounts can be accessed through passwords that the alleged speaker could have shared, or a computer and social media site may have been left logged in so that anyone with access to the computer could have posted the statements. Many people access their social media accounts through apps on their electronic devices—smartphones and tablets—and can skip entering their login name and password because the app automatically keeps them logged in. In other words, anyone who can open an app on an electronic device can post content without being the actual account holder.

Not surprisingly, courts have recognized that electronically stored information "may require greater scrutiny than that required for the authentication of 'hard copy' documents."[7] However, greater scrutiny doesn't mean the evidence won't get admitted. Courts still admit such evidence because the standard for authentication is relatively low: consider Federal Rule of Evidence 901(a), which states that a condition precedent to admissibility is "satisfied by evidence sufficient to support a finding that the matter in question is what its proponent claims."

A party who opposes introducing this kind of evidence can cite to the problems described above to try and keep the evidence out. Likewise, these same problems can be woven into your examination of witnesses and your closing argument so jurors will, one hopes, put less weight on any social media activity that's likely to come into evidence. It's important, then, to preserve your foundation objections to the evidence (e.g., not authenticated, inadmissible hearsay, unduly prejudicial) for appeal if it is admitted, because it may be reversible error.

In the context of emails and text messages for which parties have made similar arguments to exclude, courts have admitted the evidence based on circumstantial evidence and have allowed the jurors to decide, based on the parties' testimony and arguments, how much weight can be given to the evidence.[8] The extent to which social media evidence can be analogized to electronic messages such as texts and emails is not settled in the courts. Some courts have taken the position that social media should be distinguished from emails and text messages because social media

6. Lutz Finger, *Do Evil—The Business of Social Media Bots*, Forbes (Feb. 17, 2015), http://www.forbes.com/sites/lutzfinger/2015/02/17/do-evil-the-business-of-social-media-bots/#5d31e51e1104 (last visited Oct. 26, 2022).

7. Lorraine v. Markel Am. Ins. Co., 241 F.R.D. 534, 542–43 (D. Md. 2007).

8. Lorraine, 241 F.R.D. at 543 (in which the court noted that similar uncertainties exist with traditional written documents with signatures that can be forged, or distinctive letterhead stationery that can be copied or stolen).

posts are, by their very nature, shared with a larger audience, and cannot be traced back to a particular cellphone or computer as readily as emails and texts. These courts also submit that it's easier to authenticate an email or text message because the message can be compared to other messages from that person.[9] However, this is arguably true for social media activity, too, once it's established that the account holder is responsible for earlier posts. In other words, it's still worthwhile to cite cases concerning authentication of text and email messages, especially if there are similarities in how the social media activity is being authenticated.

In a 2015 criminal case in San Francisco County Superior Court in California, a juvenile was convicted of possessing firearms in violation of his probation based on a photo the defendant posted to his Instagram account showing him brandishing firearms in a room with camouflage curtains. In *In re K.B.*,[10] the court of appeal held that the Instagram photo was properly authenticated because it was obtained from a cellphone seized at the scene, appeared on the Instagram account associated with the defendant, and at the time of his arrest the defendant was wearing the same clothes and was in the same location depicted on Instagram.

However, courts of appeals have also reversed decisions where social media was admitted and later found to lack adequate foundation. In one widely discussed and cited case, *Griffin v. Maryland*,[11] the court of appeals held that the trial court should not have admitted a social media post with threatening language. *Griffin* has been cited by a number of state courts—Colorado, Connecticut, Delaware, Illinois, Kansas, Mississippi, New Hampshire, Ohio, Tennessee, Texas—because it was one of the first published cases addressing the admissibility of social media evidence. Initially, *Griffin* was cited as a case in which the social media evidence was properly admitted because the trial court decision was initially sustained by the court of special appeals. However, the decision was later reversed on a writ of certiorari by the court of appeals. In *Griffin*, a social media post that contained threatening language was admitted into evidence to explain why a witness changed

9. *See, e.g.*, Griffin v. Maryland, 419 Md. 343, 361 n. 13 (Md. 2011); Independent Newspapers, Inc. v. Brodie, 407 Md. 415, 423 (Md. 2009) (contrasting emails and instant messages with a "different category of internet communications, in which users post statements to the world at large without specification," such as on social networking sites); States v. Safavian, 435 F. Supp. 2d 36, 41 (D.D.C. 2006) (reasoning emails could be authenticated by comparison by the jury with those emails that had already been independently authenticated through the contents or in the email heading itself); Commonwealth v. Amaral, 941 N.E.2d 1143 (Mass. App. Ct. 2011) (reasoning that "[t]he actions of the defendant himself served to authenticate the emails," because one email indicated that defendant would be at a certain place at a certain time and the defendant appeared at that place and time, and in another email, defendant provided his telephone number and immediately answered when the investigator called that number); Dickens v. State, 927 A.2d 32, 36–37 (Md. 2007) (reasoning text messages received on victim's cell phone were properly authenticated because the phone number on one message showed that it had come from defendant's phone and other messages referenced the defendant's right to see the couple's minor child and their wedding vows).

10. In re K.B., 238 Cal. App. 4th 989 (Cal. Ct. App. 2015).

11. Griffin v. Maryland, 419 Md. 343 (Md. 2011).

his testimony dramatically from the first murder trial to the second trial. The trial court relied on Maryland Rules of Evidence, but noted that the state rules were modeled after the Federal Rules of Evidence and relied on state and federal cases to admit the evidence. In a MySpace post, under the profile for "SISTASOULJAH," there was a description of a twenty-three-year-old woman from Fort Deposit, with the birth date of "10-2-83," and a photograph showing a three-quarter view of a couple embracing. The threatening blurb posted on the site said:

> I HAVE 2 BEAUTIFUL KIDS. FREE BOOZY!!!! JUST REMEMBER SNITCHES GET STITCHES!! U KNOW WHO YOU ARE!![12]

The State offered this evidence to rehabilitate the credibility of a witness and to bolster his claim that the defendant's girlfriend had threatened him before the first trial.

The prosecution used the lead investigator to authenticate this social media activity, rather than asking the defendant's girlfriend similar questions when she was on the witness stand. The court of appeals held that the trial court erred in not considering the possibility that the MySpace account with these posts had been created by someone other than the defendant's girlfriend and that there was not enough evidence to overcome this possibility:

> We agree with Griffin that the trial judge abused his discretion in admitting the MySpace evidence pursuant to Rule 501(b)(4), because the picture of Ms. Barber, coupled with her birth date and location, were not sufficient "distinctive characteristics" on a MySpace profile to authenticate its printout, given the prospect that someone other than Ms. Barber could have not only created the site, but also posted the "snitches get stitches" comment. The potential for abuse and manipulation of a social networking site by someone other than its purported creator and/or user leads to our conclusion that a printout of an image from such a site requires a greater degree of authentication than merely identifying the date of birth of the creator and her visage in a photograph on the site in order to reflect that Ms. Barber was its creator and the author of the "snitches get stitches" language.[13]

The court of appeals also noted the significance that the defense had preserved its objection by objecting to the admission of the MySpace evidence.[14]

In cases where someone may be using her real name but denies that she made a particular comment or post on Facebook, the response should be that Facebook

12. Griffin v. Maryland, 995 A.2d 791, 796 (Md. App. 2010).
13. Griffin v. State, 419 Md. 343, 357–58 (Md. 2011).
14. *Id.* at 362.

gives posters the option of deleting their post or comment at any time, so the fact that the post was left for a period of time is further evidence that it was either authored or approved by the Facebook user. In the case of spam posts, for example, Facebook users who have been hacked are often alerted to it when their Facebook friends tell them they've received spam posts on their pages and the hacked user then posts an apology on their Facebook page. Similarly, people with a Twitter account, for example, have the option of posting a follow-up tweet saying they disavow a tweet as not having been authored by them. In other words, real-time activity on social media—or the lack of it—can be helpful in authenticating social media evidence.

9.3 Court Decisions on Authentication Objections

The following cases highlight different ways in which social media evidence has been authenticated to the satisfaction of a federal court and admitted into evidence. Courts address authentication issues on a fairly regular basis. Research current authentication requirements that may have been implemented in your particular circuit. The cases cited below are merely a smattering of cases that address authentication issues.

- In *United States v. Lamm*,[15] the court noted that "authentication of social media evidence . . . presents some special challenges because of the great ease with which a social media account may be falsified or a legitimate account may be accessed by an imposter. Our circuit has not yet considered what is sufficient authentication for evidence from social media accounts. Several other circuits have dealt squarely with the issue and have held that certification from the social media forum is insufficient to establish authenticity under Federal Rule of Evidence 902(11), and more extrinsic evidence is required to establish authenticity under Rule 901(a)."
- In *United States v. Hunt*,[16] the court held that "[t]he type and quantum of evidence necessary for authentication is thus related to the purpose for which the evidence is offered. Where, as here, social media content is offered for the purpose of establishing that a person made particular statements—that is, the relevance of the proffered evidence 'hinges on the fact of authorship'—a certification by a custodian in itself cannot be sufficient for purposes of authentication because, as already described, such a certification serves a limited role: it simply shows that a record was made at or near a certain time, that the record was kept in the course of a regularly conducted business activity, and that the making of the record was a regular practice of that activity. . . . Indeed, in *United States v. Vayner*,

15. United States v. Lamm, 5 F.4th 942 (8th Cir. 2021).
16. United States v. Hunt, 534 F. Supp. 233 (E.D.N.Y. Apr. 15, 2021).

the Second Circuit held that a social media profile page was not properly authenticated because the profile page's relevance turned on whether it was created by the defendant, yet the Government offered evidence only that the page existed and not that it belonged to the defendant. 769 F.3d 125, 132–33 (2d Cir. 2014). Like the Government's evidence in *Vayner,* a business-records certification shows nothing more than that a record existed or was created at a particular time and that it was regularly kept in the course of a regularly conducted business activity."

- In *United States v. Barnes,*[17] the quadriplegic defendant, Kentorre Hall, was convicted of possessing 500 or more grams of methamphetamine with the intent to distribute it and maintaining a drug-involved residence, among other crimes. Hall challenged the admission of certain Facebook messages and texts that had been attributed to him. The court of appeals held that enough of a foundation was laid with testimony from a Hall acquaintance who was familiar with Hall's Facebook posts that 1) even though Hall is a quadriplegic, he can operate a cellphone using his mouth and limited movement in his right arm, and 2) the witness, Holsen, had seen Hall use Facebook, recognized his Facebook account, and confirmed that the Facebook posts at issue matched Hall's way of communicating. Although Holsen was not certain that Hall had authored the posts, conclusive proof of authenticity is not required for the admission of disputed evidence.[18] The extent to which the evidence is reliable is for the trier of fact to decide.
- In *United States v. Souksakhone Phaknikone,*[19] the government laid the foundation for some documents from the defendant's MySpace account through a witness who admitted to robbing banks with the defendant. The witness testified that he knew the defendant had a MySpace account and that he knew defendant by the nickname "Trigga," which was also used in the MySpace subscriber report that the government authenticated through the witness. The subscriber report listed the defendant's full name as "Trigga FullyLoaded," was located in Dacula, Georgia (where the defendant resided), contained an email address of "gangsta_trigga@yahoo.com," and contained five profile photographs. Foundation for the subscriber report was laid through an employee of MySpace. Foundation was also established for two profile pictures from defendant's MySpace account: one showing the defendant dressed for a formal event with his now ex-wife, and the second showing him in a car with a gun in his hand and displaying two of his tattoos. Even though the foundation was laid for

17. United States v. Barnes, 803 F.3d 209 (5th Cir. 2015).
18. United States v. Jimenez Lopez, 873 F.2d 769 (5th Cir. 1989).
19. United States v. Souksakhone Phaknikone, 605 F.3d 1099 (11th Cir. 2010).

the MySpace evidence, the district court only allowed a redacted version of the MySpace subscriber report with the two profile pictures to come in as character evidence presenting that the defendant would be someone to rob banks by the way he casually showed himself holding a gun in one picture and by his use of the "gangsta" nickname (which the court of appeals held should not have come in, but that the error was harmless).

- In *Greco v. Velvet Cactus, LLC*,[20] the plaintiff sued his former employer and manager for sexual harassment, retaliation, and battery. Facebook posts were authenticated by declarations from the people who posted the content and by a witness who testified that he received an anonymous letter (which expressed the author's dissatisfaction with the defendant Dickinson as a general manager) in response to a post he made on the employee Facebook page for Velvet Cactus. Foundation for the anonymous letter was established, and it was admitted over hearsay objections on the grounds that it was not being offered for the truth of the matter asserted but rather, to explain the effect the letter had on the person who received it and why he decided to terminate Dickinson.
- In *State v. Assi*,[21] the state court of appeal held that there was adequate foundation that pictures on a MySpace page under the moniker also used by defendant did, in fact, depict the defendant with a variety of guns. The foundation was laid by a victim to a gang-related shooting who identified the defendant as someone he knew from MySpace as "Flaco," and by the gang unit officer who located the MySpace page for someone named Flaco from the PBS (Playboy Surenos) gang. The gang unit officer also testified that the defendant was known by the moniker of Flaco and was associated with the PBS gang. Further, the prosecution had testimony from the defendant's father, who testified that his son had a MySpace page and that he had seen some of the photographs admitted into evidence on it. The defendant objected that there is no witness who testified that the defendant himself put these pictures on his MySpace page; however, the court found that this goes to the weight of the evidence, not its admissibility, because of the foundation for identification purposes, which is how it was being used: the victim identifying defendant based on his MySpace page.
- In *Assi*, the court of appeal also discussed how defense counsel had failed to raise a foundation objection to the MySpace account evidence at trial (a mistake that none of you should make) and, therefore, the court only needed to review for "fundamental error" with respect to those pieces of evidence and that objection. Fundamental error is "error going to the foundation of the case, error that takes from the defendant a right essential

20. Greco v. Velvet Cactus, LLC, 2014 U.S. Dist. LEXIS 87778 (E.D. La. June 27, 2014).
21. State v. Assi, 2012 Ariz. App. Unpub. LEXIS 1002 (Ariz. Ct. App. 2012).

to his defense, and error of such magnitude that the defendant could not possibly have received a fair trial."[22] The burden of showing fundamental error rests with the defendant, which underscores how important it is to make your foundation objection to all social media evidence during the trial (unless you are fine with it being admitted into evidence or the objection would be without merit as a matter of law).

- In *Means v. State*,[23] the court of appeal held that the defendant was given sufficient opportunity to challenge certain Facebook evidence through his cross-examination of various witnesses and that there was sufficient evidence, taken together, to support the defendant's conviction for aggravated robbery and first-degree battery. The defendant had argued on appeal that Facebook messages were not properly authenticated to show that he was the person replying to messages sent to his account by the sister of someone who had participated in the home invasion with him. The sister sent the messages posing as her boyfriend (with the boyfriend's consent) and, in an effort to exonerate her brother, tried to engage the defendant in a conversation about the botched burglary. Ironically, the ease with which the sister could pose as her boyfriend on Facebook underscores how problematic it can sometimes be to authenticate social media evidence.

Alternatively, cases where the social media evidence was not properly authenticated are helpful to highlight lessons learned or arguments that a party can make to keep the evidence out.

- In *United States v. Winters*,[24] the court held that it was error to admit into evidence pictures from the defendant's Facebook and MySpace pages that depicted guns positioned on top of a stack of cash and wrapped packages resembling kilograms of cocaine packaged for sale. The court held that it was not enough for the government to try to authenticate the photographs by having the lead investigator testify that he found the pictures on the social media sites that defendant Winters admitted to having. No one had testified that the pictures depicted items that were possessed by or under the control of Winters.
- In *Valdez v. Virga*,[25] it appears that the court tried to unring the bell of having the jurors see social media evidence that was not properly authenticated by the prosecution, by allowing jurors to consider it in the context of the prosecution expert's testimony. In *Valdez*, an attempted murder and gang enhancement case, the prosecutor could not authenticate MySpace pages through an investigator for the district attorney's office who testified

22. State v. Henderson, 115 P.3d 601, 607 (Ariz. 2005).
23. Means v. State, 2015 Ark. App. 643 (Ark. Ct. App. 2015).
24. United States v. Winters, 530 F. App'x 390, 395 (5th Cir. Miss. 2013).
25. Valdez v. Virga, 2014 U.S. Dist. LEXIS 103018 (C.D. Cal. June 23, 2014).

that he did an internet search for "T.L.F. Santa Ana" (a gang known as "Thug Family Life") and pulled up the public pages from the defendant's MySpace account. The investigator admitted on cross-examination that he did not know 1) who uploaded the pictures or content on the defendant's MySpace page, 2) how many people had that password to access the account and post content, and 3) who created the MySpace page. Accordingly, only the MySpace profile page with a picture of the defendant was admitted into evidence based on the testimony of a witness who said the defendant's MySpace profile picture was the basis for him identifying the defendant as one of the people shooting from a car at him and his friends. However, the court allowed jurors to consider the other content from the defendant's MySpace account through the prosecution's gang expert, who testified that he formed the opinion that the defendant was an active member of the T.L.F. gang based in part on the (court-excluded) pages he reviewed on the defendant's MySpace page, including a picture of the defendant making a gang hand signal; pages with the defendant's gang moniker "Yums;" and notations that included "T.L.F.," "YUM $YUM," "T.L.F.'s 63 Impala," "T.L.F., The Most Wanted Krew by the Cops and the Ladiez," and "Yums. You Don't Wanna F wit[h] this Guy." The expert also relied on (and jurors were thus allowed to consider) what was listed under the MySpace account for "Groups" ("CO 2006, Thug Life/Club Bounc," "O.C.'s Most Wanted G's," "Viva Los Jews," and "Screaming Thug Life") and "Interests" ("Mob[b]ing the streets and hustling, chilling with homies, and spending time with my mom").[26] In other words, this case highlights what is not enough to authenticate social media content, but also provides guidance on a "backdoor" way for relying on the evidence, nevertheless, through your appointed expert.

- In *Oliver v. Oliver*,[27] the court of appeal held that the trial court was correct in excluding Facebook pictures offered to prove that the defendant husband and his current live-in girlfriend were in possession of certain pieces of furniture and decorative items that the plaintiff wife claimed belong to her. The court of appeal held that the wife did not lay an adequate foundation to admit the pictures because there was no testimony concerning where and when the pictures were taken or that the photographs were an accurate representation of the scene which they portray. Counsel for the plaintiff wife admitted that he didn't know when the pictures were taken and that they were obtained through a friend of the wife who was Facebook friends with the defendant's girlfriend, who had the pictures on her Facebook page.

---

26. *Id.* at *26.
27. Oliver v. Oliver, 2013 Ohio App. LEXIS 4626, at *32–33 (Ohio Ct. App. Oct. 1, 2013).

9.4 Tips for Laying an Adequate Foundation

- In discovery, ask the witness to verify that they posted the social media content.
- In discovery, ask the witness to produce a copy of all social media content that is discoverable and use the Bates numbered pages at trial.
- In deposition, ask the witness who denies that they posted the content at issue, why they did not delete it from their page or alert their followers that the account was hacked and posts were made that did not come from them.
- At trial, call witnesses who are familiar with identifying facts concerning a party that also appear on the social media account you wish to authenticate: nickname, pictures of the party; birthday; names of the party's girlfriend/boyfriend, spouse, or children; known affiliations (e.g., employer, social club, alma mater); city of residence or birthplace; social media account friends or followers who coincidentally are friends of the party; and identification of relatives (a feature offered by Facebook) that also happen to be relatives of the party.
- Don't make the mistake of trying to authenticate the content by simply printing it off the site and having someone testify that this is what they did. Courts will not accept this as proper authentication.[28]

9.5 Tips for Foundation Objections

If you are trying to keep this evidence out, it will be worth the time and effort to file a motion in limine asking the court to exclude the evidence and to preclude the other side from having any of their witnesses—either fact or expert witnesses—refer to the excluded evidence in their testimony or relying upon on it in any other way. If you lose your motion, don't stop there. Make your objections at trial on the record so you can preserve the issue for appeal under the abuse of discretion standard of review. Be sure to cover on direct examination and cross-examination all of the reasons why the trier of fact should give little, if any, weight to the social media evidence. Your judge may not be fluent in social media, but there's a good chance that a few of your jurors have been hacked, or know someone who was, and will appreciate that you can't always trust what you see on social media.

---

28. *See, e.g.*, Moroccanoil, Inc. v. Marc Anthony Cosmetics, Inc., 57 F. Supp. 3d 1203, 1213 n. 5 (C.D. Cal. 2014) (screenshots printed from Facebook not properly authenticated by the person printing them).

If the evidence is especially problematic to your case and you anticipate that it's coming into evidence, during voir dire ask prospective jurors if they or anyone they know 1) has had a social media accounts hacked, 2) mistakenly clicked on a link they didn't recognize and ended up with a virus on their computer, 3) received distressing messages from someone claiming to be a relative and asking them to send money because they're stranded in a foreign country without their passport, or 4) received email messages from someone with a sob story or who promised a huge windfall if they help the sender to claim prize money by fronting some money for them.[29] If your judge doesn't allow lawyers to question prospective jurors, ask that they be included in the list of questions coming from the court. All of these questions underscore the myriad ways in which the internet is being used to scam the unsuspecting and how easily people can create false identities online.

9.6 Spoofing

Spoofing refers to the practice of falsifying an email address, a phone number, a text message, etc., to make it appear to be coming from someone else. For example, a person with the phone number of (865) 555-4848 pretends he is calling from a different number such as (865) 555-1234, then he is "spoofing" the 1234 number. When a person being called sees a number on her caller ID it will display as (865) 555-1234 when he is actually calling from a different number. This is an example of "spoofing" a phone number.

While spoofing has been around for many years, only recently has it become easy for the average person to spoof phone numbers, email addresses, etc. This rather easy ability to spoof creates a challenge for authentication. While a piece of evidence may appear to be a text message from party A to party B it could, in fact, be a text message from party B (pretending to be party A) to party B.

There are a number of types of spoofing, although many of the more sophisticated types are not likely to find their way into the typical lawsuit. Some types of spoofing include falsifying email, website, internet protocol (IP), Address Resolution Protocol (ARP), Domain Name System (DNS), caller ID, GPS, and text messages. The following are the types that are most likely to be encountered in a litigation setting:

9.6.1 Email Spoofing

Email spoofing occurs when someone sends an email from a fake email address that the recipient will recognize. For example:

---

29. *See How to Recognize and Avoid Phishing Scams*, Fed. Trade Comm., http://www.consumer.ftc.gov/articles/how-recognize-and-avoid-phishing-scams (last visited Oct. 26, 2022).

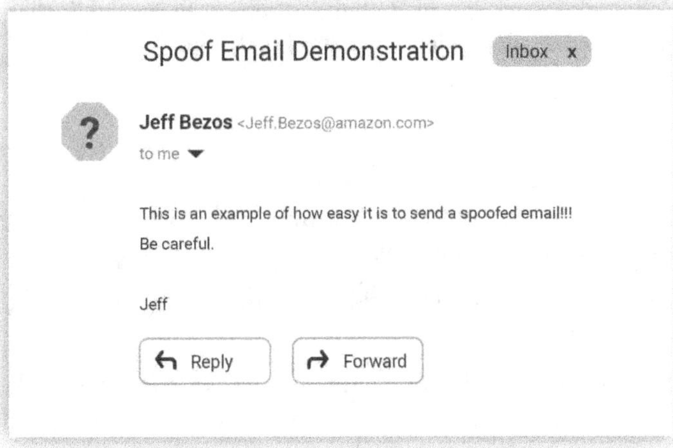

I created this email in a few seconds and sent it to myself. It was free and easy. Unfortunately, anyone can do it. Email is an open and relatively unsecure system designed to let people send and receive messages with ease. Unfortunately, this permits nefarious individuals to abuse the system and create fake messages.

In 2019 a company lost over $40,000 resulting from spoofed email messages.[30] Fortunately, email service providers are becoming more adept at blocking spoofed messages. In cases where a provider does not block a spoofed message, spotting them can be challenging. Fortunately, someone adept in the use of technology can often dig into the underlying data that accompanies an email message to determine whether it was, or was not, spoofed.

9.6.2 *Text Message Spoofing*

Much like email spoofing, text messages can be spoofed although not as easily. While text messages are much more difficult to spoof than email messages, they are also more difficult to detect because the underlying transmission data cannot be as easily accessed. This is particularly true with messages received on iOS devices.

9.6.3 *Caller ID Spoofing*

Phone numbers may be spoofed resulting in calls appearing to be coming from a known or trusted number or even a specific geographic region. This technique is

30. *Paint giant loses Rs 28 lakh in case of email spoofing*, Times of India (Jan. 18, 2019) https://timesofindia.indiatimes.com/city/mumbai/paint-giant-loses-rs-28-lakh-in-case-of-email-spoofing/articleshow/67580796.cms (last visited Oct. 26, 2022).

particularly popular among robocallers and solicitors. Much like text messages, it can be challenging to detect spoofed phone numbers. Fortunately, there are a number of apps and services that help detect and block spoofed numbers.

Key Points

Anticipate foundation objections during the discovery process, and try to get what you need to lay a foundation.

Take time laying your foundation so jurors will give the evidence the weight it deserves in their deliberations.

Social media evidence is not all the same. Courts are more likely to exclude posts by third parties appearing on the social media page of a party. Make your objections specific to each category or subcategory of social media evidence.

If you are trying to keep social media evidence out, be persistent. File motions in limine, create doubt through your examination of witnesses, preserve your objections for appeal by making them at trial, and watch for a party trying to get excluded social media evidence in through an expert who relied on it.

Be aware of spoofing and the possibility that email messages, text messages, or phone numbers could be spoofed.

Chapter Ten

Hearsay

10.1 Overview

Hearsay, traditionally, is one of the most challenging rules for judges and lawyers alike. It is often found to be difficult to apply to many situations. The language is somewhat antiquated, and the application over the years has been at best inconsistent and at worst simply incorrect. While this chapter will not pull back the curtain on the hearsay secrets (there really aren't any), it will provide a basic foundation of the rule and how to apply it in the context of social media.

In this chapter, we're assuming that you've laid a foundation for social media evidence, so now we're focusing on arguments for overcoming hearsay objections. Conversely, these same arguments will highlight ways to think about objecting to social media evidence on hearsay grounds.

10.2 The Hearsay Steps

Step One: The Prohibition

The Federal Rules of Evidence prohibit the admission of hearsay statements unless there is an exception. Rule 802 provides that "[h]earsay is not admissible unless any of the following provides otherwise: a federal statute; these rules; or other rules prescribed by the Supreme Court."

Therefore, the next step is determining whether a piece of evidence is hearsay as defined by the rules.

Step Two: The Definition

Understanding whether a particular piece of evidence is hearsay requires examining it in light of the definition set out in the rules. Therefore, first look at the evidence and determine whether it meets the definition of Federal Rule of Evidence 801(a)–(c):

> Hearsay is defined as a statement (which is a person's oral assertion, written assertion, or nonverbal conduct—intended as an assertion)

> that the declarant (person making the statement) does not make while testifying at the current trial or hearing and is offered to prove the truth of the matter asserted in the statement. *[Author's note: this is not the actual language of the rule; this is my edited version.]*

So let's unpack it with some examples:

Example 1:

John posts on his Facebook page that he is in a relationship with Jane. At trial, that Facebook post is offered into evidence. In this case, John's statement is a written statement. Let's suppose it is being offered to prove that he is in a relationship with Jane. So far, so good. It meets the definition of hearsay.

Example 2:

Wilma posts a video of a car running a red light on her Instagram account. At trial, the plaintiff offers the video into evidence. While videos can contain statements, this one does not. It is not a person's oral assertion, written assertion, or nonverbal conduct intended as an assertion. Therefore, it cannot be hearsay.

Example 3:

Danny posts pictures of him holding the money he just stole from First National Bank on his Instagram account with a big smile across his face. At trial, the pictures are offered to prove he possessed the stolen money. Here there is no verbal or written statement. What about non-verbal statements? One might argue that he is making a statement but that would be tenuous at best. Additionally, one has to be offering the statement to prove the assertion. In this case, it's likely not hearsay.

The rest of this chapter assumes that any particular piece of evidence DOES meet the definitions under FRE 801(a), (b) and (c).

Step Three: Why Is It Offered? [A Deeper Dive into 801(c)(2)]

FRE 801(c)(2) requires that a statement be offered "in evidence to prove the truth of the matter asserted in the statement." In order to assess whether a statement meets this part of the definition, the first question you should be asking yourself is for what purpose are you offering the evidence?

Do you really care if people accept as true the statements on the social media page, or are you more interested in the fact that the statements are being made? For example, in a trademark infringement case, customers coming to your corporate client's Facebook page to post complaints about a competitor's brand will be very helpful to your infringement case. You probably couldn't care less if the customers' complaints are warranted or not. Similarly, if you're suing a vendor consultant for breach of contract for not delivering on what he was contracted to do for your business client, then you may be interested in his LinkedIn page. You are not using LinkedIn to show he has years of experience in a particular field but to show that he is a fraud who's been deceiving everyone with experience and credentials he doesn't have.

If a statement is not being offered for the truth of the matter asserted in the statement, then the statement is not hearsay. If it's not hearsay, then FRE 801 does not prohibit the admission of the statement. Note—just because the hearsay rule does not exclude the evidence, it does not mean that a different rule won't keep it out.

Once you have determined that a piece of evidence meets the definition of hearsay under FRE 801(a)–(c), the next step is to determine whether the statement is "nonhearsay."

Step Four: Nonhearsay

The next question you should be asking yourself is whether the social media activity comes under the nonhearsay definitions found in FRE 801(d). The rules make this a bit confusing. We tend to call them "nonhearsay" because they are not actually exceptions. Don't concern yourself with the terminology; it's common to think of FRE 801(d)(1)–(2) as exceptions to the hearsay rule and there are two of them.

If a statement is nonhearsay, then it is not excluded under the hearsay rule. If it is, your next step is to see if the statement meets any of the relevant exceptions.

Step Five: Exceptions

The Federal Rules of Evidence have a number of exceptions to the hearsay exclusionary rule. These are found in Rules 803, 804, and 807. If a statement meets one of the exceptions, then the statement is not excluded. If a statement does not meet an exception, then it will be excluded.

10.2.1 "Truth of the Matter Asserted"

A social media post in which the person exclaims, "I am King of the World," is not being offered for the truth of the matter asserted and is, therefore, not hearsay. Rule 801 of the Federal Rules of Evidence provides in pertinent part:

> The following definitions apply under this article:
>
> (a) Statement. "Statement" means a person's oral assertion, written assertion, or nonverbal conduct, if the person intended it as an assertion.
>
> (b) Declarant. "Declarant" means the person who made the statement.
>
> (c) Hearsay. "Hearsay" means a statement that:

(1) the declarant does not make while testifying at the current trial or hearing; and

(2) a party offers in evidence to prove the truth of the matter asserted in the statement.

Here are the key takeaways from this rule. First, nonverbal conduct can be hearsay if offered for the truth of the matter asserted. This means being on the watch for hearsay objections with videos from social networking sites, including YouTube, Facebook, Vine, Twitch, TikTok, and Instagram. Second, social media activity that is not being offered for the truth of the statements contained therein is not hearsay and will come into evidence if you can lay a foundation for it—that it is relevant and is what it purports to be (a.k.a. authentication). Here are some case examples involving social media that was being offered for a purpose other than the truth of the post.

Example 1:

In *OraLabs, Inc. v. The Kind Grp., LLC*,[1] a lip balm manufacturer filed a declaratory relief action seeking to invalidate the patent of the defendant The Kind Group and to show its dome-shaped lip balm did not infringe the trade dress of the defendant.

The defendant offered Twitter posts into evidence and argued that they were offered to show the existence of them, and not for the truth of the matter asserted:

- a collection of Twitter posts from fans of musician Miley Cyrus that mistakenly identified Lip Revo products (manufactured by OraLabs) given out by Cyrus to concertgoers as EOS products (a label of The Kind Group).
- a series of Twitter posts that reflect consumers' beliefs that a photograph of a green, watermelon-flavored Lip Revo was made by EOS, which did not have a watermelon-flavored lip balm.[2]

The defendant also argued that aside from the Twitter posts not being hearsay, they should also come in under the "state of mind" exception to the hearsay rule. The court admitted the Twitter posts into evidence because courts have held that testimony that describes incidents of actual consumer confusion in trademark infringement actions are not being offered for the truth of the matter asserted.[3]

1. OraLabs, Inc. v. The Kind Grp., LLC, 2015 U.S. Dist. LEXIS 98246 (D. Colo. July 28, 2015).
2. *Id.* at *12.
3. *Id.* at *13–14.

Example 2:

In *Music Group Macao Commercial Offshore, Ltd. v. Foote*,[4] the plaintiff Music Group sued its former technology consultant for allegedly failing to secure the company against cyberattacks on its global network and communications systems, in breach of his consulting agreement with Music Group. Music Group was allowed to offer into evidence the defendant's LinkedIn profile, in which he described himself as the chief technology officer of Music Group, not for the truth of the matter asserted but that this is how defendant referred to himself.[5]

Example 3:

In *Greco v. Velvet Cactus, LLC*,[6] a hostile work environment and sexual harassment case, defendants offered a Facebook post from an employee to the owner of the defendant restaurant saying he did not observe any further inappropriate conduct with the defendant manager's performance in the year after the defendant manager returned from a suspension. The Facebook post came into evidence because it was offered to show why the owner did not take further action against the defendant manager. It was not offered for the truth of the matter asserted. The court further held that it could not come in as a present sense impression exception to the hearsay rule under Rule 803(1) because the post was referring to conduct over a year old and Rule 803(1) only applies to statements that describe or explain an event or condition as, or immediately after, the declarant perceives it.[7]

Example 4:

In *State v. Assi*,[8] the court of appeal held that the evidence depicting the defendant's MySpace page, with his gang moniker, gang affiliation, and pictures of guns, was admitted for identification purposes and, therefore, it was not hearsay evidence being offered for the truth of the matter asserted.

---

4. Music Grp. Macao Commer. Offshore, Ltd. v. Foote, 2015 U.S. Dist. LEXIS 81415, at *23 (N.D. Cal. June 22, 2015).
5. *Cf.* Tank v. Deutsche Telekom, AG, 2013 U.S. Dist. LEXIS 56096 (N.D. Ill. Apr. 19, 2013), *aff'd sub nom.* Tank v. T-Mobile USA, Inc., 2014 U.S. App. LEXIS 13135 (7th Cir. Ill., July 10, 2014) (LinkedIn profile was inadmissible hearsay in a pay discrimination case because the plaintiff was offering it to show the lack of experience of defendant's vice president of engineering and operations).
6. Greco v. Velvet Cactus, LLC, 2014 U.S. Dist. LEXIS 87778 (E.D. La. June 27, 2014).
7. *Id.* at *17.
8. State v. Assi, 2012 Ariz. App. Unpub. LEXIS 1002 (Ariz. Ct. App. 2012).

Example 5:

In *In re Marriage of Miller*,[9] the respondent ex-husband sought to end spousal support to his ex-wife by arguing that she was in a relationship that was a de facto marriage. In trying to make his case, the respondent offered various Facebook posts showing when his ex-wife became Facebook friends with her boyfriend, as well as posts chronicling holidays they spent together, trips they took together, and other things they did as a couple. The ex-wife objected on the ground that the Facebook content was inadmissible hearsay, but the ex-husband argued successfully both to the trial court and on appeal that the content was not being offered to prove the things described actually happened, but to show that this is how the couple portrayed themselves on social media. In other words, the Facebook evidence was not being offered for the truth of the matter asserted:

> We take the court at its word that it did not consider the posts for the truth of the matters asserted. And, for the majority of the posts, there is little risk that it did. Obviously, the court did not consider the truth of whether Lorena and Michael *really* played golf on a given day or ordered hotdogs with two onions and no peppers. Rather, the court was free to consider the fact in itself that Lorena and Michael were open with others about their activities and status as a couple. Sharing publicly, as opposed to keeping private, the status of one's relationship is relevant in that it suggests *some* level of commitment, the degree of which is determined by the evidence in full. Because the posts were offered and considered only to show the manner in which Lorena and Michael presented their relationship to others, and not for the truth of the matters asserted in the post, they were not hearsay.[10]

The only piece of evidence that troubled the court of appeals as being arguably hearsay was the post showing that the ex-wife and her boyfriend were "in a relationship" because this statement was being offered for the truth of the matter asserted.

Note that the trial court, in its order, said it only considered the posts by the ex-wife and her boyfriend, but not the posts from friends of the couple, such as "[g]lad you and Lori could join us for Thanksgiving yesterday." Addressing this fact, the court of appeals also held that because the trial court did not consider the content posted by third parties, it did not need to address the foundational requirements for admission of social media posts from third parties.

---

9. In re Marriage of Miller, 2015 Ill. App. LEXIS 410 (May 28, 2015).
10. *Id.* at *21.

Once it is determined that a statement is offered for the truth of the matter asserted, then the statement should be evaluated to determine whether it is non-hearsay; that is, whether the statement meets one of the requirements under FRE 801(d).

10.2.2 Nonhearsay Under the Rules

Statements that meet any of the requirements under FRE 801(d) are not hearsay under the rules. As previously mentioned, the rules make statements under this part of the rule confusing. Typically, we call these "nonhearsay" statements because the rule defines them as "not hearsay." However, it is easier to consider them as exceptions. One of the most common "nonhearsay" examples and also the most common one with regard to social media is an opposing party's statement. We find that rule in FRE 801(d)(2):

> An Opposing Party's Statement
> Rule 801(d) provides that a statement is not hearsay if—
> . . .
> (2) Admission by party-opponent. The statement is offered against a party and is:
>
> > (A) the party's own statement, in either an individual or a representative capacity, or
> > (B) a statement of which the party has manifested an adoption or belief in its truth, or
> > (C) a statement by a person authorized by the party to make a statement concerning the subject, or
> > (D) a statement by the party's agent or servant concerning a matter within the scope of the agency or employment, made during the existence of the relationship, or
> > (E) a statement by a coconspirator of a party during the course and in furtherance of the conspiracy.

The statement must be considered but does not by itself establish the declarant's authority under (C); the existence or scope of the relationship under (D); or the existence of the conspiracy or participation in it under (E).

Under the rule, if a statement meets any of the definitions under FRE 801(d)(2)(A)–(E) then the statement will not be considered hearsay and will not be excluded under the hearsay rule. Within this rule, the most common that will apply to social media is 801(d)(2)(A). That is, many statements are "an opposing party's statement [that was] made by the party in an individual . . . capacity."

If a statement that meets the definitions under 801(a)–(c) is also an opposing party's statement (801(d)), then the statement is "nonhearsay" and is not excluded by the hearsay rule. Let's examine some examples:

Example 1:

In a wrongful termination case handled by one of the authors, the plaintiff admitted on his Facebook page that he could not possibly return to work as he was still receiving life-saving treatments during the period of time he was arguing his employer should have afforded him a reasonable accommodation (such as working part time and/or from home). These Facebook posts later came into evidence as a party admission.

Example 2:

The plaintiff in a personal injury lawsuit has claimed that she cannot perform the necessary physical duties required by her job because of the injury. Subsequent to the injury, there is a social media post where plaintiff declares she just had a fabulous weekend cliff diving.

If the post is offered by the defense against the plaintiff, the statement would be considered nonhearsay. Why? It's an out-of-court statement offered for the truth of the matter asserted in the statement. So, it meets the requirements of FRE 801(a)–(c). Then you look to 801(d). Here the statement is an opposing party's statement. Therefore, it is nonhearsay.

Example 3:

In *United States v. Brinson*,[11] the defendant challenged the admission of Facebook posts in a criminal case for trafficking in child prostitution. The prosecution had laid a foundation that the Facebook account and posts by someone called "Twinchee Vanto" were made by the defendant. In establishing foundation, the court found persuasive that the Facebook account used a telephone number that was also on the bill of sale for the defendant's SUV, that two witnesses testified that "Twinchee Vanto" was the defendant's Facebook account, that the defendant was referred to as "Twin," that the Facebook account was registered to the email account tarranb@yahoo.com, and that in one of the messages at issue the poster referred to himself as "Tarran."

Example 4:

In *Vaughn v. Target Corp.*,[12] Target was able to offer a Facebook post in which the plaintiff in a slip-and-fall case referred to her fall in the Target store and stated that she was all better. The plaintiff tried to quibble with what she meant by "all better," but this goes to the weight that jurors should put on the evidence, not on whether it should come into evidence:

> In one post, Plaintiff said she "fell one year ago and hurt her bursa and they removed it! All better now" This is a statement that will

11. United States v. Brinson, 772 F.3d 1314 (10th Cir. 2014).
12. Vaughn v. Target Corp., 2015 U.S. Dist. LEXIS 17912, at *12–13 (W.D. Ky. Feb. 13, 2015).

be offered by Defendant against Plaintiff; Plaintiff made the statement on her Facebook page. Accordingly, it is not hearsay under Rule 801(d)(2).

Plaintiff also argues that it would be confusing to the jury that Plaintiff said she was "better" because "the term 'better' can mean many things."

This is something Plaintiff can explain during her direct examination, but it is not grounds to exclude the statement.[13]

Example 5:

In *Targonski v. City of Oak Ridge*,[14] the plaintiff police officer brought a civil rights action against her city employer for sexual harassment she claimed to have suffered on the job. The court admitted Facebook pages from the plaintiff's account as admissions by a party opponent. The city offered the posts as evidence that the plaintiff couldn't actually be offended by the sexually based rumors an officer was allegedly spreading about her because she was saying very similar things on her Facebook page. The Facebook pages were authenticated by the plaintiff, who acknowledged in her deposition that they came from her page. The plaintiff also argued that the Facebook comments were jokes between her and her friends, unlike the rumors that she claimed were embarrassing and humiliating to her because they were being spread to people in the workplace who don't know her very well. Again, the court ruled that this argument goes to the weight of the evidence, not its admissibility.

Much of the social media evidence you'll offer into evidence will fall into Rule 801(d)(2)(A) or 801(d)(2)(D), with either the social media evidence being posted by an individual party or the social media evidence being taken from the account of a business entity and being posted by someone authorized to post content on its behalf.

10.3 Hearsay Exceptions

Once you have determined that a statement is hearsay, for the statement to be admitted, it must meet an exception. The Federal Rules of Evidence contain a total of twenty-nine exceptions. The vast majority of these, however, do not apply in a social media context. This book sets out the ones that are most common with regard to social media.

Three rules contain all of the exceptions: FRE 803, 804, and 807. Federal Rule of Evidence 803 contains what are informally called the "strong" exceptions. The reason for this is that they will apply anytime the provision of the exception

13. *Id.* at *12–13.
14. Targonski v. City of Oak Ridge, 2012 U.S. Dist. LEXIS 99693 (E.D. Tenn. July 18, 2012).

applies. For example, if a statement is made that describes an event when it happens (i.e., "that car just ran a red light") then the exception will apply. Rule 803 contains twenty-three exceptions. On the other hand, rule 804 contains what are informally called the "weak" exceptions. The reason they are referred to as weak is that a prerequisite is required before the exception will apply. And finally, the last exception is the "weakest" although it is only referred to by its name, the residual exception. It is the weakest because courts rarely find the circumstances justify the application of the exception. We begin the discussion with the strong exceptions.

10.3.1 The Strong Exceptions

Rule 803 sets forth twenty-three different exceptions to the hearsay rule, none of which depend on the declarant's availability to testify. Of these exceptions, the first three are probably the most relevant for getting social media activity into evidence because they capture all aspects of the "selfie era" in which we find ourselves with social media:

The following are not excluded by the hearsay rule, even though the declarant is available as a witness:

1. **Present Sense Impression.** A statement describing or explaining an event or condition, made while or immediately after the declarant perceived it.
2. **Excited Utterance.** A statement relating to a startling event or condition, made while the declarant was under the stress of excitement that it caused.
3. **Then-Existing Mental, Emotional, or Physical Condition.** A statement of the declarant's then-existing state of mind (such as motive, intent, or plan) or emotional, sensory, or physical condition (such as mental feeling, pain, or bodily health), but not including a statement of memory or belief to prove the fact remembered or believed unless it relates to the validity or terms of the declarant's will.

- **Present Sense Impression**

Is the social media describing certain events while they're happening? If yes, then the evidence may be admissible under Rule 803(1): "Present Sense Impression: A statement describing or explaining an event or condition, made while or immediately after the declarant perceived it." Availability of the witness for trial is irrelevant for this exception to apply.

For statements to come in under this hearsay exception, the statement must be made near in time to the event that is being described. In *Greco v. Velvet Cactus,*

LLC,[15] a hostile work environment and sexual harassment case, an employee's Facebook message observing how the defendant manager had been conducting himself during the year after the employee came back from a job suspension could not come into evidence as a present sense impression because it concerned events over a year's time.[16]

- **Excited Utterance**

Social media posts made in the excitement of the moment and recounting the person reacting to what's happening around them may come in under the excited utterance exception to the hearsay rule. Rule 803(2) defines an excited utterance as a "statement relating to a startling event or condition made while the declarant was under the stress of excitement caused by the event or condition." Availability of the witness for trial is irrelevant for this exception to apply.

In a civil action under the American with Disabilities Act, the court held that statements by a minor child to his parents could have come in as either an excited utterance or under the residual hearsay exception. In *Doe v. Darien Board of Education*,[17] the defendant school district was being sued in connection with the alleged sexual abuse of the plaintiff child, who suffered from Down syndrome, by his paraprofessional aide in the classroom. In considering the admissibility of the boy's statement to his parents that the paraprofessional took out his penis and told the boy to touch it, the court went through what courts consider when applying this exception to the hearsay rule:

> Factors that a "trial court must weigh in determining whether . . . offered testimony is within the 803(2) exception" include: "[t]he lapse of time between the startling event and the out-of-court statement," "the age of the declarant, the physical and mental condition of the declarant, the characteristics of the event and the subject matter of the statements." *United States v. Iron Shell*, 633 F.2d 77, 85–86 (8th Cir. 1980). "In order to find that 803(2) applies, it must appear that the declarant's condition at the time was such that the statement was spontaneous, excited or impulsive rather than the product of reflection and deliberation." (*Id.* at 86).[18]

In the context of social media, factors cutting against admitting a post may include how many versions of a photo or video were taken before settling on the one that was finally posted, how much planning went into the post, and how many people collaborated on the post. In other words, social media content that is essentially

15. Greco v. Velvet Cactus, LLC, 2014 U.S. Dist. LEXIS 87778 (E.D. La. June 27, 2014).
16. *Id.* at *17.
17. Doe v. Darien Bd. of Educ., 2015 U.S. Dist. LEXIS 66699 (D. Conn. May 21, 2015).
18. *Id.* at *12.

staged is neither spontaneous nor impulsive; it should not come into evidence under this exception to the hearsay rule.

- **Then Existing Mental, Emotional, or Physical Condition**

Remember the Facebook feature that allows users to share how they feel as they make their post—the posts that begin with, "How are you feeling?"—where users volunteer how they feel at that specific moment?

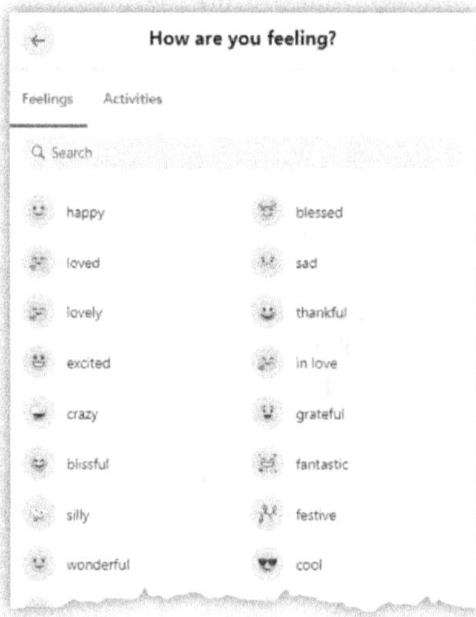

This social media seems ripe for coming in under the hearsay exception for existing state of mind, Rule 803(3):

> **Then Existing Mental, Emotional, or Physical Condition.** A statement of the declarant's then-existing state of mind (such as motive, intent, or plan) or emotional, sensory, or physical condition (such as mental feeling, pain, or bodily health), but not including a statement of memory or belief to prove the fact remembered or believed unless it relates to the validity or terms of the declarant's will.

Availability of the witness for trial is irrelevant for this exception to apply.

In a product liability crashworthiness action against the manufacturers of car airbags and seat belts, pages from Facebook and other social media sites of the plaintiff came into evidence over the plaintiff's objection that they were irrelevant and prejudicial. The plaintiff in *Thompson v. TRW Automotive, Inc.*[19] argued that the social media posts unfairly masked the emotional distress she was suffering.

19. Thompson v. TRW Auto., Inc., 2014 U.S. Dist. LEXIS 75562, at *25 (D. Nev. June 2, 2014).

The court held that social media posts can be relevant to someone's emotional or physical condition, and that the same rules of admissibility apply to them as to other evidence:

> Evidence of social networking postings is not subject to heightened admissibility standards simply because of its nature. Photos and similar postings about Thompson's physical and emotional condition and lifestyle are relevant to her claims, and If [*sic*] TRW can demonstrate its admissibility under the rules of evidence, this material may likely be admissible. However, some limitations on this evidence is appropriate to ensure that it does not unduly delay the trial.

There was no hearsay objection to this evidence because it was offered by defendants.[20] However, some of the evidence, as described by the court, is also a good example of evidence that could be admitted under Rule 803(3) if it was close in time to when the plaintiff was feeling the emotion or physical condition.

In addition to sharing how the user is feeling, Facebook also invites users to give a number of other real-time updates, with relevant drop-down menus for each:

And then offers users the opportunity to provide even more details. Under Celebrating, for example, there are a number of activities to choose from:

20. Fed. R. Evid. 801(d)(2).

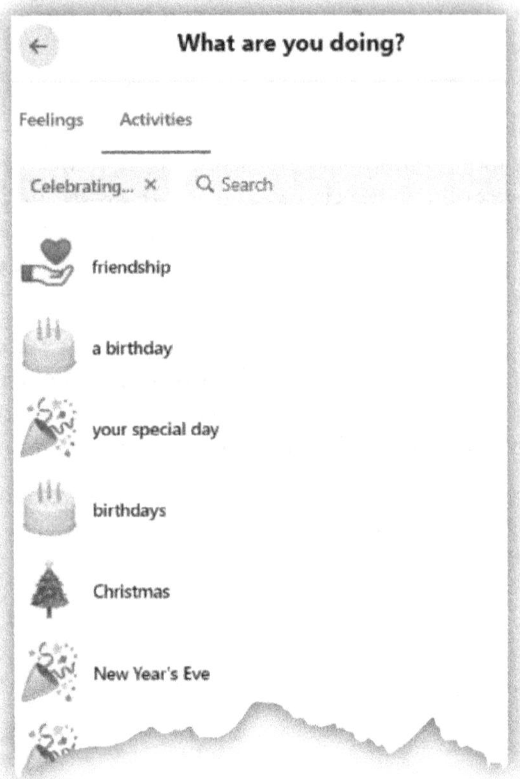

In personal injury cases and cases in which the plaintiff is seeking emotional distress damages, you can probably imagine the relevancy of these posts, as well as being able to argue that they are party admissions that are not inadmissible hearsay.

10.3.2 The Weak Exceptions

There are also exceptions to the hearsay rule that requires the declarant (a.k.a. the speaker) to be unavailable as a witness. To use any of these exceptions, the declarant (speaker) must be unavailable as defined by the rule.

Under Federal Rule of Evidence 804(a), a witness is considered unavailable for any of these reasons:

(1) is exempted from testifying . . . because [of a] privilege. . .;
(2) refuses to testify . . . despite a court order to do so;
(3) testifies to not remembering the subject matter;

(4) cannot be present or testify at the trial or hearing because of death or a then-existing infirmity, physical illness, or mental illness; or

(5) is absent from the trial or hearing and the statement's proponent has not been able, by process or other reasonable means, to procure:

(A) the declarant's attendance, in the case of a hearsay exception under Rule 804(b)(1) or (6); or

(B) the declarant's attendance or testimony, in the case of a hearsay exception under Rule 804(b)(2), (3), or (4).

Once it has been established that a declarant is "unavailable" under the rule, then one of the exceptions under rule 804(b) may apply. With regard to social media, only 804(b)(3) is a likely candidate.

- **Statement Against Interest**

For something to be admitted as a "statement against interest," the person making the statement must be unavailable as a witness. Further, the statement needs to be made under circumstances supporting its trustworthiness. Specifically, Rule 804(b)(3) provides:

(b) The Exceptions. The following are not excluded by the rule against hearsay if the declarant is unavailable as a witness:

(3) Statement Against Interest. A statement that:

(A) a reasonable person in the declarant's position would have made only if the person believed it to be true because, when made, it was so contrary to the declarant's proprietary or pecuniary interest or had so great a tendency to invalidate the declarant's claim against someone else or to expose the declarant to civil or criminal liability; and

(B) is supported by corroborating circumstances that clearly indicate its trustworthiness, if it is offered in a criminal case as one that tends to expose the declarant to criminal liability.

Example 1:

In a high-profile murder trial in Tennessee, the defense attorney asked for the victim's social media activity to be preserved. Defense attorney Joe Brandon, Jr. wanted to use the posts to argue that his client Shanterrica Madden killed her roommate, Middle Tennessee State University ball player Tina Stewart, in self-defense.[21] The defense attorney argued in court pleadings that Stewart made postings on Twitter, MySpace, and/or Facebook, including one on Twitter that said, "I just called police on my roommate. I feel like a snitch, but I don't like

21. State v. Madden, No. M2012-02473-CCA-R3-CD (Tenn. Crim. App. Mar. 11, 2014).

that b—h." In response, an unknown person posted, "[d]on't hurt her."[22] This is a good example of a statement against interest because it gives the defense room to argue that the murder victim started the violent altercation that sadly resulted in her own death.

Example 2:

In *SEC v. Sirianni*,[23] the court, in an unpublished opinion, held that statements made by Sirianni's co-defendant Morgan to an SEC witness were admissible as statements again interest because they concerned an alleged kickback scheme, in which the defendant was accused of recommending a stock to clients without telling them about the kickbacks he was allegedly receiving from the stock's promoter. Morgan's statements concerned the role of kickbacks in the "pump and dump" scheme involving the stock, which Morgan allegedly helped orchestrate.

Example 3:

It's no far stretch to see how social media evidence may come into evidence under this exception. Law enforcement gathers evidence by monitoring public accounts, creating fake accounts to "friend" people and get access to their private pages, and/or serving criminal subpoenas for private pages. In one case, New York police arrested someone whose public page showed him flashing gang gestures, but it was his private pages (provided to police by his social media "friends") that were even more incriminating:

Take Melvin Colon, who faced charges of murder, along with weapons and narcotics-related crimes. The suspected New York gang member posted public photos on Facebook that showed him flashing gang signs but privately made more incriminating posts, including references to past violent crimes and threats against others.

Unfortunately for Colon, one of his Facebook friends agreed to give police access to Colon's "private" information, and on August 10, 2012, a federal judge ruled Colon lost all claims to privacy when he shared those details with friends.[24]

Example 4:

One can also imagine this hearsay exception in the context of civil cases. For example, Domino's Pizza had its brand image damaged by two employees who

22. Sam Stockard, *Attorney in Stewart case wants Twitter notes saved*, The Daily News Journal, printed in USA Today (Mar. 10, 2011), http://usatoday30.usatoday.com/sports/college/womensbasketball/2011-03-10-middle-tennessee-stewart-twitter_N.htm (last visited Oct. 26, 2022).
23. SEC v. Sirianni, 2009 U.S. App. LEXIS 12822 (2d Cir. June 16, 2009).
24. Heather Kelly, *Police embrace social media as crime-fighting tool*, CNN (Aug. 30, 2012), https://www.cnn.com/2012/08/30/tech/social-media/fighting-crime-social-media (last visited Oct. 26, 2022).

posted a fake video of them doing disgusting things while making sandwiches for customers in April 2009. The employees were charged criminally, and had Domino's gone through with a threatened civil suit, the video possibly could have come into evidence as a statement against interest.[25]

10.3.3 The Residual Hearsay Exception (The Weakest Exception)

And, finally, there is what I like to refer to as the "kitchen sink" hearsay exception that gives courts some latitude to admit hearsay evidence that it finds is trustworthy under the circumstances, which is fundamentally the public policy behind all of the hearsay exceptions. Rule 807 provides that a hearsay statement may be admitted if:

(a) In General. Under the following conditions, a hearsay statement is not excluded by the rule against hearsay even if the statement is not admissible under a hearsay exception in Rule 803 or 804:

(1) the statement is supported by sufficient guarantees of trustworthiness—after considering the totality of circumstances under which it was made and evidence, if any, corroborating the statement; and

(2) it is more probative on the point for which it is offered than any other evidence that the proponent can obtain through reasonable efforts.

Example:

In *Ministers & Missionaries Benefit Board v. Snow*,[26] the court admitted Facebook pages printed from the account of the decedent Flesher, whose estate was being administered by Snow, because the pages were authenticated by someone close to the decedent, were corroborated by other documents, and could not be obtained by other means because the Facebook account user was deceased. The court also noted that the other side was on notice of the Facebook evidence because it was provided to them through discovery.

10.4 Red Flags that May Draw Objections

Recognize that there will be some social media evidence that just does not fall within any exception. One red flag should be social media posted by third parties on the social media pages of another party. Another red flag is double hearsay, where the social media post purports to state what someone else said to them, or the

---

25. Stephanie Clifford, *Video Prank at Domino's Taints Brand*, New York Times (April 15, 2009), http://www.nytimes.com/2009/04/16/business/media/16dominos.html?_r=0 (last visited Mar. 28, 2022).
26. Ministers & Missionaries Benefit Bd. v. Snow, 45 N.E.3d 917 (S.D.N.Y. 2014).

post is comprised of sharing what was posted by someone else and the original page is inadmissible hearsay. It is by no means impossible, but it will be more difficult to get this evidence admitted over a hearsay objection. If you're trying to keep social media activity out of evidence, be on the alert for these red flags so you don't miss making your hearsay objection.

10.5 Plan Ahead—Whether You Are Making or Responding to Hearsay Objections

We've spent a lot of time in this book discussing how to gather social media evidence through formal and informal discovery methods. You've seen examples of how social media can be used in a wide range of cases. Social media can be very effective in getting cases settled, trying cases to a jury, and shifting public opinion. In some cases, it may be your most persuasive evidence—which is why you should know in advance how you're going to respond to hearsay objections so you're never caught off-guard at trial. Be creative. The discussion above was designed to highlight the various ways in which social media posts can come into evidence. However, the facts and issues in your case will afford you more arguments. Remember to establish preliminary facts that you may need to show for certain hearsay exceptions, such as unavailability of the witness, or that the social media post was made in close proximity to when the speaker was feeling that way. Otherwise, you may have collected some terrific social media evidence that you won't get before a jury. You should be thinking of how you are going to get social media into evidence from the start of discovery. If you're prepared, then there's a very good chance you can win with social media.

Key Points

Don't automatically assume that social media is subject to some hearsay objection. If the social media activity is relevant regard less of whether it's true, you're not offering it for the truth of the matter asserted and it's not hearsay.

There isn't a different standard of admissibility for social media evidence. There's a good chance one of the hearsay exceptions will fit your evidence, especially because social media evidence tends to reflect real-time posting. (Think "selfie era.")

If it is social media activity by an opposing party or someone acting on its behalf, it should come in as a party admission.

If the social media activity is posted by a third party or shares content posted by another speaker, don't miss your opportunity to object to the evidence as inadmissible hearsay.

Chapter Eleven

Digital Tools

There are numerous tools for accomplishing almost anything you can imagine when you want to capture, retain, or even manipulate digital information. This second edition of this book was written in 2022. The following tools may or may not still exist; they may exist in a different form; and, most importantly, there may be tools that are better than those that follow. The programs and apps identified represent the ones that the authors are familiar with and in many cases use. While no endorsement is offered for any particular solution, most offer trial versions and it is highly recommended that you try more than one tool and use the one that offers the features you desire, the usability that fits your experience, and the price that you are comfortable paying. The following lists offer a number of solutions. The top-most reference is the one that either the authors use or find to be the most beneficial. Each reference also indicates which operating systems for which the solution is available. The authors have found these tools useful but we have no affiliation with the manufacturers in any way.

11.1 Screen Capture

There are many tools to capture what appears on a computer screen. Some offer simple options while other offer complexities such as capturing a scrolling window and editing captures within the program itself.

Snagit	www.techsmith.com/snagit
Greenshot	https://getgreenshot.org/
PicPick	https://picpick.app/en/
ShareX	https://getsharex.com/
Lightshot	https://app.prntscr.com/en/
Awesome Screenshot	https://www.awesomescreenshot.com/

The above offer solutions for capturing information found on a computer screen. Oftentimes, information found on the screen of a device (a phone or a tablet) must be captured. You can often do this using the built-in functionality of the device itself. Check the instructions for the particular device and operating system to determine how to capture a screen.

For example, on an iPhone 14 with iOS 16.1, the user merely needs to simultaneously press the power button and the volume up button. The device will take a snapshot of whatever is on the screen. That screen shot may then be transferred to another device using a variety of methods, such as email, text message, or using a variety of apps loaded onto the device itself.

11.2 Device Data Extraction

Some information is not easily transferred to from devices such as phones and tablets to a more easily used (and displayed) form. For example, text messages can be powerful evidence. But how is that evidence best presented? In a recent trial involving an indictment for murder, the prosecution offered text messages between the accused and her boyfriend. The messages were intended to show, among other things, that the accused was racist. The messages were displayed to the jurors using an overhead projector and presented in the format of a table.

Although the information comes across, some of the effectiveness may be lost in the way it is presented. Jurors are not accustomed to reading messages in table form. It comes across as a cold, sterile, presentation of the information. And most importantly, this presentation looks completely unfamiliar.

Timestamp	Party	Description	Deleted
2018-01-15 9:53:43 AM(UTC-6)	To: +12 Misty	You working this parade?!	
2018-01-15 10:10:30 AM(UTC-6)	From: +13 Blevins	he grandsons on the other side if she can get through lol	Yes
2018-01-15 10:10:32 AM(UTC-6)	From: +13 Blevins	What's Justin's number. Can you ask him if he told this lady with I	Yes
2018-01-15 11:34:36 AM(UTC-6)	From: +12 Misty	Hell on! I worked it for ten years. I'm good. Lol	
2018-01-15 11:34:41 AM(UTC-6)	From: +12 Misty	No!	
2018-01-15 11:36:18 AM(UTC-6)	To: +12 Misty	Lol! Dang! Yep you deserve to have it off. Was hoping you were just to say hi. Miss ya!!	
2018-01-15 11:36:48 AM(UTC-6)	From: +12 Misty	Miss you too!!	
2018-01-15 12:14:01 PM(UTC-6)	From: +13 Blevins	When does this end lol	Yes
2018-01-15 12:18:47 PM(UTC-6)	To: +13 Blevins	When MLK is dead... oh wait...	Yes
2018-01-15 12:19:56 PM(UTC-6)	From: +13 Blevins	HA	Yes

Table of Text Messages

Now consider messages in the case against Michelle Carter, accused of causing the victim to commit suicide. The accused had sent many messages to the victim encouraging him to kill himself, which he ultimately did. The prosecution offered the messages sent between the accused and the victim in the form that appeared as they had when originally sent and received. The effect is familiar and gives a sense of immediacy. Although this version of the evidence contains less information than the previous version (such as individual dates and times for each message), this can be provided by the attorneys through the appropriate witnesses to the extent they feel it is necessary.

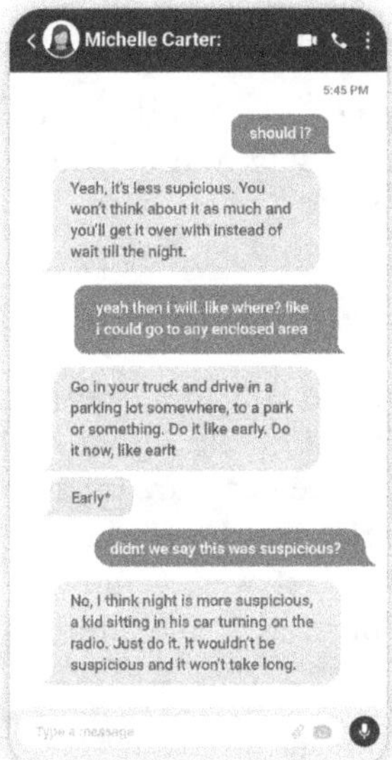

Screenshot of Text Messages

Unfortunately, displaying this information often presents a different problem. How does one extract the information from these devices and in a usable form that can be made into an effective exhibit (digital or print)? And although text messages are the common problem, much of the information on portable devices can be difficult to extract. And the greatest difficulty comes from iOS devices.

Fortunately, there are some solutions. One such solution is iMazing. This program which is specifically designed for iOS devices (which are some most difficult devices from which to extract data). There is a free version and a paid version which offers more robust features. The application may be found at www.imazing.com. Other solutions include:

- iMobie — www.imobie.com
- Dr.Fone — drfone.wondershare.com
- iBackup Extractor — wideanglesoftware.com

Android phones and tables are less challenging. D from these devices can be more easily extracted than those from iOS devices, and third-party software packages can facilitate the tasks more easily. Here are some of the solutions for Android Devices:

- FoneDog — www.fonedog.com
- MobiKin — www.mobikin.com
- Droid Transfer — www.wideanglesoftware.com

These tools merely scratch the surface of those available for extraction of various types of data. A keyword search using your favorite search engine will undoubtedly reveal numerous additional tools.

11.3 Video Capture

Capturing video is a close cousin to capturing screen data. And, just like screen capture tools, there are numerous options. One of the leaders in the field also produces one of the top screen capture programs: TechSmith. In fact, their screen capture program, SnagIt, can also capture video. However, the video capture capabilities of TechSmith's software Camtasia, specifically designed to capture video, is much more robust. This and similar tools may be found as noted below:

- Camtasia — www.techsmith.com
- Debut — www.nchsoftware.com
- BandiCam — www.bandicam.com
- FlashBack — www.flashbackrecorder.com

11.4 Browser History

Retrieving one's browser history can provide valuable information to be used for evidentiary purposes. Generally obtaining the history is straightforward. Although most commands are uniform, one might have to play around in various settings to bring up the browser history. The standard command to retrieve browser history is CTRL + H. Once the history is up, it can often be saved as a PDF or at the very least printed. I suggest "printing" as a PDF if you cannot save it directly in that format. As a PDF, you can easily create the necessary trial exhibits.

Appendices

A. Primary Social Media+ Checklist

B. Secondary Social Media+ Checklist

C. Dating Sites Checklist

D. Witness Preparation Checklist

E. Authentication of Facebook Pages

F. Authentication of Twitter Posts (Tweets)

G. Authentication of Instagram Posts

H. Authentication of LinkedIn Posts

I. Authentication of Text Messages

J. Generic Authentication Checklist for Social Media

K. Checklist for Contents of Litigation Hold Letter

APPENDIX A

PRIMARY SOCIAL MEDIA+ CHECKLIST

Please list each and every one of your username(s) for each social media, messaging and other accounts below. If you have more than one account, please indicate accordingly. Use as many sheets as necessary. If you have accounts for platforms not listed, please fill in the name of the platform and each of your usernames. If the username has a zero in it, please signify by using a zero with a slash through it: "Ø". Please be clear as to whether a letter is uppercase or lowercase. Write NEATLY or type.

SOCIAL MEDIA SITE/ PLATFORM	1ST USER NAME	2ND USER NAME	3RD USER NAME
Discord			
Facebook			
Facebook Messenger			
Flickr			
iMessage			
Imgur			
Instagram			
LinkedIn			
Meetup			
Microsoft Teams			
MySpace			
Nextdoor			
Photobucket			
Pinterest			
Quora			
Reddit			
Skype			
SnapChat			
Telegram			
TikTok			
TruthSocial			
Tumblr			
Twitch			
Twitter			
Vine			
WeChat			
WhatsApp			
YouTube			
Zoom			
Additional platform name			

APPENDIX B

SECONDARY SOCIAL MEDIA+ CHECKLIST

Please list each and every one of your username(s) for each social media, messaging and other accounts below. If you have more than one account, please indicate accordingly. Use as many sheets as necessary. If the username has a zero in it, please signify by using a zero with a slash through it: "Ø". Please be clear as to whether a letter is uppercase or lowercase. Write NEATLY or type.

SOCIAL MEDIA SITE/ PLATFORM	1ST USER NAME	2ND USER NAME	3RD USER NAME
23Snaps			
8tracks			
Academia.edu			
ASmallWorld			
Athlinks			
Band			
beBee			
Blind			
Caffeine			
Classmates			
DailyMotion			
DeviantArt			
Houseparty			
Likee			
MeetMe			
Meerkat			
Mix			
Peanut			
Periscope			
ReverbNation			
Shutterfly			
Steemit			
Tagged			
ThisLife			
Triller			
Untapped			
Veoh			
Vimeo			
Yogile			
Vube			

APPENDIX C

DATING SITES CHECKLIST

Please list each and every one of your username(s) for each dating site or platform below. If you have more than one account, please indicate accordingly. Use as many sheets as necessary. If the username has a zero in it, please signify by using a zero with a slash through it: "Ø". Please be clear as to whether a letter is uppercase or lowercase. Write NEATLY or type.

DATING SITE/ PLATFORM	1ST USER NAME	2ND USER NAME	3RD USER NAME
#open			
Adam 4 Adam			
Align			
Ashley Madison			
Badoo			
Bumble			
Chappy			
Christian Mingle			
Clover			
Coffee Meets Bagel			
Datefit			
Dig			
Dine			
Do I Date			
eHarmony			
Elite Singles			
Facebook Dating			
Fantasy			
Feeld			
Fetlife			
Grinder			
Growlr			
Happy Hour			
Hater			
Her			
Hily			
Hinge			
How About We			
Inner Circle			
JDate			

APPENDIX C

DATING SITES CHECKLIST continued

KinkD			
Kinkoo			
Loosid			
Minder			
OK Cupid			
Our Time			
Pickable			
Plenty of Fish			
Quiz Date Live			
Raya			
Ship			
Tastebuds			
The League			
Tinder			
Whiplr			
Zoe			
Zoosk			
Additional platform name			
Additional platform name			
Additional platform name			
Additional platform name			
Additional platform name			
Additional platform name			
Additional platform name			
Additional platform name			
Additional platform name			
Additional platform name			
Additional platform name			

APPENDIX D

WITNESS PREPARATION CHECKLIST

The following rules will assist witnesses when they testify, regardless of whether they are testifying about social media or otherwise. Covering the rules with prospective witnesses in advance of trial will often improve the accuracy of their testimony. The list is presented in such a format that you may copy and print out for your witnesses. Please retain all copyright information on the copies distributed.

Best Practices for Witness Testimony

By Professor Sydney Beckman

1. Listen carefully to the question asked.
2. Do not rush. Pause (take a breath) before you answer.
3. Think about your answer before you speak.
4. Only answer questions when you fully understand what is being asked.
5. Answer only the question asked. Do not volunteer information.
6. Tell the truth.
7. Do not guess.
8. Do not exaggerate.
9. Do not "spar" with the lawyer. Be professional but human.
10. Respond orally and clearly.
11. If you forget a question (i.e., after a lawyer objects), ask for it to be repeated.
12. Do not explain, justify, or apologize for your answer.
13. Pause for objections.
14. Remember to breathe.

APPENDIX E

AUTHENTICATION OF FACEBOOK PAGES

Note: Facebook pages frequently consist of many elements, for example, pictures, posts, photographs, links, and advertisements. Depending on what portion of the page is being offered, each element may require different evidence to fulfill the authentication requirements. Courts generally accept a wide range of extrinsic evidence to establish authentication. Conclusive proof of authenticity is not required.

☐	1	**Mark the exhibit** (the best practice is to have it premarked).
☐	2	Present the exhibit to the witness.

Have the witness do the following:

☐	3	**Identify** the exhibit (i.e., it's a printout of a Facebook page).
☐	4	Identify **where/how** the exhibit was created. (i.e., witness's printer).
☐	5	Identify **when** the exhibit was created.
☐	6	**Witness/User:** If the witness is the user, authenticate the exhibit by asking the witness whether the exhibit is a true and accurate copy of their Facebook page. If the witness is not the user, continue with step 7; otherwise go to Step 9. 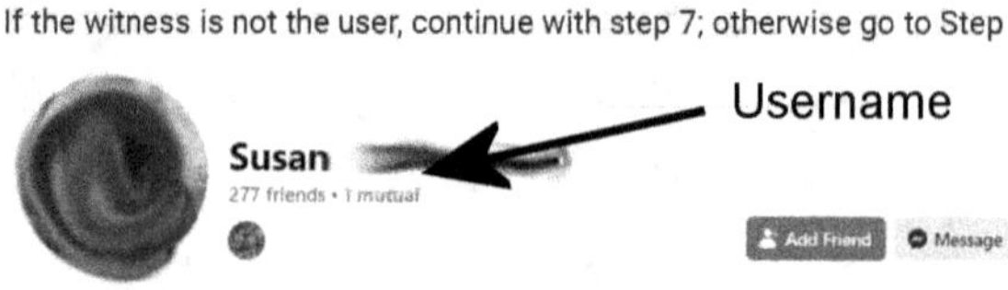
☐	7	**Witness/Not User:** Identify the username.
☐	8	**Describe** how the witness connects that username with a particular individual. Examples: • Witness has seen the user using Facebook and recognizes their Facebook page. • Witness recognizes the user's Facebook page (and describes how). • Witness recognizes the user's style of communicating as reflected in messages.
☐	9	If necessary, authenticate individual elements on the page (i.e., photographs).

APPENDIX F

AUTHENTICATION OF TWITTER POSTS (TWEETS)

Note: Tweets may contain more than one element in addition to the text string. For example, pictures and videos may appear in addition to the "tweet." If the additional elements are being offered, each element may require different evidence to fulfill the authentication requirements. Courts generally accept a wide range of extrinsic evidence to establish authentication. Conclusive proof of authenticity is not required.

☐	1	**Mark the exhibit** (the best practice is to have it premarked).
☐	2	Present the exhibit to the witness.

Have the witness do the following:

☐	3	**Identify the evidence** as a printout (or digital display) of a tweet (or multiple tweets).
☐	4	Identify **where/how** the exhibit was created. (i.e., the page(s) were printed from the witness's printer).
☐	5	Identify **when** the evidence (printout) was created.(i.e., the printout was made on <date>).
☐	6	**Witness/User:** If the witness is the user, authenticate the exhibit by asking the witness whether the exhibit comes from their Twitter account. If the witness is not the user, continue with step 7; otherwise go to Step 9.
☐	7	**Witness/User:** Witness can testify that the printout is a true and accurate copy of their tweets. If the witness is not the user, continue with step 8; otherwise move to Step 12.
☐	8	**Witness/Not User:** Identify the username. 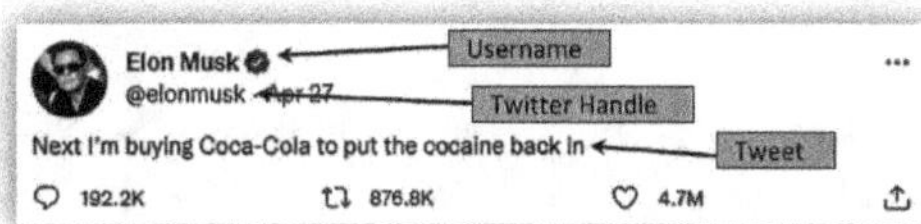
☐	9	**Describe** how the witness connects that Twitter username with a particular individual. • Witness has seen the user using Twitter and recognizes their username. • Witness recognizes the user's Twitter username (and describes how). • Witness recognizes user's style of communicating as reflected in tweets on the page. • If the witness cannot identify the username, continue with step 10; otherwise move to Step 12.

APPENDIX F

AUTHENTICATION OF TWITTER POSTS (TWEETS) continued

☐	10	**Witness/Not User:** Identify the Twitter handle.
☐	11	**Describe how** the witness connects that Twitter handle with a particular individual. • Witness has seen the user using Twitter and recognizes their handle. • Witness recognizes the user's Twitter handle (and describes how). • Witness recognizes user's style of communicating as reflected in tweets on the page.
☐	12	If necessary, authenticate individual elements on the page (i.e., photographs or video).

Tweets will often involve hearsay. Even though evidence is properly authenticated it will require, if necessary, overcoming hearsay objections.

Tweets may often be "retweets" or retransmission of someone else's statement. Although this will likely not impact authentication, it may impact a hearsay analysis. If the particular retweet comes from a party opponent, it may fit the definition of 801(d)(2)(B): an opposing party's statement that is offered against an opposing party and "is one the party manifested that it adopted or believed to be true." It may be argued that by "retweeting" the statement, the party manifested that it adopted the statement or believed the statement to be true.

APPENDIX G

AUTHENTICATION OF INSTAGRAM POSTS

Note: Instagram evidence frequently consists of video, pictures, and posts. Depending on what is being offered (one element or all elements), each element may require different evidence to fulfill the authentication requirements. Courts generally accept a wide range of extrinsic evidence to establish authentication. Conclusive proof of authenticity is not required.

☐	1	**Mark the exhibit** (the best practice is to have it premarked).
☐	2	Present the exhibit to the witness.

Have the witness do the following:

☐	3	**Identify the evidence** as a printout (or digital display) of the portion of the Instagram post you are offering. Obviously, if it is a video, it will be digital.
☐	4	Identify **where/how** the exhibit was created. • i.e., the page(s) were printed from Witness's printer or the video saved to the Witness's flash drive • i.e., you might need to authenticate the webpage as being pointed to the Instagram URL
☐	5	Identify **when** the evidence (printout, or video) was created. • i.e., the printout was made on <date>. Note: this will not apply of using the live website and displaying the video or other evidence
☐	6	**Witness/User:** If the witness is the user, authenticate the exhibit by asking the witness whether the exhibit comes from their Instagram account.
☐	7	**Witness/User:** Witness can testify that the printout/video is a true and accurate copy of their Instagram post If the witness is not the user, continue with step 8; otherwise move to Step 10.
☐	8	**Witness/Not User:** Identify the username. 

APPENDIX G

AUTHENTICATION OF INSTAGRAM POSTS continued

☐	9	**Describe** how the witness connects that Instagram username with a particular individual. • Witness has seen the user using Instagram and recognizes their username. • Witness recognizes the witness's Instagram username (and describes how). • Witness recognizes user's style of communicating as reflected in comments on the page.
☐	10	If necessary, authenticate additional elements on the page (i.e., comments).
☐	11	Identify any other relevant facts that help authenticate the exhibit.

Note: Instagram comments will often involve hearsay. Even though evidence is properly authenticated it will require, if necessary, overcoming hearsay objections.

APPENDIX H

AUTHENTICATION OF LINKEDIN POSTS

Note: LinkedIn pages frequently consist of many elements, for example, pictures, posts, photographs, links, and advertisements. Depending on what portion of the page is being offered (or the entire page), each element may require different evidence to fulfill the authentication requirements. Courts generally accept a wide range of extrinsic evidence to establish authentication. Conclusive proof of authenticity is not required.

☐	1	**Mark the exhibit** (the best practice is to have it premarked).
☐	2	Present the exhibit to the witness.

Have the witness do the following:

☐	3	**Identify the evidence** as a printout (or digital display) of a LinkedIn page or pages.
☐	4	Identify **where/how** the exhibit was created. (i.e., the page(s) were printed from the witness's printer.)
☐	5	Identify **when** the evidence (printout) was created.(i.e., the printout was made on <date>.)
☐	6	**Witness/User:** If the witness is the user, authenticate the exhibit by asking the witness whether the exhibit is a true and accurate copy of their LinkedIn page. If the witness is not the user, continue with step 7; otherwise move to Step 9.
☐	7	**Witness/Not User:** Identify the username.
☐	8	**Describe** how the witness connects that username with a particular individual. • Witness has seen the user using LinkedIn and recognizes their LinkedIn page. • Witness recognizes the user's LinkedIn page (and describes how). • Witness recognizes user's style of communicating as reflected in messages on the page.
☐	9	If necessary, authenticate individual elements on the page (i.e., photographs).
☐	10	Identify any other relevant facts that help authenticate the exhibit.

APPENDIX I

AUTHENTICATION OF TEXT MESSAGES

Note: Courts generally accept a wide range of extrinsic evidence to establish authentication. Conclusive proof of authenticity is not required.

☐	1	**Mark the exhibit** (the best practice is to have it premarked).
☐	2	Present the exhibit to the witness.

Have the witness do the following:

☐	3	**Identify the evidence** as a printout (or digital display) of text message(s).
☐	4	Identify **where/how** the exhibit was created. (i.e., it is a photo taken of the screen of an iPhone 13.)
☐	5	Identify **when** the evidence (printout) was created.(i.e., the photo was taken on <date>. Note: This is not the date the messages were sent. See Step 12.)
☐	6	[Optional] Authenticate the photograph (some courts might not require this step as it is somewhat 'built in' to the authentication of the instant messages.)
☐	7	Identify the number from which the message was sent (Sender).
☐	8	Identify who owns the number (Sender).
☐	9	Offer evidence as to how the witness knows the number is associated with the owner.
☐	10	Identify the number which received the message (Recipient).
☐	11	Identify who owns the receiving number (Recipient).
☐	12	Identify the date(s) the messages were sent.
☐	13	Identify any other relevant facts that help authenticate the exhibit.
☐	14	It may be necessary to reveal previous edits, if available. (iPhones running iOS 16 or later retain the previous edits but hide them; they remain available to see.)

APPENDIX J

GENERIC AUTHENTICATION CHECKLIST FOR SOCIAL MEDIA

Note: Courts generally accept a wide range of extrinsic evidence to establish authentication. Conclusive proof of authenticity is not required. Although different platforms may be laid out differently or have different elements on them, they will contain many similarities.

☐	1	**Mark the exhibit** (the best practice is to have it premarked).
☐	2	Present the exhibit to the witness.

Have the witness do the following:

☐	3	**Identify the evidence** as a printout (or digital display) of the picture/video/message/etc.
☐	4	Identify **where/how** the exhibit was created.
☐	5	Identify **when** the evidence was created.
☐	6	Identify the **source/username/handle** etc.
☐	7	Identify if the witness is the user.
☐	8	If witness is not the user, identify how the witness knows the source/username/handle is connected to the individual.
☐	9	If applicable, identify the recipient.
☐	10	Identify the date(s) of the content.
☐	11	Identify any other relevant facts that help authenticate the exhibit.

APPENDIX K

CHECKLIST FOR CONTENTS OF LITIGATION HOLD LETTER

☐	**1**	List the social media sites by name.
☐	**2**	List known usernames for each social media site (even with usernames are identical between sites.
☐	**3**	Include generic requests for unknown social media sites.
☐	**4**	Include generic requests for all usernames.
☐	**5**	Cite cases in which as party was sanctioned for not preserving social media activity.
☐	**6**	Summarize the type of content requested for each site.
☐	**7**	Request written confirmation that the other party will comply.

INDEX

www.ingramcontent.com/pod-product-compliance
Lightning Source LLC
LaVergne TN
LVHW080049210926
848481LV00011B/3312

* 9 7 8 1 6 0 1 5 6 9 3 4 9 *